Disorienting Politics

Disorienting Politics

*Chimerican Media and
Transpacific Entanglements*

Fan Yang

UNIVERSITY OF MICHIGAN PRESS
ANN ARBOR

Published in the United States of America by the
University of Michigan Press
Manufactured in the United States of America
Printed on acid-free paper
First published June 2024

A CIP catalog record for this book is available from the British Library.

Library of Congress Cataloging-in-Publication Data

Names: Yang, Fan, author.
Title: Disorienting politics : chimerican media and transpacific entanglements /
    Fan Yang.
Description: Ann Arbor : University of Michigan Press, 2024. | Includes bibliographical
    references and index.
Identifiers: LCCN 2024000444 (print) | LCCN 2024000445 (ebook) |
    ISBN 9780472076796 (hardback) | ISBN 9780472056798 (paperback) |
    ISBN 9780472904464 (ebook other)
Subjects: LCSH: China—Civilization—American influences. | United States—
    Civilization—Chinese influences.
Classification: LCC DS779.23 (print) | LCC DS779.23 (ebook) |
    DDC 327.51073—dc23/eng/20240206
LC record available at https://lccn.loc.gov/2024000444
LC ebook record available at https://lccn.loc.gov/2024000445

DOI: https://doi.org/10.3998/mpub.12838895

Open access funding for this publication was provided by The Dresher Center for the
Humanities at the University of Maryland, Baltimore County (UMBC).

The University of Michigan Press's open access publishing program is made possible
thanks to additional funding from the University of Michigan Office of the Provost and
the generous support of contributing libraries.

Cover illustration: *Chimerica*, Almeida Theatre, London, 2013 (set design by Es Devlin,
photograph by Finn Ross). Used by permission.

For Adeline

Contents

Acknowledgments

I have always thought of "Acknowledgments" as a meaningful way to disrupt the myth of individual authorship. So many colleagues, friends, and family members have inspired and supported me in the decade of writing this book. I want to take this opportunity to express my gratitude to each person as specifically as possible, though omissions are inevitable given the magnitude of the task.

I am most grateful for the nurturing environment at the University of Maryland, Baltimore County (UMBC), where I have the best colleagues. Their brilliance informs my thinking about US (racial) politics on a daily basis. In the Department of Media and Communication Studies, interactions with Jason Loviglio, Elizabeth Patton, Tracy Tinga, and Donald Snyder have taught me much about American studies, media history, and US/global popular culture. My engagement with Asian American studies benefited a great deal from conversations with Tamara Bhalla in UMBC's Department of American Studies, with whom I co-taught the humanities seminar "Re-orienting Culture" in 2016. Theo Gonzalves, the former chair of American Studies who started the Asian and Asian American Faculty and Staff Council at UMBC, of which I was also a founding member, is an exemplary scholar-activist whom I aspire to model through my own work. Kimberly Moffitt, now the dean of UMBC's College of Arts, Humanities, and Social Sciences, pointed me to important resources regarding the intersections of race, class, and gender in American media and continues to inspire me to explore the political possibilities for humanities scholarship to address systemic inequalities.

The Dresher Center for the Humanities at UMBC has been an amazing interdisciplinary space that encourages the kinds of intellectual conversations this book seeks to promote. Jessica Berman, the center's director, has been an incredible scholarly and professional mentor. Rachel Brubaker deserves extra recognition for helping me figure out ways to describe the project in an early stage. A Dresher Center Residential Fellowship in fall 2020—coinciding with the first full "virtual" semester during COVID-19—provided me with the crucial time necessary to complete the manuscript. The "Fellows and Others" workshops and the "Currents" work-in-progress discussions in which I participate on a regular basis, as well as various writing and faculty working groups, offered tremendous opportunities to learn from colleagues in other departments/ fields/institutions, especially Courtney Hobson (the Dresher Center); Derek Musgrove, Brian Van Wyck, Nianshen Song, Christy Chapin, and Michelle Scott (History); Preminda Jacob and Irene Chan (Visual Arts); Sharon Tran and Emily Yoon (English); Nicole King (American Studies); Christine Mallinson and Craig Saper (Language, Literacy, and Culture); Constantine Vaporis, Christopher Tong, and Meredith Oyen (Asian Studies); Dawn Biehler (Geography and Environmental Systems); and Carole McCann (Gender + Women Studies), among others. I am also particularly grateful for the Dresher Center Advisory Board for awarding me a Scholarly Completion Fund in fall 2023 to support the open access publication and indexing of this book.

Inclusion Imperative Fellows at the Dresher Center, such as Gina Lewis (Bowie State University), Teresa Chisu Ko (Ursinus College), Will Youmens (George Washington University), Krista Johnson (Howard University), and Theresa Runstedtler (American University) also offered many inspirations. I enjoyed and benefited from my exchange with May Chung, my first PhD advisee, regarding the practices of Chinese learning in the United States. My undergraduate students, many of whom conduct timely research on topics related to media, communication, and social justice, have been wonderful interlocutors as well.

Beyond UMBC, anthropologists Ralph Litzinger and Louisa Schein are two important mentors in thinking about critical approaches to contemporary China in transnational contexts. Cowriting various pieces with them has transformed me as a cultural studies scholar (and an anthropologist wannabe). (A special shoutout to Louisa for pushing me to more clearly articulate the key interventions of the project!) Lily Wong (my DC writing group partner), Rebecca Adelman (my former colleague and "intellectual playmate"), and Cara Wallis and Silvia Lindtner (my cultural studies "partners in crime" in the China field) offered thoughtful feedback on various chapters. At an earlier stage of developing the project, Viviana McManus kindly invited me to join a DC-based writing group in 2015–16, which allowed me to gain valuable insights from her and her friends, Dixa Ramirez-D'Oleo and Chelsea Stieber; I also enjoyed learning from their own brilliant scholarship. During the pandemic, the online meetings of the Coronavirus Multispecies Reading Group, organized by Eben Kirksey, became an indispensable space for intellectual exchange. I have fond memories of visiting Eben's family farm and obtaining both fresh produce and fascinating ideas from our conversations. Several online sessions organized by the Critical China Scholars network during the pandemic also offered many clarifying moments of reflection.

I was fortunate to have convinced Paul Smith, my advisor back in George Mason University's Cultural Studies PhD program, to see the play *Chimerica* at Studio Theater in Washington, DC, in 2015. The fact that he talked with me about the (problems of) the play for hours afterward only solidifies what a pleasure it always is to see and learn from him. Numerous fellow scholars of Chinese descent living and teaching in North America, especially in the DC area, many of whom I first met online during the pandemic, are now close friends with a shared commitment to carving out new spaces for intellectual dialogue across the Pacific. These include Yang Zhang, Duo Jiang, Li Chen, Ruoyun Bai, Yuanchong Wang, Xin Fan, Yan He, Dewen Zhang, Junliang Huang, Ling Zhang, Lihong Liu, Meng Li, Peng Xu, Dandan Chen, Yige Dong, Shuang Chen, among others. Several discussions held with this group of friends on the sound-based platform Clubhouse in 2020–21, including one right after the 2021 Atlanta shootings, a discussion attended by hundreds, lent meaning and peace at a time of political and emotional turmoil. Ying Zhang, with whom I enjoyed hosting "Piano and Poetry" sessions on Clubhouse, brought me (back) to Ohio State University to talk about the book as part of the Sino-US Relations: New Perspectives series. I'm grateful for Ying's warm hospitality as well as the invited discussant Jennifer Hubbert's insightful comments.

I was also lucky to have shared my work in progress with many colleagues both within and beyond the United States. I recall presenting some preliminary ideas at the Athens Institute for Education and Research (thanks to an International Forum on Asian History and Asian Studies co-organized by Constantine Vaporis), an early version of chapter 2 at the 2016 Marxist Literary Group meeting in Montreal, and other chapters at several other international conferences. I appreciate Samirah Hassan's help in swiftly handling my travel arrangements to attend these events. Part of chapter 3 was presented at the University of North Florida, upon the kind invitation of Nicholas de Villiers, with whom I have long had stimulating conversations. I thank Ying Qian for the invitation to discuss the introduction to this book with the engaged participants at the Modern China Seminar series at Columbia University in 2021, especially Ying Zhu (the discussant), Britta Ingebretson (who read and suggested references for chapter 3), and Nicholas Bartlett. Thanks also to Roger Lancaster for the opportunity to share some ideas from the project with the faculty and (prospective) students at the 2022 recruitment event for the Cultural Studies PhD program at George Mason University.

An early version of chapter 2 appeared in the *Journal of Asian American Studies*, volume 19, issue 3, in 2016. I'm grateful for Anita Mannur's expert editing and the anonymous reviewers' helpful suggestions. Indeed, the Asian American studies community has become another important intellectual home where I have found a new kind of scholarly kinship. I thank Christopher Fan, Aimee Bahng, Yu-Fang Cho, Minh-ha Pham, Lisa Nakamura, Grace Wang, David Roh, Rachel Lee, Peter Feng, Joseph Jeon, Vincent Pham, Kent Ono, Lori Lopez, Michelle Huang, Douglas Ishii, Hee-Jung Serenity Joo, Nandini Dhar, Tina Chen, and many others for welcoming me to this community with their brilliance and generosity.

Sara Cohen at the University of Michigan Press expressed an interest in my work as early as 2016. She has set new standards for efficiency and responsiveness during the review process. I couldn't be more thrilled to work with her and her colleagues to bring the book into this world. Several anonymous reviewers, including the media studies member as well as others of the Faculty Executive Committee at the Press, offered valuable feedback for further improving the book in the final revision stage. I am of course responsible for any remaining imperfections.

Friends and family are often underrecognized coproducers of academic knowledge. I'm deeply indebted to Ann Arbor and John Rosenwald, whom I met in my first year of college in Shanghai when they were on a Fulbright Fellowship. It was they who first encouraged me to study "culture" in the United States and eventually brought me to the Great Mother and New Father Conference in Maine in 2022—a magical encounter with many beautiful souls that reinvigorated my aspiration to foster more awareness of global interconnectivity. John's editing help for an earlier version of the introduction and conclusion was much appreciated. I'm also grateful to Kate and Ryan for their unique perspectives as fans of *Firefly*, especially for Kate's helpful comments on chapter 3. My neighbors Dan and Judy, among others, offered warm friendship and company over many meals. I also appreciate Dan's careful reading of chapter 4 on *House of Cards*. Katy and Lia are always there when I need them. Ann Yee first told me to see *Chimerica* in London when I was visiting Vicky Watts there in 2013, and I'm grateful to them both for the inspiration. Conversations with Gil Rodman and Maria Repnikova in the streets of DC during the last moments of revision also provided much encouragement to finish the book. It was also in those streets that I recall having stimulating conversations during a 2018 protest with Maria, Louisa Lim, Bin Xu, Yan Long, and Christian Sorace, from whom I learned a great deal. Under the pandemic conditions, I could not imagine completing this book without the help of Marc and Tracy in household and child-care duties. It is to the "fruit" of our collective labor, Adeline, that I dedicate this book.

Introduction

In late 2019, a novel coronavirus quietly began to spread in the Chinese city of Wuhan. Some local doctors and officials tried to sound the alarm bell, while others fed the public with misinformation and even moved to repress the news.[1] On January 20, 2020, Xi Jinping, the president of China, first publicly acknowledged and vowed to contain the outbreak.[2] Three days later, Wuhan, a city of 11 million, went into quarantine mode. What the World Health Organization (WHO) came to call COVID-19, a highly contagious and unpredictable disease caused by the virus, officially became a global pandemic on March 11, 2020. Within months the virus spread to most countries, often with exponential intensity. Governments and citizens around the world had to drastically reorder social life so as to cope with the explosive contagion, which went on to claim millions of lives.

The first case in the United States was confirmed on January 21, 2020, a day after the Chinese government locked down Wuhan.[3] For the weeks that followed, President Donald Trump's administration denied the severity of the outbreak while proclaiming that the situation was under control. Nonetheless, a travel ban from China was issued on January 31, restricting Chinese nationals from entering the United States. Lacking explicit federal guidance, different state and local entities took it upon themselves to adopt various measures to limit the spread of COVID-19. On March 13, President Trump declared a national emergency. Within two weeks, the number of identified cases in the United States surpassed that of China, lending an eerie meaning to the "America first" slogan popularized by the Trump campaign.

President Trump referred to the virus as having "started in China" in his first national briefing and, along with his supporters, continued to emphasize its Chinese origin.[4] This emphasis appeared to be more intentional than accidental, even though scientists confirmed that the strain of the virus that caused the majority of cases in New York City actually came from Europe.[5] On March 19, *Washington Post* photographer Jabin Botsford snapped a picture of the president crossing out the term "corona" and replacing it with "Chinese" in his speech.[6] An insistence on using "Chinese virus" instead of "China virus," as David Frum writes in *The Atlantic*, "subtly shifts the blame from the state of China to Chinese people, including people of Chinese descent living in the United States."[7] Perhaps not coincidentally, the Western world in general and the United States in particular have seen a surge in the number of racist attacks against people of Asian descent.[8]

Meanwhile, the Chinese state remains a prominently targeted culprit. Some have singled out the authoritarian state's initial lack of transparency as the main cause for the global spread of the disease.[9] Others have blamed the government, led by the Chinese Communist Party (CCP), for the continuous censoring of information, particularly that of the death toll, which created a false impression about the virus's severity.[10] In February 2021, a team led by WHO and Chinese experts began to investigate whether the virus was engineered in or accidentally released from the Wuhan Institute for Virology (WIV), known for international collaborative research, not far from the seafood market first thought to be its originating spot.[11] On May 26, 2021, President Joe Biden ordered the intelligence community to further inquire into the origin of the virus in Wuhan and report back within ninety days. The inconclusive evidence of this "Wuhan lab" investigation, however, did not stop Fox News from reporting that the virus "likely started as an attempt by the Asian country to show its virological capabilities."[12]

Emerging from these US outbreak narratives was the figure of the People's Republic of China (PRC) as a powerful agent that manifested contradictory political effects.[13] First, the communist party-state appeared to excel at controlling the spread of information, especially at the beginning of the outbreak.[14] Later it also seemed quite efficient in containing the spread of the virus, exemplified first by the lockdown of Wuhan and later still by the centralized coordination of relief efforts, which kept the numbers relatively low compared to more developed nations like the United States (at least prior to the ending of the zero-COVID policy in December 2022). Speculation about China's underreporting undermined the notion that the powerful Chinese state has contained the virus as effectively as claimed. At the same time, such speculation also reinforced the image of the CCP as a masterful manipulator of information.

This contradictory presence of the Chinese state in American public discourse forms the central object of study in *Disorienting Politics: Chimerican Media and Transpacific Entanglements*. To be entangled, feminist philosopher Karen Barad tells us, "is not simply to be intertwined with another . . . but to lack an independent, self-contained existence."[15] In this interdisciplinary book, I examine a set of media artifacts and processes that enact what I call *transpacific entanglements*. At once economic, political, cultural, and ecological, these entanglements of China and the United States are constantly brought into view through audiovisual media that stem from the American context but traverse national boundaries in their production, circulation, and consumption. I shall argue that the prevailing tendency among wide-ranging cultural producers and commentators to render the Chinese state an Other in ideological opposition to the United States[16]—a process I term *racialization*—precludes the possibility of engaging these entangled relations as grounds for imagining politics anew.

Nowadays, it is not uncommon for Euro-American journalists and academics alike to describe China as a "rising" power. Oftentimes, these depictions of China combine myth and reality to conjure a chimera of sorts that straddles the realms of materiality and imagination. A case in point is the above-mentioned Fox News attribution of the coronavirus's origin to China's "virological capabilities." While the scientific grounding for the "lab leak" theory remains disputed, US media reportage of this kind has contributed to the heightened public perception about China's role in creating and spreading the coronavirus pandemic.[17] Meanwhile, evidence has surfaced that the US National Institutes of Health (NIH) provided long-standing funding for the New York–based nonprofit Eco-Health Alliance, which distributed part of the grant to the WIV (the "Wuhan lab" in question) to "study bat coronaviruses collected in the wild and examine their potential to jump to humans."[18] What ostensibly demonstrated the virological prowess of China turned out to be a conjoined effort involving both American and Chinese entities.

Pandemic-generated narratives of this kind crystallize the construction of the Chinese state as an actor *co-constituted* with the myriad processes that extend beyond geopolitical boundaries to bring the two superpowers into at times an uncomfortable unity. A more critical inquiry into the making of "rising" China in the first two decades of the twenty-first century in US media, which culminated in the "China virus" rhetoric of the COVID-19 moment, therefore demands a more precise set of analytical vocabularies for illuminating the complex interactions between border-crossing media and place-bound politics. Indeed, terms like "American media" and "US politics" are ultimately inadequate in depicting the media artifacts and processes at work in enabling the figure of "rising" China to exert political impact. For this reason, I've found it necessary to define several key terms deployed in this study that would help us unpack the transpacific entanglements of the two superpowers captured by the term "Chimerica."

"Rising" China and Chimerica

What motivated me to adopt "Chimerica" to describe US-China entanglements is my observation that the particular mode in which the PRC manifests itself in contemporary American life cannot be simplistically examined *as representation.* For one thing, the figure of "rising" China frequently assumes an *absent presence* in American-originated media, exerting an influence even when invisible.[19] A case in point is a *Huffington Post Entertainment* video released on its YouTube channel on August 28, 2015, starring the then Republican presidential hopeful Donald Trump.[20] The three-minute clip, which cuts together Mr. Trump seeming to chant the word "China" 234 times with little additional content, went on to garner over 17 million views. While the mash-up implies China's increased presence in US politics, "China" does not appear here in the form of images but as a repeated sonic gesture. This manner of appearance does not immediately figure the geopolitical entity of the PRC, since the invocation of "China" is devoid of any concrete references to the nation-state. Nonetheless, the segment is distilled from an ongoing media discourse that positions China as the source of US problems, to which Trump's campaign contributed in no small part. Indeed, this absent presence of a sonically rendered "China" stems from the profound material connections that have entangled the two superpowers, especially in the first two decades of the new millennium.

These connections prompted economists Niall Ferguson and Moritz Schularick to coin the term "Chimerica" in 2007 as a way to reference the symbiotic relation between China and the United States.[21] Evocative of the mythological figure of chimera, the portmanteau has been subject to insightful critique (see chapter 1) and perhaps even become more problematic during the Trump-era trade war and the subsequent delinking efforts that escalated since the onset of the pandemic. Nonetheless, the term is continuously invoked among US-based China scholars and watchers alike, suggesting the persisting potency of the coinage in capturing the multiple ways in which China and America have been bound up, even at a time when decoupling has become the dominant narrative.[22]

For instance, when James Palmer from *Foreign Policy* used "Chimerican dream" in an essay about the American-born skier Eileen Gu, who won gold for China during the 2022 Winter Olympics in Beijing, he meant to invoke a clashing rather than an alignment of values that threatened to pull a married couple apart. Yet his description of Gu as an offspring of "the Chimerican elite" clearly stems from the profound interconnectivities between the two nation-states.[23] After all, Gu's mother, Yan Gu, is the daughter of a Chinese government official who emigrated to the United States three decades ago and once worked as a venture capitalist in San Francisco specializing in China-related investment. Eileen Gu, the (then-to-be) Stanford student, spent much of her time growing up traveling back and forth between the two countries. She also has sponsorship deals with numerous Chinese and American companies, including China Mobile and Victoria's Secret. She is even more popular on the Chinese social media site Weibo than she is on Instagram and has frequently appeared on the state-run China Central Television.[24] Behind Gu's success story, therefore, are myriad border-crossing movements of people, money, goods, and images that render it nearly impossible to distinguish her solely as an American or a Chinese. Indeed, the media frenzy surrounding her stardom across two sides of the Pacific has made "the Chimerican Dream" a most apt caption for Palmer's piece, despite the uncertain prospects of US-China relations.[25]

For this reason, I have appropriated "Chimerica" as a shorthand for the multiple entanglements that connect the two superpowers, whose most salient manifestations can be found in the first two decades of the twenty-first century. As I discuss in chapter 1, despite the apparent mystification in its coinage, the term, which among other things has become the title for an award-winning play analyzed in this book, can be usefully deployed less as a descriptor of economic symbiosis than as an imaginary construct.[26] To many, "Chimerica" evokes the figure of chimera from Greek mythology, a fire-breathing beast with a lion's head, a goat's body, and a serpent's tail. This is a figure that feminist scholar Donna Haraway has also employed in her classic formulation of the cyborg—"a condensed image of both imagination and material reality" for our "fabricated" existence that fuses machines with organisms.[27] Hybrid and ephemeral, "Chimerica" offers a powerful metaphor to capture the ways in which "rising" China manifests its racialized presence in twenty-first-century America. It is a most apt term to capture a conjoined mode of being that binds the two superpowers in these two decades, signifying the multifaceted entanglements that can be discerned through what I call transpacific media.

Chimerica through Transpacific Media

In the United States, the first two decades of the twenty-first century may be remembered as a period that began with the September 11 terrorist attacks in 2001, the 2008 subprime mortgage crisis, and the COVID-19 outbreak. The same period is also marked by China's 2001 entry into the World Trade Organization (WTO), the hosting of the 2008 Beijing Olympics, and the US-China trade war in 2019. Juxtaposing these events may readily invoke a common sentiment among the Sino-American scholarly community that a "declining" America now confronts the ascending superpower that is "rising" China. Nevertheless, attending to the proliferating, border-crossing media forms that shape and are shaped by the increased presence of China in America offers a rather different picture.

Chimerican entanglements through media, to be sure, had existed well before the beginning of the twenty-first century. Literary scholar Richard Jean So, for instance, has noted the role of communication technologies such as telegraphy and radio in the interwar decades (1930s–1940s) in "heightening the feeling that the two nations existed within a shared, simultaneous reality."[28] Likewise, the first two decades of the twenty-first century saw the rapid expansion of internet-based media, particularly social media and online streaming, on both sides of the Pacific. Despite the persistence of the digital divide, or the uneven distribution of access to digital tools, personal media devices such as mobile phones have penetrated many parts of the world, leading to what is often dubbed the "supersaturation" of media. According to philosopher Mark Deuze, we literally "live *in* media," and this "media life includes much more than media hardware, software and content—it is also everything we do with and in response to media."[29] During the COVID-19 pandemic, the meanings of media life have arguably become more keenly felt. Many of us are now accustomed to participating in social life through media in newly configured time and space, maintaining relationships with distant family and friends, communicating with coworkers from afar, engaging in education and entertainment, and experiencing (mis)information overload.

Deuze's definition of media life resonates with what other media theorists have come to call *mediation*—the idea that media are better thought of as processes, not things (see chapter 1). If the meanings of media have always been heterogeneous, the rethinking of media as mediation also highlights the fact that the digital media landscape we inhabit is made up of material objects that shape and condition our encounters with seemingly immaterial media contents.[30] With this in mind, it is hard not to notice the ubiquitous presence of "China" in twenty-first-century American media life. The majority of our cell phones, laptops, tablets, and other personal technologies bear the "Made in China" label, albeit accompanied by "Designed in California" in the case of Apple products.[31] Likewise, China provides numerous invisible infrastructural elements that underpin our internet connectivity, from cables to routers, from wires to electricity outlets. Arguably, these elements become visible only during such controversies as the US decision to perceive the Chinese telecommunications company Huawei as a national security threat and ban its 5G networks. Until recently, China has also been a primary destination for recycling global e-waste, often generated from functioning electronic gadgets that are deemed obsolete.[32] Contributing to this are the accelerated cycles of planned obsolescence promoted by corporate tech giants like Apple.[33]

These material conditions of a media life permeated by "rising" China call for a re-conception of media that does not simply understand them as textual representations of a "rising" China already pre-formed. To be sure, media that bring Chimerica into visibility often take the form of conventionally understood media contents, encompassing such artifacts as election campaign ads, popular films, shows, and journalistic accounts. Yet much like Trump's "China chanting" video, they do not always make visible the figure of China directly; neither are they necessarily the collaborative results of Chinese and American people, businesses, and governments. Rather, they stem from the material entanglements that bind the lives of so many people in the two countries even as these media appear to have originated from the United States. As such, they manifest the co-constitution of "rising" China as a figure shaping and shaped by transpacific mediation.

A key aspiration of this book, then, is to deepen the conversation between cultural studies and new materialisms. Informed by the desire to carefully engage nonhuman agents and the material world—the hallmark of new materialisms—*Disorienting Politics* remains dedicated to a cultural studies approach to the production of meanings within a globally uneven power matrix. At the same time, it also seeks to unpack how the materiality of media helps shape the discursive construct of China as a racialized Other in the US context. As such, it echoes film and media studies scholar Caetlin Benson-Allott's observation that media discourses "are deeply 'entangled' in material culture."[34] It is with the sensitivity toward this entanglement that I have come to theorize media that manifest Chimerica as a kind of *transpacific* media. That is, they *capture* the complex mediation processes that characterize the Pacific as a space of Chimerican—among other Asian and American—encounters.

Unlike "transnational media," a more commonly used term to denote media contents and technologies that move across geopolitically defined national borders, transpacific media are artifacts and processes that emanate from the Pacific Ocean as a "contact zone" of voluminous "traffic in peoples, cultures, capital, and ideas between 'America' and 'Asia.'"[35] If the transnational often reifies the national framework even as it seeks to destabilize it, the "oceanic framework" that is the "transpacific," as literary scholar Lily Wong argues, de-emphasizes "the authenticity of national or cultural origins, since currents are produced collectively and through the process of contact."[36] Much like anthropologist Monica DeHart's study of the multiple development efforts of the PRC, Taiwan, and the Chinese diaspora in Central America, I embrace such a "transpacific analytic" because it "illuminates not only much more complex, diverse histories and experiences but also more capacious visions of the future worlds they might engender."[37] Instead of highlighting the movement of media across nation-specific territories, as does the phrase "transnational media," the concept of "transpacific media" draws attention to the co-constitution of media and their agents of production.

In this book, I use "Chimerican media" to describe a particular genre of transpacific media that bring Chimerica into visibility. These media, congealing myriad processes of transpacific mediation, help to produce Chimerica, an imaginary place without a real geographical referent. As such, they enact the "imaginable ageographies" that literary scholar Tina Chen discusses in "(The) Transpacific Turns," an epistemic "remapping" that breaks through the limits of the territorial nation-state to invite new critical inquiries into previously "understudied relationships."[38] Embodying the interactions between state-bound politics and transpacific media, "Chimerica" simultaneously gives shape to and stems from the powerful agency of the Chinese state. Its mythological reference to chimera is also evocative of the not infrequent characterization of "China" as an antihuman (rights), subhuman, or superhuman actor in US media reportage of the party-state's actions, not least those during the COVID-19 pandemic, exhibiting what Asian Americanist Belinda Kong calls "bio-orientalism."[39] Indeed, the coronavirus crisis has cast into sharper relief this elusive and yet racialized presence of the Chinese state, reflecting a kind of "transpacific asymmetry" that Chen stresses.[40] This moment perhaps prompts a more urgent need than ever to critically examine the material and discursive making of Chimerican media and the ideological work they perform in co-constituting the figure of China in US media life.[41]

Racialization and Orientalism

Chimerica, in other words, invites us to scrutinize the complex processes of amalgamation that have helped to construe the Other that is "rising" China. My engagement with this "animation" of the figure of the Chinese state thus echoes cultural critic Mel Chen's project in *Animacies* to seek "productive openings" for rethinking "notions of governmentality, health, and race beyond a national framework."[42] Chimerican media artifacts offer a glimpse into the transpacific entanglements that challenge the dominant understanding of the state as a self-contained body politic in international relations.[43] And "rising China"—with "rising" suggestive of a masculine undertone—as a figural formation that is entangled with the American body politic, in turn facilitates the racialization of the disembodied entity that is the Chinese state. To be sure, the state is routinely represented by its leader in real politics, even as its bureaucratic components take nonhuman forms.[44] But for this study, I wish to emphasize that the racialized formation of the Chinese state in American media life connects to but also *exceeds* the immediate embodiment of the state in the (male) leader representing it.[45]

A prescient artifact that enacted this racialization during the COVID-19 outbreak was the slogan "China lied, people died." Reminiscent of the phrase "Reagan lied, people died" from the 1980s AIDS pandemic in the United States, the phrase appeared as a hashtag on Twitter and Instagram. It also became the name of a Facebook group dedicated to boycotting Chinese goods. T-shirts with the phrase available for sale on Amazon were even rumored to be manufactured in China. In one version of the T-shirt, the five golden stars on the Chinese national flag are rendered in the shape of the widely circulated image of the coronavirus.[46] The potency of the Chinese state, as implied by its position as a "liar," is conflated with the virus itself, while the attribution of deaths to China's act of lying obscures the numerous structural reasons that have caused the loss of so many lives in the United States.

One can easily dismiss this slogan as another example of the anti-China rhetoric promoted by right-wing media and political pundits. But the tendency to heighten the authoritarian character of the Chinese state is much more widespread, as may be seen in the *New York Times*'s coverage since the beginning of the Wuhan lockdown.[47] Conventionally, "Sinophobia" has been the default name for politically charged "fear of China," though much like "homophobia," such "fear" often manifests itself through hatred. This perception of China as a geopolitical menace, as historian Gordon Chang argues, is long intertwined with Yellow Peril, the stereotyping of the Chinese/Asian population as an economic and cultural threat.[48] The critique of Sinophobia, however, often falls short in offering a satisfying explanation as to how the revulsion against the Chinese state, which has seen a spike during the pandemic, impacts racism against people who reside in or are perceived to have come from China.

A case in which Sinophobia and Yellow Perilism are inadequate categories when analyzed in isolation was the nationwide protest against anti-Asian racism in the aftermath of the Atlanta spa shootings on March 16, 2021. Scholars such as sociologist Kimberly Hoang have insightfully linked the tragic death of eight individuals, including six women of Asian descent, to the long-standing racialization and sexualization of Asian women in the United States.[49] But the incident, as cultural studies scholar Juan Alberto Ruiz Casado points out, also took place at a time of rampant "dehumanizing anti-China narrative."[50] The critique of the attack and its surrounding media coverage through either the lens of Yellow Perilism or Sinophobia appears insufficient in accounting for the historically specific context in which it occurred—namely, a moment of "rising" China. For this reason, I contend that the distinctive ways in which the PRC manifests its presence in Chimerican media demand greater analytical precision. I have opted to use *the racialization of the Chinese state* to describe the dominant mode in which China appears here, with the awareness that it is distinguishable but not separable from the racialization of Asian people.

The term "racialization" typically describes the process by which a dominant group differentiates a subordinate population from themselves as a basis for systematized discrimination, subjugation, oppression, and colonization. It operates through the ideological (and often visible) construction of nonwhite bodies as different from, and therefore inferior to, normative whiteness.[51] While the Chinese state is commonly represented by the leader figure in international affairs, it more often manifests itself in American media life through nonhuman or disembodied forms. How, then, can this adoption of the term "racialization" be justified?

In this book, my use of the term "racialization" refers to a mode of address predicated on a dichotomous understanding of the American Self and the Chinese Other. Informed by an ideological opposition between liberal democracy and authoritarianism, this mode of talking about China operates through the naturalized assumption that between the political norms set by the US state and the party-state of China, there are fundamental if not irreconcilable differences. While many would trace the lineage of this othering of China to the Cold War, I argue that introducing the analytic of race—which is about the relation *between people*—to the realm of international politics helps to illuminate the uneven power dynamics *between nation-states*. Naming this othering as racialization lends a degree of precision to the formation of "rising" China in American media life in the first decades of the twenty-first century. Propagating this racializing discourse are not only right-wing media and political commentators but also wide-ranging cultural producers based in, affiliated, or interacting with institutions in the United States, regardless of their national origins. Here, I am less interested in identifying and accounting for the kinds of actors who partake in this racializing discourse than in mapping a rhetorical pattern that bespeaks its ideological potency. Tracing the historically specific formation of "rising" China in the beginning years of the new millennium, my goal is to explore how this figure presents diverging effects on our political imagination within the United States and beyond. Herein lies a key layer of meaning for "disorienting" in the book's title—that is, the figure of China to some extent defies the long-standing, well-rehearsed framework of Orientalism.[52]

Postcolonial theorist Edward Said famously devised "Orientalism" to examine a "style of thought" that shaped nineteenth-century European and twentieth-century American representations of people in the Middle East.[53] These representations, from novels and paintings to journalistic reportage, served as a means to justify colonial conquests and occupation. As I show in chapter 2, the lens of "Orientalism" and its updated variations regarding Euro-American representations of Asia remain useful in discussing the presence of "rising" China in Chimerican media.

Nonetheless, the framework is limiting in that it often presumes the object of representation to be a static entity.[54]

In conversation with Said's legacy, cultural studies scholar Dan Vukovich, among others, has delineated a China-specific Orientalism at work in post–Cold War US Sinological knowledge production. What Vukovich calls "Sinological-orientalism" corresponds to the period from the 1970s to the 2000s, which saw "a confluence of capital, China, and Sino-Western relations and flows."[55] If this form of Orientalism operated through an implicit assumption that China ought to become the same as the West, Vukovich has discerned, in his subsequent *Illiberal China*, a refusal on the part of the Chinese state to adopt "the liberal universalist model or norm."[56] Echoing Vukovich's careful consideration of "China" as a *dynamic* entity, *Disorienting Politics* observes the phenomenon of "rising" China in the first decades of the twenty-first century primarily from the US context. My approach therefore resonates with sociologist Ching Kwan Lee's call for China studies to "abandon its methodological nationalism" and expand its "empirical boundary" to encompass places "beyond China's territorial borders."[57] Acknowledging that the examination of Chimerica in the Chinese context would deserve a separate treatment beyond this book, I nonetheless pay attention to the ways in which Chinese entities, from state actors (chapter 3) to media audiences (chapter 4), also partake in enacting Chimerican entanglements. No longer merely an object that awaits orientalist (mis)representation, "China" at once participates in the making of Chimerican media and appears prominently therein as a racialized Other. What I term the "racialization" of the Chinese state thus simultaneously invokes the making of a *subject* and highlights its frequent *object*ification.

COVID-19 and the (Chinese) State

To further discern the workings of this racialization, it is important to turn closer attention to the US media obsession with China as *the place* where the pandemic began. On March 18, 2020, a reporter at the White House news conference questioned President Trump about his use of the term "Chinese virus" on the basis that "ethnicity" does not cause virus. Trump responded, "It is not racist at all . . . it comes from China. . . . That's why . . . I want to be accurate."[58] Here, the understanding of China as a place of origin for the virus legitimizes the use of "Chinese" as a modifier. The latter lends itself to the interpretation that the entity of China—encompassing the state and its people—has had some sort of role to play in causing the virus. It is telling that immediately afterward, Trump declared that he would not tolerate what "China tried to say at one point," that "American soldiers" created the virus: "That can't happen. Not as long as I am president."[59] His emphasis, then, has the effect of attributing agency—that of the creator of the virus—to the Chinese counterpart of the US military, namely the Chinese government.

In subsequent public speaking, Trump clarified that he had no intent to antagonize Asian Americans: "These are incredible people. They love our country."[60] The inadvertent use of "they" versus "our country" betrays the long-standing ideological depiction of Asian Americans as perpetual foreigners, despite their presence in the nation since the nineteenth century. Asian American scholars and activists have painstakingly demonstrated the othering effects of this ideology—among them the 1882 Chinese Exclusion Act as the first race-based immigration ban—across a wide spectrum of cultural productions, both historically and in the present.[61]

While the intensified racism against Asian Americans in the COVID-19 crisis and beyond warrants continuous attention, the racialization of the Chinese state calls for an equally careful but somewhat different scholarly treatment. As is the case with President Trump, it has become common practice to condemn the racial stereotyping of the Chinese/Asian American people while maintaining the accusation against the Chinese state. "Blaming the Chinese for the Coronavirus is racism, blaming the Chinese government for it is not,"[62] says Johns Hopkins University sociologist Ho-fung Hung, echoing a sentiment shared by many. President Joe Biden, during his 2020 campaign, also released an ad with the tagline "Trump didn't hold China accountable."[63]

This widely circulated "hold China accountable" narrative deserves some unpacking. Hung, for instance, asserts that racial stereotyping may be "counterproductive to the effective containment of the disease," but such a recognition "should not prevent us from discussing the China-origins of the virus and blaming the Chinese government for causing this global public health crisis." Drawing a comparison between China's Great Famine of 1959–1961 and the coronavirus outbreak, Hung centers his critique on the "draconian censorship" of the authoritarian state. He also references the successful containment of the disease in Taiwan, highlighting the role played by its democratically elected government. "Holding Beijing and the political system it represents accountable is not Sinophobia," Hung continues. "It is our responsibility if we want to prevent similar global disasters from ever again starting in China or any other authoritarian country."[64]

Not unlike Trump's statement that casts China as a virus creator, the emphasis on authoritarianism here attributes agency to the Chinese state. Yet by highlighting that the US government should "*hold* China accountable," the narrative also shifts the power back to the American, liberal-democratic state. A global public health crisis, then, is recast as a political contention between Chinese authoritarianism and American democracy, rehearsing a long-standing dichotomy dating to the Cold War. Yet how exactly China can be held responsible for the suffering and loss of American lives remains unclear. The headline "Trump Blames China for Acting Too Late in Coordinating US Coronavirus Response," on the satirical news site *The Onion*,[65] is telling of this deflection of responsibilities, given that the head of the Chinese Center for Disease Control—modeled on the American entity—had reportedly notified his US counterpart about the uncontrollable tendency of the outbreak as early as January 3, 2020.[66]

Certainly, the obfuscation of COVID-19-related information on the part of Chinese authorities—whether in the interests of avoiding public panic or driven by the desire to manage the nation's global image—is a subject to critique in its own right. In the US context, however, it is important to note that the "hold China accountable" narrative also obscures other alternatives about what the state's role can and should be in a global pandemic. One such alternative, for instance, may point to the capacity of the Chinese state to effectively contain the virus within Wuhan in 2020, which contrasts with what writer George Packer called "a failed state" in the United States.[67] It may also reference Taiwan's National Health Insurance system and state-organized contact tracing, which, as cultural studies scholar Catherine Liu argues, not only provided the infrastructural foundation for combating the spread but also boosted "public confidence in science and the government's commitment to social welfare."[68] The condemnation of the authoritarian character of the CCP regime, which also operated as a dominant framing device for reporting the Wuhan lockdown,[69] works to suppress a different vision for the state that the figure of "rising" China also helps to produce—namely, as a force for securing the public good (see chapters 2 and 3).

As the word's Greek etymology implies, "crisis" invites decision on the part of an agent. The "hold China accountable" narrative circulating in the COVID-19 crisis, which paints the Chinese state as a creator of the virus, a censor of information, a regulator of economic mobility and personal freedom, works to solidify the American state as *a particular kind of agent* in response to a global health crisis. Naming the foreign origin of the virus—a conventional tactic of the outbreak narrative that "articulates community on a national scale"[70]—helps to justify the early travel ban from China, which strengthens the image of the Trump administration as a protector of national sovereignty and economy. Calling out China's suppression of information also helps to exonerate the Trump administration from potential charges against its lack of early response. What these accounts leave open are questions about the state's responsibility in a public health crisis in particular and its role in the national community more generally.

The lesson of COVID-19, then, is that a place as distant as China may not be so distant after all. Indeed, the making of Chimerica—as the convergence of a distant place and a space created by mediation—prompts us to recognize the "intimacies" (to borrow a term from American studies scholar Lisa Lowe) between the two superpowers.[71] Recognizing this entanglement, I argue, is crucial for envisioning politics in *relational* terms. Such recognition, for one thing, might have served as a substitute for the disregard for sufferings in a faraway place like Wuhan.[72] The US response to the crisis might have also looked a little different if "China" had been approached as less a racialized Other than a politically relevant place quite close to home.

Relational Politics and Racial Capitalism

What I set out to argue in *Disorienting Politics*, again, is that the political implications of a racialized Chinese state are no less important than those of overt racism against Asian Americans. One way to discern the effects of "China" in contemporary America, as I show in chapter 1, is to analyze the production of Chimerica in transpacific media. This imaginary place, much like the media that give shape to it, is not characterized by fixity. Rather, it is better understood as constellations of the dynamic forces that I have come to call Chimerican entanglements. As part of the "transpacific entanglements" formulated by Asian Americanists Yến Lê Espiritu, Lisa Lowe, and Lisa Yoneyama, Chimerican entanglements invite "us to link apparently separate subjects, contexts and issues whose connections have been rendered unavailable by existing geographical, political, and disciplinary boundaries."[73] Such a sensitivity to transpacific relationality encourages an approach to "China" not as a preformed object to be represented but as an agent that helps to produce Chimerica. A careful engagement with the emergence of this agent, therefore, may allow us to *disorient* politics—that is, to imagine a political elsewhere.

Like media, the meanings of politics are also heterogeneous. Typically, politics with a capital "P" finds disciplinary homes in political science, international relations, and public policy, encompassing electoral and other activities associated with the state. Meanwhile, politics with a lowercase "p" more often concerns humanists and interpretive-minded social scientists focused on investigating how uneven power relations in society are perpetuated along such differences as class, gender, race, ethnicity, sexuality, and disability. More often than not, the ways in which these power relations are maintained have to do with how dominant groups help make the world appear in a manner that perpetuates the hierarchical status quo. In this sense, politics is ultimately a project of world making, informed by competing understandings and representations of the world order.[74]

In my interdisciplinary vision, "Politics" and "politics" are deeply intertwined. Politics with a capital "P" is almost always shaped by particular locales, whether local, regional, or national. From electing government representatives to street protests for social justice, from voting on local legislation to the defense of homeland against foreign enemies, what mobilizes these forms of political engagement is often a specific connection to a place, geographically defined. At the same time, scholars of globalization have long paid attention to the effects of transnational media on politics with a small "p." As communication scholars such as Manuel Castells and Terhi Rantanen have argued, when we experience other places through media, our sense of belonging often becomes less tied to the places we inhabit and more dependent on the spaces created by communication.[75]

This "deterritorialization" of identities, national or otherwise, has profound implication for politics with a "P." Anthropologist Arjun Appadurai has spoken of globalization's effect on politics as a "disjuncture" between the nation and the state, since various "-scapes"—flows of media, technologies, finance, people, and ideologies—have come to defy the territorial bounds of Politics and politics.[76] Building on this idea, I have argued elsewhere that we should pay attention not only to the morphing of national identities in globalization but also to the cultural effects of globalization on the state.[77]

The presence of "China" in the United States enacts a case in which place-based Politics becomes imbricated with deterritorialized politics. The numerous accounts about China's role in the COVID-19 crisis can be seen as part of an expansive repertoire of Chimerican media that, I argue, offer competing visions of the state. In chapter 2, for instance,

I trace the portrayal of the Chinese government as an owner of US national debt in popular media and campaign ads after the 2008 financial crisis. The depiction of China as a socialist Other through what I call "fiscal orientalism" has also come to function in the COVID-19 crisis as an ideological alibi for the lack of, among other things, a health care system that delinks public well-being from private profits.

It is in this sense that the racialization of China in Chimerican media takes place at the intersection of place-bound Politics and deterritorialized politics. The nonhuman entity of the Chinese state can be othered precisely because its entanglement with the American body politic is manifested through complex processes of mediation. Appearing in multifarious forms, the chimerical presence of China in these seemingly American-originated media generates different understandings of what the state means for the nation and what a national community might look like once the role of the state is thus reimagined.

The imagination of the national community has long been associated with media.[78] In this book, I am interested in how "rising" China produces political effects when the place of the nation becomes entangled with the space created by transpacific media. "Space and place," as Mark Deuze reminds us, "are best understood as under permanent construction . . . something continuously and concurrently made, sustained, remixed and taken apart by the very people and things that make up that ecosystem."[79] This conjoined making of space and place is clearly manifested in the COVID-19 outbreak, when Trump's constant invocation of the "China virus" enables a distant place to threaten the American body politic, even the body of the president himself.[80]

What the transpacific space of Chimerica offers is precisely "an index of space of contestation and dissensus" that, according to sociologist Andrew Barry, defines "the political."[81] This spatial understanding of the political is instructive for connecting a place-bound Politics of the state with the politics of world making (see chapter 4). As communication scholars Kent Ono and Jiao Yang suggest, "If real democracy is to thrive, nations and scholars must create an open, peaceful, social and discursive environment in which disagreements exist rather than seek a world without differences."[82] The re-conception of the state as a cultural formation, therefore, encourages us to discern the *different* possibilities of politics beyond the limiting framework of the nation, which retains a default status in shaping how we think about the political.

Disorienting Politics therefore joins other transpacific scholarship in the hopes of contributing to the global project of decolonization.[83] The transpacific, as Richard Jean So puts it, "is a place in motion, filled with people, ideas, objects, technology, and texts."[84] In Tina Chen's words, the "transpacific turns," with "turns" invoking "both things and action," can activate a more critical sensibility toward "some of the uneven and overlapping histories, power dynamics, and cultural forms that collectively compose the transpacific."[85] The word "disorienting" is thus meant to highlight the ways in which the liquid environment of the Pacific challenges our terrestrial understanding of places as default grounds for politics (see the conclusion).[86]

The meanings of "disorienting politics" in this book are twofold and intersect cultural studies scholar Sara Ahmed's *Queer Phenomenology* in significant ways. First, as Ahmed points out, referencing postcolonial theorist Frantz Fanon's encounter with the white gaze, racism produces a feeling of disorientation among people of color when the space of interaction is normalized around whiteness. Specifically, "Orientalism involves the transformation of 'farness' as a spatial marker of distance into a property of people and places."[87] It is by facing this direction of the Orient—in this case the "far east" that is China—that the nation (such as the United States) "coheres" into a collective.[88] In this sense, "disorienting politics" *describes* the racializing effect that the othering of China produces within the American context, as may be seen in the attack against Asian bodies perceived to be from China—and therefore "out of place"—during COVID-19. At the same time, Ahmed suggests that "disorientation can move around; it involves not only bodies becoming objects, but also the disorientation in how objects are gathered to create a ground, or to clear a space on the ground."[89] The second meaning of "disorienting politics" therefore reflects my aspiration to challenge the ground on which place-specific forms of identity politics are often based so as to create different kinds of collectivities. The book is, in other words, an invitation to consider the transpacific linkages of places, people, media, and environment as a fluid basis on which to construct what I call *relational politics*.[90] So why should we focus our attention on an emerging, if not much-fetishized, hegemon in the transpacific when the framework is meant to generate more investigations into counterhegemonic formations and alternatives?

It is important to note that the motivation for inaugurating the field of "transpacific studies," for American studies scholars Janet Hoskins and Viet Thanh Nguyen, is in part to address the impact of "rising" China on "the rapid transformation of what transpacific competition and struggle means" in light of new formations such as the Trans-Pacific Partnership

(TPP)—the US agreement with twelve countries in the Pacific region—to contain China.[91] Anthropologist Biao Xiang, a contributor to Hoskins and Nguyen's volume, has used the term "the Pacific paradox" to describe the "deeply intertwined and mutually enhancing" aspects of Sino-American "socioeconomic integration," on the one hand, and "political, ideational, and military tensions," on the other.[92] In the Chinese context, the Pacific paradox gave rise to a distinctive perspective, what Xiang calls "neo-statism," which "sees the state as the primary and unquestionable frame within which society should be organized," in the process taking the state as "the central referent in making sense of the world.[93]

There is, therefore, an intricate link between the Pacific—what literary scholar Yunte Huang calls "an absolute, abstract, contradictory and differential space"[94]—and the geopolitical outlooks on the part of the two superpowers engaged in regional imaginings. "Cross-Pacific tensions," Xiang reminds us, "do not stem from the fact that China and America are too different, but from the fact that they are too similar; not because the two are too far apart, but because they are tightly connected."[95] If the Pacific indeed points to the inseparability of these two geopolitical entities, how transpacific media—of which Chimerican media is part—inform specific refashioning of the state in the US context is precisely what *Disorienting China* intends to investigate.

To be sure, the failure for Obama's White House to ratify the TPP and the withdrawal of the United States from the trade deal in 2017 provided perhaps yet another indicator of America's "decline" vis-à-vis China's "rise" in the Asia-Pacific wherein the latter's effects can be quite viscerally felt.[96] Meanwhile, even as China has applied to enter the TPP in 2021, there are visible efforts on the part of the Chinese state to carve out a China-centered world order through, for example, the "One Belt, One Road" initiative officially launched in 2013 seeking to build up infrastructural, communicational, and financial networks in Asia, Africa, and Europe. At this particular conjuncture, it has become rather difficult to still cast China in the position of the subaltern, one that awaits the representation of the dominant power. It is for this precise reason that I have attempted to offer the alternative perspective that the figure of "rising" China is co-constituted with Chimerican media, as an actor *and* as an object.

At the same time, rethinking China as an agent does not mean that Chinese and American entities are on an equal footing in generating Chimerican media artifacts. After all, aside from those related to Chinese language learning (see chapter 3), there are almost no Chinese-produced media contents that have circulated and gained as much mass popularity in the United States as the Netflix show *House of Cards* has in China (discussed in chapter 4). Furthermore, the racialization of the Chinese state in the COVID-19 outbreak clearly demonstrates that the uneven power relations embedded in Chimerican entanglements work to privilege certain visions generated by "rising" China over others.

As Tina Chen reminds us, attending to the "uneven contestation" of the transpacific can enable us to discern how it may create "the conditions for both the perpetration of injustice and the possibility of pursuing a more just world."[97] A desire to account for the asymmetrical power matrix indeed informs my decision to limit the choice of my objects to those that primarily originate from the American context, though in a manner that does not take for granted the national boundaries of their production, circulation, and reception. In so doing, I wish to unpack the racialization of the Chinese state in what Taiwan-based cultural studies scholar Kuan-Hsing Chen calls "the imperial center" that is the United States.[98] My approach therefore resonates with Ivan Franceschini and Nicholas Loubere's understanding of "Global China as method," which regards "China as intimately entangled with global histories, processes, phenomena, and trends."[99] Meanwhile, by drawing specific attention to Chimerican entanglements as key components of these global interconnectivities—or what the late historian Arif Dirlik calls "complicities,"[100] I also wish to shed light on how the PRC figures in the workings of US imperialism. As Ho-fung Hung notes, "China's low-cost manufactured exports and investment in US government debt under the Chimerica formation became an ever more important economic and fiscal foundation of US empire-making."[101] Examining the presence of "rising" China in America in the two decades of the new millennium is one way to delineate a path toward deimperialization from within the United States in conjunction with the movement for decolonization more broadly.

In the spirit of bringing the often incommensurable transpacific entanglements into a dialogue to produce new decolonizing visions, I argue that the racialization of the Chinese state can be usefully engaged as part of the long-standing workings of racial capitalism. For Lisa Lowe, "The term racial capitalism captures the sense that actually existing capitalism exploits through culturally and socially constructed differences such as race, gender, region, and nationality, and is lived through those uneven formations."[102] Drawing on disparate archives in the late eighteenth to the early nineteenth centuries, Lowe's account reveals how the freedom of the "human" promised by Western liberalism is predicated on the dehumanizing subjugation of people of color in Africa, Asia, and the Americas through colonialism, slavery, and imperialism. Following historian Cedric Robinson, she argues that the practice of racial capitalism "refuses the idea of a 'pure' capitalism external to, or extrinsic from, the racial formation of collectivities and populations, or that capitalism's tendency to treat labor as abstract equivalent units does not contravene its precisely calibrated exploitation of social differences and particularities."[103] Capitalism, in other words, has always been racial capitalism in that its social organization relies on the systematized subjugation and oppression of racial others.

While the understanding that capitalism is racially organized has been eclipsed in the Asian/China studies fields until recently,[104] Asian American studies, a critical-activist academic formation in the 1960s, has long engaged the question of difference as it relates to capitalist production, American imperialism (in Asia, among other Third World sites), and US citizenship. Relatedly, communication scholars such as Robeson Taj Frazier have come to connect the revolutions in China to a global anti-imperialist, decolonizing movement in which African American radical intellectuals like W.E.B. and Shirley Graham Du Bois actively participated.[105] In light of these disparate but interconnected struggles against racial injustices, the transpacific turn can be productively engaged for approaching "China" as a site of political alterity, one that disrupts the normative understandings of politics along the lines of Sino-US relations.[106]

Bringing "rising" China together with the critique of racial capitalism helps to illuminate not only how the racialization of the Chinese state results in overt racism against people of Asian descent in Euro-America but also how it aids in the deflection of government responsibilities for those already subject to preexisting systemic inequalities. In the United States, members of the working class, many of whom are people of color, are disproportionately vulnerable to the threat of infection because their employment in such essential entities as grocery stores and hospitals require their physical presence. Many are also more likely to bear the brunt of long-term economic consequences for lack of savings, paid leave, and access to affordable health care. While these preexisting unequal conditions have not solely stemmed from the effects of China's "rise," neoliberal globalization has certainly played a role in enabling corporate decisions to offshore much of the manufacturing base in America to China, subjecting the Chinese workers—also people of color—to the global system of exploitation.[107]

Amid the COVID-19 crisis, the rhetoric of decoupling between China and America begins to surface more prominently in official and popular accounts alike. Yet as economist Isabella Weber suggests, the breakup of the Chimerican economic interdependence means no less than "a complete reorganisation of a large chunk of the world's production," given that even in the aftermath of the US-China trade war, China still supplied 45 percent of computers and tablets as well as 54 percent of mobile phones globally.[108] The (aspiringly) emerging post-pandemic moment therefore also becomes an opportune one to reflect on the chimerical presence of China in American media life. "Self-isolation is key if we are to stop the pandemic," writes historian Kate Brown, "and yet the need for isolation is, in itself, an acknowledgement of our deep integration with our surroundings."[109] In similar ways, any attempt to delink America from China also implies the recognition of the deep entanglements of the two superpowers in the decades leading up to the pandemic. As Richard Jean So observes in comparing the twenty-first century to the interwar period of the last century, "Once again, the relationship between America and China appears to define our notion of the Pacific as an essential region for imagining the fate of the world."[110] At the time of this writing, many of us in the United States are again able to experience the long-suspended sensation of breathing each other's air. The recent memory of our physical distancing and the ongoing reality of our mediated communication may well instruct us to more deeply reflect on the transpacific entanglements of China and America through Chimerican media.

Overview of Chapters

Chapter 1 lays out the theoretical foundation for this book by examining British playwright Lucy Kirkwood's 2013 award-winning play, *Chimerica*. A fictional account about an American photojournalist who took the famous "Tank Man" picture on Tiananmen Square in 1989, the play's twisted plotline allegorizes the asymmetrical power matrix that continues to shape the racialized (and gendered) visibility of China in America. Drawing particular attention to what I call a "disorienting affect"—an embodied response—generated by *Chimerica*'s London production, which featured a rotating cube with projections on its exterior, I analyze the enactment of *relational space* in the play to explain how the nonrepresentational presence of China disturbs the place-bound notion of politics. The chapter mobilizes key scenes in the play to illustrate the ways in which media emerge as dynamic processes rather than as static entities that serve as instruments of (mis)representation. Delineating the play's critique of individualism, I highlight its vision for a collective citizenship whose emphasis on breathing connects the Black Lives Matter movement in the United States and anti-pollution activism in China, a point that returns in the book's conclusion. My analysis thus points to Chimerican entanglements as a basis for imagining politics beyond the dichotomy of democracy versus authoritarianism. It provides the conceptual road map that prepares the reader for the subsequent chapters, each of which more closely examines the economic, cultural, political, and ecological facets of Chimerica.

Chapters 2, 3, and 4 take up economic, cultural, and political Chimerica as different aspects of Chimerican entanglements, with the understanding that these facets are closely intertwined even as they are separated here for analytical purposes. Chapter 2 focuses on economic Chimerica by analyzing the discourse of US national debt owed to China in popular films like *The Martian* and political campaign ads that invoke a menacing "Chinese future." I propose *fiscal orientalism* as a new framework–supplementing the techno-orientalist one centering on Japan in the 1980s—for understanding the racializing logic underlying this discourse, as it perpetuates a historically specific form of *indebted* citizenship. Probing the political-economic conditions that gave rise to these accounts, I argue that the economic interdependencies invoked by Chimerica masked the continual subjugation of the Chinese economy to the dollar regime during this time. The othering of the Chinese state as a foreign creditor in fiscal-orientalist discourses thus aided in offering an ideological fix for a crisis of the US state under neoliberal financialization. This othering discouraged alternative means of imagining the national community and the role of the state within it.

Moving from economic to cultural Chimerica, chapter 3 focuses on the transpacific imagination of the Chinese language as a future lingua franca. On the one hand, the performative display of Chinese fluency by an increased number of white figures—from Mark Zuckerberg to Arabella Kushner—in US media culture reflects elite Americans' desire to equip themselves and their offspring with the linguistic currency of Chinese so as to secure a future dominated by China. On the other hand, politicians and political commentators have perceived China's establishment of Confucius Institutes as a cultural "invasion" of the United States. Yet this state interest in building a "linguistic power" by promoting Mandarin learning globally is informed by the American-originated concept of "soft power." The instrumentalization of language in both is linkable to the neoliberal ethos of privatization, which has not only internalized individual self-help as a primary means to secure one's future but also reduced the budget for language education in US public schools, rendering them more willing to accept the influx of Chinese funds. Contrasting these practices is the cult sci-fi TV series *Firefly* (2002–2003). Set in an Anglo-Sino future of 2517, this short-lived production from the early years of economic Chimerica (i.e., after China's 2001 WTO entry) features a group of space outlaws who communicate occasionally in mixed Chinese dialects. Continuing to accrue fans through streaming sites and a film sequel over the years, the show conjures a different relationship between language, culture, and power. As a Chimerican media artifact, its playful linguistic crossing and fandom bring forth an alternative vision of culture that reflects and challenges the deficit of collectivity under neoliberal globalization.

Chapter 4 turns to political Chimerica by analyzing the Netflix political drama *House of Cards* (2013–18) with an emphasis on its linkages to China. My study of the show and its engagement with China highlights the workings of Chimerican media in enacting a relational space. This space can be discerned through the multifaceted ways in which *House of Cards* is received in China and how "China" manifests itself in the series, especially in season 2. The emergence of Netflix as a distinctively globalizing data-driven media platform with a keen interest in entering the Chinese market has informed the production, distribution, and reception of *House of Cards*, reflecting the co-constitution of "rising" China with transpacific media. Symptomatic of the logic of surveillance or platform capitalism, predicated on the extraction of data for profit, the show points to the depoliticization of politics that corresponds to the individual, consumerist ideology of neoliberal globalization. My analysis of the transpacific encounters enacted in the show also illuminates media as not just an instrument for representing politics but an environment in which politics takes place. Recognizing this political entanglement of the two superpowers, then, encourages a rethinking of politics as the making and enactment of reality in a media environment permeated by algorithms.

In the conclusion, I engage the ecological entanglement of the two superpowers as a way to connect the previous three chapters and to further situate the racialization of the Chinese state in the global context of racial capitalism. To do so, the chapter focuses on breathing, a bodily act so often prematurely denied to people of color globally, as seen in the making of "I can't breathe" as a slogan for Black Lives Matter and in the deadly effects of air pollution in China. Connecting China's pollution to its manufacturing of communication technologies in America's media life, including the smartphone, which became a central artifact in various social movements in both countries during the pandemic, I turn attention to the materiality of air, which crosses the Pacific to bring China and America into an eco-unity. I argue that the Pacific, like the Chimerican media examined in this book, can also be grasped as a media environment that enacts Chimerican entanglements. These entanglements invite a relational approach to politics that more carefully considers the interconnectivity between the body and the world in envisioning new forms of state and citizenship.

CHAPTER 1

Chimerica and Chimerican Media

I first saw Lucy Kirkwood's award-winning *Chimerica* at London's Almeida Theatre, where it premiered in June 2013. The set, as I recall, consisted of a giant, revolving white cube with multiple sliding panels. As the play went on, the panels opened and closed, allowing the inside of the cube to be turned into different interiors—an apartment in Beijing, an office in Manhattan, the backstage of a strip club, and a fish stall, among others. During scene changes, the spinning cube seemingly worked as a vessel transporting the audience from one geographical location to another, from one moment in history to the next. The external surfaces of the cube often became screens onto which multiple press photos were projected. Sometimes they offered clearly identifiable markers of places, whether it was a factory in China or Chinatown in New York City. Other times red ink marks likening editorial traces were superimposed over the pictures, as if to accentuate their status as products of photojournalism.[1]

The staging of *Chimerica* was among the most memorable experiences of my trip to London for the annual meeting of the International Communication Association that year. The play struck me as a clear enactment of media's role in shaping the experience of globalization. After all, journalistic photographs, among other media artifacts, enable their audience to travel to different places without actual physical movement. Ideas like the "global village," "time-space compression," and "time-space distanciation" are among the best-known academic terms to describe this feeling of being brought closer to events that are happening afar.[2]

What is now known as the Tank Man photo is one such artifact that has brought China and America into closer, even if imagined, proximity. The picture, showing a lone protester facing down a row of parading tanks during the mass protests at Tiananmen Square, Beijing, first appeared on the *Los Angeles Times* front page on June 5, 1989, before becoming featured on the cover of *Time* magazine and in other media outlets. On both the poster for the play *Chimerica* and the cover of its published script, this iconic image is a looming backdrop for the title—a term Kirkwood has borrowed from historian Niall Ferguson's book *The Ascent of Money*.[3] The coinage, amalgamating the English names of the two superpowers, immediately brings to mind the elusive, hybrid creature in Greek mythology, with a lion's head, a goat's body, and a serpent's tail. It also references the Tank Man picture as "a photograph of one country by another country,"[4] an artifact that enacts a representational relationship between the two superpowers. China was the place where the photograph was taken. Yet it is by way of American journalists and media corporations that it achieved tremendous global circulation.

The Tank Man photo, therefore, is a paradigmatic example of what I call "Chimerican media" artifacts in this book.[5] These are objects congealing the processes that bring the entanglements of the two superpowers— signified by the term "Chimerica"—into greater visibility. Naming them Chimerican media, however, does not imply that they are an outcome of equal and mutual exchange between China and the West. After all, the play, the source of inspiration for its name, and the Tank Man photo are all products of Euro-America even as they feature China, implicitly or explicitly. London as a long-standing cultural capital of world stature also provides a privileged backdrop for cultural productions of this kind. As communication scholar Yuezhi Zhao points out, the discursive environment that has prefigured Kirkwood's play and its success on the London stage is very much in line with "the transnational media's initial framing of 1989 as a Chinese struggle for American-style liberal democratic capitalism."[6]

American hegemony, in other words, shaped the milieu from which the Tank Man emerged as an iconic sign. After all, "The recursive mark of man and tank" in the picture, as media studies scholar Bishnupriya Ghosh suggests, "naturalized a culturally particular aspiration (the demand for political rights from a regime that had lost its revolutionary horizons) into a universal human condition (everyone wants democracy)."[7] Its status as a "news photo" lays claim to "the image's ground of representation" by offering the viewer a "sense of being present in Tiananmen Square." Bespeaking "China's location in the political imaginary of the United States," the man in the picture, "embodying racial difference in constant ekphrastic descriptions of the slight man, would affirm the geopolitical unevenness necessary for neoliberalism's vision of progress."[8] Highlighting the structural asymmetry of America vis-à-vis China, Ghosh's analysis echoes the assessment of communication scholars Robert Hariman and John Louis Lucaites that the Tank Man photo "subordinates Chinese democratic self-determination to a liberal vision of global order," thereby "limiting the political imagination regarding alternative and perhaps better versions of a global society."[9] The uneven relations of power that condition who gets to represent whom and on whose terms, well documented especially in wide-ranging scholarship informed by Edward Said's *Orientalism*, is there from the start.[10]

At the same time, the sense of amalgamation that the term "Chimerica" evokes also disturbs the default national frames we often bring to media and cultural analysis. Much like the revolving cube in the London production, Chimerican media artifacts like the Tank Man photo conjure Chimerica as a hybrid entity that interweaves the *place* of the nation with the *space* created by transpacific communication. As such, they generate what feminist theorist Sara Ahmed calls "moments of *disorientation*"; phenomenologically, they "can offer us the hope of new directions."[11] Kirkwood's play, therefore, provides methodological inspirations for approaching Chimerican media as sites through which to better discern the economic, cultural, political, and ecological entanglements of the two superpowers. These entanglements point to the specific ways in which "rising" China manifests itself in contemporary American media life. Crucially, the play as a performative artifact aptly reveals the distinctive appearance of China in Chimerican media beyond the framework of representation, as its absent presence is more often *enacted* rather than represented. Moreover, the play's plot allegorizes the uneven relations of power that continue to shape the visibility of China in America, as a hypermasculine subject but also racialized object whose agency is always intertwined with transpacific mediation.

Chimerica/Chimera

Chimerica, as drama scholar Christine Kiehl describes, is a "three-hour long political epic" that "covers two decades of intricate Sino-American relations in five acts and thirty-eight scenes, portraying thirty-three convincing characters in no fewer than twenty-seven settings."[12] Despite its complexity, it is not the only theatrical production inspired by the "rising" China discourse in twenty-first-century Euro-America. Other examples include *China: The Whole Enchilada*, written by Mark Brown, which won the Outstanding Musical Award of the 2008 New York International Fringe Festival, and renown Asian American dramatist David Henry Hwang's *Chinglish*, which opened in New York in 2011.[13] Nonetheless, what I found most inspiring in *Chimerica* is its more explicit engagement with media life as it is lived across the Pacific when compared to other plays. After seeing it in London before it moved to the West End for a sold-out run, I then had the opportunity to see *Chimerica* again in Washington, DC, in 2015, where it was restaged. Various subsequent productions also took place in other cities outside the UK, such as Chicago (2016), Sydney (2017), and Vancouver (2019). A thoroughgoing comparison between the play and others of similar concerns certainly deserves a detailed treatment on its own. My intent here, though, is to mobilize the visually and conceptually stimulating production in the UK as a means to introduce and clarify a set of vocabularies that I find useful for examining the figuring of China in twenty-first-century American media life.

The play's title, while inspired by Ferguson's work, clearly departs from its original coinage, if not "invalidates" it as a utopian fantasy.[14] As a portmanteau, Chimerica first appeared in a coauthored piece by Ferguson and Moritz Schularick, who used it to describe a paradoxical condition. The inclusion of Chinese (and other Asian) labor into the global economy, the authors argue, has increased not only the profit margins of US corporations but also Chinese excess savings. The latter, when combined with exchange rate depreciation, has helped to keep US and global interest rates low, which in turn benefits international businesses.[15] After the 2007–2009 financial crisis, Ferguson and Schularick pronounced that this "financial marriage" previously deemed "perfect" must come to an end in order to bring back the "equilibrium" within the global economic system.[16] In 2018, when President Trump started a trade war with China by announcing a series of tariffs on Chinese imports, Ferguson coauthored (with Xiang Xu) another piece titled "Make Chimerica Great Again." Suggesting the emergence of "Chimerica 2.0," now a "marriage of equals" more than "a marriage of opposites,"[17] the authors argue that China must concede to the trade war in order to avoid a divorce of Chimerica, which would negatively affect not only the two largest economies but also the world at large.[18]

Given the prescriptive undertones in Ferguson's accounts, the neologism is more usefully seen as an ideologically laden product of its time than as an accurate prophecy of a new world order to come. As Yuezhi Zhao suggests, not only does the notion of Chimerica obscure "the historical status of the US dollar as a global reserve currency backed up by US global military power," but it also mystifies "the nature of transnational production in the neoliberal global economy."[19] Adopting a "nationalist" framing that reifies the saving or lending habits of so-called East and West Chimericans, the conception leaves little room for "thinking about the transnational class interests or social divisions within the nation-state."[20] Much like the figure of chimera that it evokes, the concept mystifies more than it illuminates, even though its potency can still be felt in the "decoupling" narratives that ensued amid escalating US-China tensions.

While Kirkwood has adopted Ferguson's neologism as the title, she makes no pretense that her play is a work of the imagination: "It is a fact there was a Tank Man. It is a fact that photographs were taken of him. Beyond that, everything that transpires in the play is an imaginative leap."[21] The term "Chimerica" is not once invoked in the script; its absence perhaps serves as an invitation for the audience to partake in the wide-ranging possibilities of meaning making that this neologism can set in motion. Likewise, the Tank Man photo that is the centerpiece of the puzzle also retains a sense of instability. "There are at least six recognized versions," according to Kirkwood, aware that several journalists took different but similar pictures of the Tank Man back in 1989. The protagonist Joe Schofield, an American journalist who took the original picture in the play, she insists, is "purely a fictional construct," just as "the play takes place in an imagined universe."[22]

The play's twisted plot mirrors these shifting identities of the Tank Man, its maker, and indeed "Chimerica" itself; their referents are hard to pin down and seemingly always in the making, not unlike what literary scholar Tina Chen has noted about the transpacific as a "fluid" terrain.[23] Joe was a nineteen-year-old intern in Beijing when he captured the Tank Man on camera. Now in his forties, he finds himself covering the 2012 US presidential election for a major American newspaper (unnamed in the script but quite likely referencing the *New York Times*). Upon learning from Zhang Lin, an old friend from Beijing, that the Tank Man may still be alive and has moved to America, Joe is determined to find the man so that he can complete a follow-up story. In the process, Joe falls in love with Tessa Kendrick (Tess), a British business consultant he met on a plane to China. As Joe's search for the Tank Man continues in New York City, he confronts a series of ethical dilemmas and even resorts to blackmailing a progressive female senator in order to track down a source of donation to her campaign. His obsessive action also results in the criminalization of two undocumented Chinese immigrants living in Chinatown. Meanwhile, Joe's friend Zhang Lin in Beijing battles the haunting memory of his lost wife while attempting to expose the government's corruption in regulating air pollution. Zhang's activism on- and offline ultimately leads to his imprisonment when the American company hosting the site for his online post nonchalantly reveals his identity to the Chinese police.

At the end of the play, Joe's effort ends in vain, for he discovers that all this time he has been tracing a different "unknown hero"—the soldier in the tank who disobeyed the order to kill the man in front of it—a figure within the Chinese state apparatus that is, one may add, almost entirely absent in US discourses surrounding the Tank Man photo.[24] Joe's "voyeuristic impulse and possessive instinct" to "capture" the Tank Man again also unwittingly disrupts his relationship with Tess,[25] who helped a Western credit card company profile its potential consumers in the much-coveted Chinese market before turning to offer free publicity aid to the Occupy movement. On the eve of a New York gallery opening for a show featuring Joe's work, he receives a personal recording of Zhang Lin from Zhang's nephew. As the recording reveals, the Tank Man is none other than Zhang Lin himself, and the plastic bags he carries in the picture contained the clothing of his pregnant wife, who died on June 4, 1989.

For those who have seen a live performance of the play, a summary like the above hardly does justice to this densely packed "thriller," as Kirkwood herself described it.[26] One London critic, among others, pointed out that the "revolving white cube set with superimposed logos, slogans, video film and location shots that transcends time" generated "seamless scenes which are so fast paced, and, at times, barely digestible."[27] Matching this layering of images was the play's blending of numerous themes and genres. In the words of another critic, *Chimerica* "takes the formula of the romantic comedy, gives it a bittersweet twist, and plants it in the arid terrain of international politics."[28]

With its complex and nonlinear plotlines, *Chimerica* understandably invited criticism. As Paul Levy wrote in his review of the play in the *Wall Street Journal*, its "virtue is that it doesn't simplify—but that is also a fault of this remarkable play."[29] On the one hand, "The characters are complicated: Is Joe an idealist artist or a self-serving hack?"; on the other, "So many things are going on and being said that you can really only get all of them by reading the script."[30] The problem appeared to be more severe in its restaged version at the Studio Theatre in Washington, DC. "After three-hours-plus of lumbering exposition," Peter Marks wrote in the *Washington Post*, "you leave the playhouse on 14th Street no more enlightened about the sprawling piece's host of 'serious' concerns than when you arrived."[31]

Among these diverging responses, a feeling of disorientation—or what may be called a *disorienting affect*—appears to be quite commonly shared. This visceral reaction indeed resonates with my own viewing experience of the play's London and DC productions. In fact, I found the dazzling, affective intensity of the London performance—conveyed through its distinctive stage set—to be largely lost in the US version, where projections were limited to a few small and discrete flat screens on the stage. The mesmerizing layering of images and cinematized movement between locations in the London production appeared to have offered a boost to the dynamism of the plot twists and shifting identities of the characters. Without the sense of being transported to different places and times, "the subtleties of how the Chinese and American governments and people see each other" felt indeed "oversimplified" in DC.[32]

This disorienting affect, as I will argue, is a key characteristic of Chimerican media that Kirkwood's play encourages us to recognize. Numerous moments in *Chimerica* produce such affective features by way of *enacting*, and not just *representing*, Chimerican entanglements. "It is important [the Tank Man] is Chinese . . . but we cannot see this from the photograph," writes Kirkwood. "It is important it was taken by an American . . . but we cannot know this simply by looking at it."[33] The entanglement of the image and its producer, Kirkwood seems to suggest, is not immediately visible from the artifact itself. The Tank Man, then, is an American-produced artifact that is nonetheless Chimerican; its making allegorizes the ways in which China manifests itself in Chimerican media. No longer a mere object to be represented, China herein emerges as an actor whose agency is entangled with Chimerican media. To grasp this particular mode in which China appears in Chimerican media, however, requires a rethinking of media as mediation—that is, less as things than as processes. The play *Chimerica*, again, provides some cues for such a methodological reconsideration.

Media as Mediation

In their 2012 book, *Life after New Media*, Sarah Kember and Joanna Zylinska propose mediation as a "key trope for understanding and articulating our being in, and becoming with, the technological world, our emergence and ways of interacting with it, as well as the acts and processes of temporarily stabilizing the world into media, agents, relations, and networks."[34] Central to this intervention is the inversion of the relationship between media as objects and the mediation process. Conventional scholarship on mediation, as summarized by communication scholars Nick Couldry and Andreas Hepp, tends to presuppose a separation of media and society.[35] Reversing this "static model" of mediation as "an intermediary layer" between the two, Kember and Zylinska propose the alternative that "mediation is the originary process of media emergence, with media being seen as (ongoing) stabilizations of the media flow."[36] Photography, among other media forms, is therefore recast as "an active practice of cutting through the flow of mediation."[37] It is not merely a technological instrument independent from life that transforms social events into objects but is rather part of the process that "*produces* life forms."[38] This refiguration of photography as a vital site of becoming is vividly displayed in *Chimerica*.

Notably, what drives the plot of the play is the photographer's knowledge that the Tank Man in the picture is *alive*. It is Joe's quest for this "unknown hero" now living in the United States that sets in motion a series of events that enact the numerous entanglements of China and America. These events are themselves animated by a vast array of media technologies, networks, platforms, and institutions that co-constitute the relations among distant people and places. In this sense, the absent presence of Chimerica in the play points to the historically distinct mode in which the figure of China is enmeshed in American media life.

To be sure, the mediated presence of China in the United States has a history that dates far back before 1989. The twentieth century, indeed, has seen continuous news reportage of China in the American press, with President Richard Nixon's 1972 visit there being among the most recognized moments. Nor did the 1989 Tiananmen Square incident initiate China's reintegration into the global economy, which can be traced to the 1978 beginning of the Dengist policies of Reform and Opening Up.[39] Nonetheless, for communication scholar Guobin Yang, June 4 was a "defining moment of China's entry into the age of global media."[40] As sociologist Craig Calhoun points out, during this time the "China story" achieved "the single most sustained visibility of any Third World country ever in the press of Western Europe and the United States."[41] Understandably, "the awareness of a global audience was an important factor in keeping the student protestors in the Square."[42] Global news media did not just transmit pre-constituted events in Tiananmen Square but contributed directly to their making. Rather than serving as static representations of reality, the media coverage of the events is better seen as engaging in a process that has partaken in the creation of Chinese reality.

An early "split-screen" scene in the play *Chimerica* points us toward such a rethinking of media as mediation. On June 5, 1989, nineteen-year-old Joe, overlooking Tiananmen Square from a hotel room window, telephones his mother, Susannah, as she watches the news on television in the United States. When Susannah questions Joe about his decision to go to China during this turmoil, Joe relays his experience from back in Philadelphia, where the protest "looked like it was a party or something" on TV.[43] When Susannah is informed (by Walter Cronkite) that "three hundred people" have been "gunned down by their own government," Joe contends the death toll is a "Hell of a lot more than" reported.[44] Right at this moment, Joe spots a man carrying grocery bags standing in front of the dozen tanks that are rolling in. He begins to take pictures as Susannah worries for his safety. Only minutes before a group of Chinese soldiers storm in to smash the camera, Joe manages to hide the roll that contains the Tank Man photos in the bathroom after replacing the film with another.

At first glance, this scene conveys a sense of the intense danger faced by Western journalists at the hands of ruthless Chinese soldiers. It also reflects a long-standing obsession with the death toll in the square, something that remains disputed among historians and journalists alike.[45] Rather than dwelling on this politics of death, however, Kirkwood has portrayed Joe as being lured to Beijing by the "party-like" protests on television. In instances like this, Joe is no longer positioned as a "user" of media set out to "document" the event. Instead, his agency is activated within a "technological environment" of which he is part.[46] The photographer, much like the event itself, emerges through a "co-constitution" with global news media.[47]

The plot of *Chimerica* also goes on to undermine Joe's privileged status as a Western photojournalist in relation to the pictures he takes. During a scene in Joe's apartment after Barack Obama's winning of the 2012 presidential election, Joe and Tess engage in a conversation about the waning "heroism in the world."[48] "You can't shock anyone into any-thing, not any more [*sic*]—" Joe says, lamenting that horror movies have rendered young people "inert."[49] When Tess responds with sarcasm, Joe continues to rationalize his search for the Tank Man:

The idea that horrifying people can change anything is, it's bankrupt, it's been disproven, so I'm just looking for a, a different angle. A different kind of picture. Not of darkness, but light. I think that could be a, a *good* thing.

[*pause*]

Those pictures I showed you, they make noises, at night. I don't mean ghosts, not Scooby Doo, ectoplasm, all that crap. But they do make noises. Sometimes I think I'll just burn them . . .[50]

Here, the pictures that Joe has taken—of the Tank Man, of a trade unionist in Colombia, and of a Palestinian woman in protest—are depicted as taking on lives of their own. Their "noises" disturb, even motivating their ethically conflicted creator to go on a quest for the Tank Man so as to capture that hero in a new light.

Photography is thus not so much tied to "the passage of time and death" as conventionally understood; instead, it is to be thought of "more productively in terms of vitality, as a process of differentiation and life-making."[51] As if to demonstrate photography's "proximity to life itself,"[52] after the conversation about the burning of the pictures in *Chimerica*, Joe and Tess make love and Tess becomes pregnant as a result. Photography is thus rendered as a force that *makes* life, enacting mediation "as another term for 'life,' for being-in and emerging-with the world."[53]

The afterlife of the Tank Man photo in the age of the internet, which extends far beyond China's geopolitical confines, perfectly illustrates the vitality of photography. As is well known, the Chinese state has long been censoring the "June 4th" discourses across wide-ranging media platforms within the real and virtual borders of China. Yet the Tank Man image continues to return in multifarious forms and via online circulation, especially during commemorations of 1989. Cultural studies scholar Margaret Hillenbrand has argued that the Tank Man "lives on in China as the grit in the clam of the public secret for the very reason that his remakes are more or less unsearchable."[54] Reappearing in transmedial "photo-forms," often orchestrated by diasporic Chinese artists, "Tank Man may be more iconic in the nooks and crannies of digital China, the place that has supposedly 'forgotten' him, than anywhere else."[55] Elsewhere, the Tank Man icon has also been appropriated or referenced in political cartoons,[56] even appearing in the publicity of such mass protests as the Occupy movement and in media coverage of Black Lives Matter (BLM) in the United States. In 2019, not long before the thirtieth anniversary of the June 4 events, the German camera company Leica released a controversial commercial named "The Hunt" that depicts the "heroic" role of Western photojournalists in documenting non-Western social injustices. Prominently featured in the ad is none other than the Tank Man photo, though it only appears at the end of the commercial as a reflection in the lens of the camera.[57]

Such a transnationally vibrant afterlife of the Tank Man picture epitomizes Kember and Zylinska's notion that "it is only with globalization that media become truly moving, that they gain a new level of intensity, that they are 'lively' at last."[58] Mediation, understood in this way, offers an analytic to examine the relationship between Chimerican media and Chimerica in this book. If Chimerica names the multiple entanglements of the two superpowers, Chimerican media are artifacts, practices, and discourses that capture the mediation processes that bring these entanglements into being. They point to a *co-constitution* between the agents of media production—whether it's the Chinese state or American news organizations and journalists—and the media products themselves. In this sense, they reflect an understanding of entanglement that cultural theorist Rey Chow describes as the "relativization of agency," which rests on the complicated "relationships among things, among things and humans, and among different media," especially "in the age of digitization."[59]

What, then, does this conception of Chimerica as entanglement offer in terms of thinking about the political implications of China as a "rising" figure in America? "One outcome of entangled relationships," for Chow, "would be the fuzzing-up of conventional classificatory categories due to the collapse of neatly maintained epistemic borders."[60] Turning attention to Chimerican media is one way to challenge such conventional "epistemic" borders separating (Asian) American studies and China/Asian studies, echoing the critical possibility of "the transpacific turns."[61] Approaching Chimerican media as a process of transpacific mediation allows us to disrupt the geopolitical and ideological distinction between the two superpowers that, as I have discussed in the introduction and further analyze in the remainder of this book, delimits China's global visibility. This approach relies on a critical engagement with the changing relationship between politics, place, and space. The making of *relational space* in the play *Chimerica* indeed corresponds to the elusive presence of "China" in American media life, a figural formation that exerts political effects in conjunction with Chimerican media.

Chimerican Media and Relational Space

Writing within a decade of the 1989 events, anthropologist Ralph Litzinger suggested that an important question raised by the Tiananmen Square protests was "how to theorize the place of the transnational media in the cultural politics of 1990s China."[62] The term "place" appears to contrast sociologist Craig Calhoun's understanding of the protests as simultaneously tied to Tiananmen Square as a physical location while being extended to the "placeless (or 'metatopical') space of the international information flow."[63] These diverging views point to communication scholar Terhi Rantanen's observation that mediated globalization has increasingly enabled space and place to overlap with each other, creating "*splace*" as a result.[64]

Echoing this notion of "splace" is cultural studies scholar Scott McQuire's concept of "relational space," a daily experience that came about "with the intensive development of media and communication technologies in the second half of the century." Relational space, for McQuire, refers to "the social space created by the contemporary imperative to actively establish social relations 'on the fly' across heterogeneous dimensions in which the global is inextricably imbricated with the face-to-face."[65] Contemporary media life and the communicative space it affords, in other words, enable a kind of openness to interconnectivities beyond one's immediate locales. With this in mind, the layering of images on the exteriors of the white cube in *Chimerica* can be seen as enacting the process by which Chimerican media render the boundaries of inhabited places malleable, whether it's Beijing or New York, China or America. What potentially results are new ways to establish social interactions beyond one's geographical confines.

The encounter between Joe and Zhang Lin toward the beginning of *Chimerica* offers a glimpse into this production of relational space in Chimerican media. In this scene, Joe meets Zhang Lin at Tiananmen Square, in front of the giant Mao portrait, having just returned from his assignment to a Chinese factory. He asks Zhang Lin if he has "been to one of those places," where women are found "earning like fifty dollars a month, working fifteen-hour days, sleeping on the floor." In response, Zhang Lin shares the story of his brother, who has moved up to the position of a foreman and even has a son attending Harvard.[66] Upon hearing how "guilty" Joe still feels, Lin sneers and says, "We all blame you too," stating that "a girl leaves a village in Hubei to work on a production line. . . . It's not because she has a burning passion for supplying Americans with telephones. It's because where she's coming from is worse and where she's going to is better." Joe continues: "Sure and getting sick, and mistreated, and sleeping twenty to a room, having to leave their loved ones behind on the way—" "Like on the Mayflower," replies Zhang Lin. Joe disagrees: "But they're not travelling to a whole new country, / this isn't a—" to which Zhang Lin responds, "Of course they are. It just occupies the same part of the atlas as the old one."[67]

Here, the dormitory-factory compound in which rural-to-urban migrants in China reside—indicated by the photograph of a building façade on the surface of the white cube—is a peculiar kind of space. This is a space in which what communication scholar Jack Qiu calls "iSlaves" work overtime to churn out large quantities of First World consumer electronics.[68] While the products they assemble enjoy global mobility, their lives are more often characterized by "immobile mobility," which media studies scholar Cara Wallis has used to describe "a means of surpassing, but not erasing, limiting material conditions to gain inclusion in expanded and enriched social networks."[69] The exchange between Zhang Lin and Joe here at once recognizes the migrant workers' upwardly mobile potential—documented in popular accounts like journalist Leslie Chang's *Factory Girls*—while pointing to the price and limit of their mobility. Interestingly, as Zhang Lin insists, the workers are indeed "moving to a new country." That "country," it would appear, is none other than "Chimerica," an imaginary space without a real geographical referent, despite the fact that it "occupies the same part of the atlas" as China.

Resonating with Tina Chen's notion of the transpacific as less terrestrial than oceanic remapping that invites attention to power asymmetry,[70] this making of Chimerica as a relational space is fraught with tensions. Chinese migrant workers' capacity to "travel" to Chimerica without leaving China goes hand in hand with their subjection to the excruciating exploitation of the global electronics industry, which the Chinese state indirectly supports; the immediate economic benefit offered by their job opportunities is hardly justified by the inherent uneven power relations that condition their mobility. A subsequent plotline on Joe's attempt to place the new "Tank Man" story in the newspaper for which he works similarly reveals these tensions. At first, Joe's boss, Frank, refuses to feature the new "Tank Man" story in the weekend edition of his paper, a media outlet that is increasingly under the commercial pressure to focus on "Lifestyle and leisure."[71] Joe's colleague Mel then comes to the rescue, proposing that they "take a whole 'God Bless America,' 'land of the free home of the et cetera' angle." Mel's pitch below piques Frank's interest because it can now become a story "about America":

"because this man, strike that, this *hero*, brave, noble, persecuted, he escapes from this supposedly superior country, and where does he go? Not London, not Mumbai, not Moscow. He comes to New York. To the States. Because so what if our economy's stalling, our power is ebbing, one thing won't change: America means freedom, it means rights, set down in a constitution, to speak, to protest, to be an individual, it is, and will always be, the homeland of heroes."[72]

In this segment, a profit-driven American media outlet's initial disinterest in the Tank Man as a "Chinese" hero is salvaged by its potential transformation into a news piece about the economically troubled United States as a defender of rights and freedom. Yet a later segment works to offset this attempt at reconstituting America's national subject position, increasingly perceived by many to be in decline.

This follow-up scene takes place in Washington Square Gardens, where Frank, a previous anti-Vietnam-War-protester-turned-cynical-newsman, demands that Joe and Mel drop the "Tank Man" story. The reason given is that Verico, the company that owns Frank's newspaper, is looking to expand in Asia and would not want to jeopardize its plans to obtain Chinese "investment capital." Outraged by this "collusion," Joe accuses Frank of scheming "to run a newspaper with less transparency than the *People's Daily*" when he is "supposed to be a guardian of a free fucking press."[73]

As Kirkwood reminds us via Frank's reminiscence, Washington Square Gardens is the locale for anti–Vietnam War protests in Frank's youth. This reference echoes Joe's comment in another scene that "the Vietnam War wasn't lost on the battlefields of Vietnam" but "was lost in the living rooms of America" and "because of photographs."[74] Joe's belief reflects a widely circulated nostalgia for an "uncensored war,"[75] a myth that is debunked by recent scholarship.[76] Yet the invocation of the Vietnam War nonetheless points to the imbrication of the politics of place and the politics of space within the imaginary landscape of Chimerica. The protests in Washington Square Gardens and Tiananmen Square against the actions of their respective national governments are both place-specific expressions of political dissent. Yet as the enactment of mediation in *Chimerica* has shown, this kind of place-bound politics has become increasingly intertwined with the communicative space created by mediation. In both cases, the materiality of the square as an infrastructural foundation of the public demonstration is to some extent dematerialized as the events themselves become mediatized, much like the superimposition of photos on the exterior of the cubed stage transforms physical boundaries into portals to other places and times. This imbrication of the mediated space and physical place creates a precondition for the making of relational space.

Furthermore, the Washington Square Gardens scene allegorizes the subtle ways in which "rising" China manifests its presence within the relational space of Chimerica. Though fictional, the role of Verico in the play indexes the real-world deal struck by Rupert Murdoch with the Chinese party-state when attempting to expand the Chinese market for News Corp.[77] The extraterritorial entity that is China, therefore, is positioned as an agent who impinges upon the US national public sphere by means of its lure as a booming marketplace. Importantly, this agent does not appear as an object of representation but works to produce an *erasure*—that of the Tank Man. Such a practice is not uncommon in Hollywood's negotiation with Chinese censorship, among other global media productions, where contents deemed "sensitive" by China's censorship bureau are asked to be removed so as to ensure approval for release in China.[78] The Verico scene, much like the "Mayflower" segment that came before, thus inspires us to critically engage China's *absent presence* in Chimerica, which does not always manifest itself in direct representational forms (see chapters 3 and 4).

This absent-present mode in which China appears has important political implications. For one thing, it departs from the dominant narrative of China "rising" stemming from both sides of the Pacific, whose distinctively masculine undertone I will examine further in chapter 4. In this way, it introduces a gender lens that illuminates the uneven power relations shaping China's appearance in Chimerican media, which I theorize as a form of *racialization* in this book (see the introduction). This gender lens is also latent in Kirkwood's play in ways that resonate with––even complicate—Rey Chow's argument that Tiananmen 1989 was a moment in which "China as a spectacle . . . becomes, in its relation to the West, 'woman.'"[79]

Reflecting on the "overdetermined" relationship between Western media and the student protests—what I have suggested as a form of mediation, Chow invoked what she called the "King Kong syndrome" to describe the mediated event in which China became "the site of the 'raw' material that is 'monstrosity,'" one that works to affirm the notion that "ideology exists only in the 'other' (anti-U.S.) country."[80] This production of a "Third World" spectacle for "First World" TV viewers reinforces the dichotomy between China and the West by creating an othering effect predicated on "what China 'lacks': democracy."[81] In Kirkwood's play, set in the United States nearly three decades later, the idea of China as a gendered Other is simultaneously reckoned and challenged, particularly through the actions of the female characters. If the "Chimerica" title is imbued with a sense of monstrosity reminiscent of King Kong in its reference to chimera, its hybrid form also invites a rethinking of China less as a distinctive Other than a formation entangled with Chimerican media.

Gendering "Rising" China

In *Chimerica,* Joe first obtains the lead that helps him locate the Tank Man via two ads placed in a domestic Chinese newspaper by Feng Meihui and Jimmy Wang, two diasporic Chinese living in New York City's Chinatown. One ad reads, "In memory of the mothers who lost on 64" and the other, "To Wang Pengfei. The Unknown Hero of the Square."[82] As referenced on the accompanying website for the play, Kirkwood appears to have drawn on an actual news story back in 2007, which reported that a "June 4th" ad was able to surpass censors due to the ignorance of a young editorial staff member.[83] This young journalist is reincarnated in the play as Mary Chang. Having lost her job and fallen for a scheme of human traffickers, Mary Chang later came to New York and worked as a stripper in the Garment District. Wishing to obtain a job offer at Frank's newspaper, she eventually became his mistress.

The soundtrack that accompanies Mary Chang's stage entry—as a dancer in silhouette—is tellingly the parodied "oriental" guitar tune from David Bowie's 1983 hit song, "China Girl." Here, the categories of "China" and "woman" converge in interesting ways via mediation. Ostensibly, Mary Chang's geographical displacement from China is followed by the subjection of her body to the ready-made exotica of "China Girl" in America, which Bowie's lyrics subtly critique. Yet her stage appearance is an intriguing amalgamation between body and screen, sound and image. This synthetic entrance brings to mind literary critic Anne Anlin Cheng's "ornamentalism," a term she uses to describe a distinctive mode in which the "yellow woman" is racialized as "a human figure that emerges as and through ornament."[84] Departing from the well-rehearsed critique of racialization as objectification, dehumanization, and commodification, Cheng draws attention to the ways in which a "peculiarly synthetic, aggregated, feminine, and non-European" subject comes to challenge the "modern Western personhood" normalized in the form of "a biological, organized, and masculine body."[85] Seen in this way, Mary Chang as "China Girl" is endowed with a *thingified* agency, at once an object put on display for the strip club patrons (and the theater audience) and a *subject* intent on getting her journalist job back—she even hands Joe a copy of her resume to be delivered to Frank just before she gets ready to perform "China" as part of a "United Nations" show booked by a male client.

This reading of Mary Chang's onstage presence is instructive for thinking about the agency of "rising" China in conjunction with Chimerican media. On the surface, the plotline has attributed Mary Chang's departure from China to the role of the Chinese state in exerting information control. This corresponds to the censorship framework typically brought to the study of contemporary Chinese media in general and that of the Tank Man in particular. As Margaret Hillenbrand argues, such a framework, much like the "amnesia" trope that often accompanies it and is displayed in the play through Mary Chang's ignorance of June 4th, ascribes more power to the Chinese state than it deserves, as it reifies the efficacy of the censorship regime at the expense of recognizing the collective work that goes into keeping the Tank Man a "public secret."[86]

Meanwhile, Mary Chang's arrival in America, while seemingly liberating her from a repressive state apparatus, also subjugates her to the classed, racialized, and gendered relations of power long present in the "land of the free"—a myth also challenged in the earlier exchange between Mel and Frank about covering the Tank Man's move to New York. The ethnicization of Mary Chang's body in the synthetic form of the "China Girl," then, departs from the masculine assurance of "rising" China promulgated by the Chinese state—implied by the rhetoric of "*jueqi*/崛起" (rising)—and the widespread perception among the American public of China as a powerful player, if not a threat. The fact that she is asked to perform "China" as a member of the "United Nations" further invites a reading of China as feminized and racialized, especially when its global visibility results from the conjoined workings of the Chinese state (via "censorship") and the transpacific processes of mediation, workings that are enacted through the placing of June 4 ads within China by two Chinese people living in the United States.

Inspired by this scene, I hope in this book to grasp the figure of China as an inversion of the ornamentalist representation of Mary Chang's "China Girl." The Chinese state is a nonhuman entity that can be racialized because it can be simultaneously embodied and dehumanized. Its agency stems from the embodiment—in the form of a censoring agent, for example—but is also conditioned by the racialized and gendered relations of power that permeate the transpacific communications network and invariably shape its global visibility. There is, therefore, heuristic value in conceptualizing "rising" China as an entity coproduced by the Chinese state and Chimerican media. Because of its emergence at the nexus of state actions and transpacific mediation, "rising" China is best seen as a subject that also remains a racialized and feminized object in American media life. As an increasingly powerful agent, the figure of China partakes in the production of its own absent presence, which is shaped by the asymmetrical power matrix embedded in transpacific media.

Disorienting Politics

As a play that inspires a rethinking of media as mediation and the co-constitution of media producers and their artifacts, *Chimerica* provokes an important and disorienting affect that corresponds to the gendering of China. Not only does this gendering disrupt the masculine myth of "rising" narratives across the Pacific, but it also cuts through the ideological framing of the Tank Man photo as symbolic of an authoritarian China presumed to be marching toward American-style democracy. Numerous plot twists in the play work to challenge this dominant framework, at once prompting us to reflect on the break between the ideals and practices of democracy in the United States and the supposed authoritarian character of the Chinese government. Engaging with these moments of disorientation as they are entwined with mediation, then, points to some ways in which we may, in the words of Litzinger, "unleash the political from the nation-state, to understand power as it traverses and crisscrosses different local, national, and global spaces," and to discern "forms of power and oppression within particular national boundaries" simultaneously.[87] In other words, an affect of disorientation produced by Chimerican media can enable us to envision a relational politics beyond the dichotomy of "us" versus "them" or "democracy" versus "authoritarianism."

One such moment of disorientation arrives when the British woman, Tess, after spending the night with Joe in New York when she is impregnated, appears in front of her corporate client the next day to deliver a well-rehearsed PowerPoint presentation. In this scene, Tess begins by citing a number of Western-originated multinational companies that have "failed" to succeed in the Chinese market due to the misconception that "China was looking over the fence wanting to be America."[88] In contrast, for those companies that have succeeded, the secret "lies in the fact they made themselves Chinese enough in a country that values the supremacy of its culture above all else."[89] She continues to list a number of additional success cases, having mentioned the strategically sound localization of "Starbucks, McDonald's and KFC":

> You walk in Givenchy or Hermes in Paris, the staff speak Mandarin, because those companies understand that China is not the drunk girl at the frat party. She's the business major with an A-plus average, and really great hair. She's in charge of this brave new economic world, you bend to her or you die trying.[90]

Tess's explicit feminization of China as a "business major with . . . really great hair" echoes the gendering of the China figure in the Mary Chang segment. Here, "rising" China's agency is refashioned more specifically as a sort of consumerist spending power long associated with femininity—"how are those Chinese tourists paying for . . . their ostrich-skin handbags?"[91] Tess then introduces herself as someone who would help the credit card company better "understand the Chinese consumer" so as to capitalize on their love for shopping. She brings up an oversize photo of the Tank Man on screen, with two red circles around the two plastic bags in his hands—"there he is, in the middle of a political protest, a guy who's just been to the store."[92] At the precise moment when she reframes the Tank Man's heroism in terms of consumerism, Tess's self-assurance appears to evaporate. She reluctantly goes on to showcase her "seven customer segmentations," grouped under such categories as "The Rural Dreamer" and "The Luddite Shopper." With a shaking hand, she messes up the order of the slides, which no longer matches her presentation.

In the subsequent moment of chaos, Tess bursts into a rant:

> China's moving faster than we can collect the data. I mean, this is a nation that's gone from famine to Slim-Fast in one generation. I know some of you've been out there, I mean, did you see the smog? My last trip, it rained one way, the puddles were black, the sky was yellow, they're growing so fast you can see it in the air! And, you know, in the fact there are like thousands of babies who can't breathe properly, but

anyway . . . I'm sorry if this is—but have we really thought about what happens when you turn one-point-three billion economic pragmatists into people who think about money like us? I mean, we're still breaking our nails on a recession now[,] right? But, what is it going to be like if one-point-three billion Chinese renege on their mortgages and credit-card payments? . . . [It's like] you're about to get into bed with someone you don't really understand which is, it just seems a bit . . . lunatic, because, you know, this is the future. . . . And we don't understand. And I think that might [be] a problem, Right? [*sic*]"[93]

In this scene, Tess's breakdown enacts what film scholar Homay King describes as "the lost girl"—a female protagonist who is disoriented in a surrounding foreign to her.[94] By this point Tess has already returned from China to the United States. But the disorienting impact comes less from the "foreignness" of America than from the breakdown in the linearity of the PowerPoint presentation, a visual record of her findings from China, the distant land. She is "lost" in a self-staged presentation that is supposed to orient her client to a nation imagined as its future market. And yet the idea of a future China shaped in the image of the consumerist, credit-driven society that is America has all of a sudden become less certain as a destination. Tess's uneasiness with the determinacy of this destination appears to be prompted more immediately by the disordering of the PowerPoint slides, whose opening image of the Tank Man mysteriously returns at the end of her rant.

Tess's self-questioning therefore comes to exhibit "a willingness to inhabit and valorize transitional spaces over and against destinations, an openness to what is new and different, and a sense of the external world as present and affecting."[95] It is important to note that the grocery bags in the Tank Man's hands are key objects from that "external world" that affects Tess. These are objects that cultural studies scholar McKenzie Wark has compared to an image produced by the media. "An image," like a bag, "carries things from one place to another"; it "is a displacement, literally a changing of place."[96] Tess's apparent inability to follow the guidance of the PowerPoint slides, and indeed her refusal to carry out the task assigned by her client, point to the capacity of the Tank Man to induce a sense of disorientation that defies the trajectory of transforming China in the image of America.

What is rehearsed here is none other than a re-conception of Chimerican media as mediation. The "changing of place" enabled by this mediation has rendered the Tank Man's bags, and in turn Tess, as "the conduit for a reciprocal movement between two locations, a negotiation of the old and familiar and the new and strange."[97] It is perhaps no surprise that when Joe and Tess meet again, Tess is six months pregnant but immaculately dressed, working under a new contract with the British company Tesco while helping the Occupy movement with their publicity pro bono, an act that Joe perceives as "schizophrenic."[98] As philosophers Gilles Deleuze and Félix Guattari tell us, "Schizophrenia is not the identity of capitalism, but on the contrary its difference, its divergence, and its death."[99] Tess's disorientation, therefore, enacts this difference-making possibility and self-reflexively challenges what cultural studies scholar Dan Vukovich calls a form of "Sinological-orientalism" specific to the PRC, which projects China to be on a path to becoming the same as America/the West.[100]

Importantly, Tess's speech in many ways echoes communication scholar Yuezhi Zhao's critique of the myth of "Chimerica" in its masking of "China's massive social deficits," from "the suppression of wages and social spending" to "environmental degeneration."[101] The environmental cost of China's high-speed growth is also salient in other parts of the play and indeed shapes the destiny of Zhang Lin, whom we discover later to be the man in front of the tank back in 1989. In numerous scenes set in Zhang's apartment, he hears the coughing of his neighbor Ming Xiaoli, a retiree and former "poster girl for the Party,"[102] now suffering and later dying from "Beijing lung."[103] Outraged by the official corruption over issues of pollution, Zhang wrote a piece about Ming's death, hoping that Joe would publish it in an American newspaper. After Joe rejected him, saying, "The story was too small, Americans can't even solve their own problems," Zhang released the story online anonymously. When the piece invited the party's attention, the officials requested Zhang's information from the American company Mytel, headquartered in Silicon Valley. Mytel's Beijing office, "required to comply with Chinese law," offered the information to the Chinese authority without "any assurance as to what this data will be used for."[104] This led to Zhang's arrest, shown through a simultaneously staged scene in his apartment.

The plotline here points to the complicity of global tech firms in shoring up the Chinese state's censorship regime as identified by communication scholar Rebecca McKinnon.[105] Just like Joe's discovery that the crucial Tank Man he had searched for was the soldier in the tank rather than the protester in front of it, unexpected twists like this arguably reinforce the play's capacity to produce a disorienting affect. Together they work to complicate a monolithic understanding of the Chinese state as an all-powerful agent. Instead, what emerges is a deeply imbricated relationship between China and the transpacific media processes that are stabilized in Chimerican media. Joe's inability to recognize Ming's death from "Beijing lung" as a story worthy of the American audience's attention, then, serves to caution against the dichotomous framing of "our problem versus theirs" typically applied to the reportage of China's pollution, which I have elsewhere called (along with Ralph Litzinger) "Yellow Eco-peril" (see the conclusion).[106] In his obsession with an imaginary "unknown hero" fighting for the ideal of democracy, Joe has failed to see the on-the-ground activism of Zhang Lin in advocating the right to breathable air.

In a memorable scene months after Zhang Lin's arrest and subsequent torture by the Public Security Bureau, he addresses a protesting crowd:

> We call for a Party that refuses to get rich on our blood. We call for a Party that puts its people over its profits. We call for a Party that does not turn a blind eye as young men walk wheezing upstairs. We call for these things, at the top of our voices, while there is still breath in our lungs to do so.[107]

Zhang Lin's invocation of "we" as a pronoun here echoes an earlier exchange he had with Joe, who laments that the extent of Chinese state censorship of online searches like "Tiananmen Square" means "the Tank Man is dead in more ways than one."[108] In his response, Zhang Lin asks, "What are you—you want to reduce this to one man? There were a hundred thousand of us, Joe, we're not dead!"[109] This implicit critique of individualism as an idealized value celebrated in neoliberalism is also present in one of Tess's comments—"No such thing as an individual"—before she goes on to successfully categorize Joe's colleague Mel,[110] using the "profiling system" for marketing that Mel detests.[111] What is brought to the surface in these segments, then, is the tension within neoliberal globalization between *consumerism* masking as individualized political agency and *citizenship* as a form of collective participation. Zhang Lin's protest and Tess's breakdown, seen together in this light, can be said to offer an alternative vision for citizenship that does not privilege the individual consumer as a default political actor under neoliberal globalization. Instead, what is conjured is a collective subjectivity that aims to hold the state accountable for public good—an ideal that has become seemingly more difficult to put into practice in both China and America today (see chapter 4).

In 2019, Channel 4 aired a four-part miniseries based on the play, updating its events to the year 2016. Donald Trump's unexpected presidential win in the United States and Xi Jinping's tightened control in China now served as the backdrop for the "Tank Man" story.[112] In an interview about this adaptation, Kirkwood says, "Brexit and the Trump election in particular complicated the play's assumptions that Western democracy is a superior system in a way that was really interesting to me . . . The extent to which Western democracy proved to be vulnerable to demagoguery really blindsided me in 2016." On the Chinese side, Kirkwood continues: "Xi Jinping has been a great agent of positive change as well as an agent of corruption." She goes on to highlight the issue of pollution, sharing the view that "it's not worth your economy growing if the health of your citizens is suffering in such a profound way, but what has changed is that the Chinese government are now dealing with it." Interestingly, Kirkwood describes the show as "a love letter to the power of protest" that conveys "the energy and thrill of being gathered with lots of other people to express the same emotion, the same thought." Indeed, she "wanted [the series] to be an aspirational portrait of people stepping beyond the individual, into the collective."[113]

Kirkwood's words were well worth reflecting upon in the year 2020, when the murder of George Floyd amid the COVID-19 pandemic led to the largest ever mass-scale BLM protest in America. Even before this most recent round of demonstrations against racially charged police brutality, journalists and citizens alike had captured photos of individual BLM protesters confronting the state machine in the same manner as the Tank Man on Tiananmen Square.[114] Most famous among them was perhaps the picture of Ieshia Evans, a New York City resident who calmly stood in front of two policemen in full riot gear during the protests in Baton Rouge, Louisiana, after the local police shot and killed Alton Sterling.[115] And hashtags such as "#Tiananmen SQ Tank Man 2015" received wide circulation on social media.[116] In moments like this, it is hard not to think of anthropologist Jennifer Hubbert's claim that the "Tank Man" photo, once a symbol of Chinese state oppression, has come to "speak less about the absence of political liberalism and democracy in China . . . than [it does] about their absence in the contemporary United States."[117]

At first glance, the deaths of Trayvon Martin, Michael Brown, Tamir Rice, Freddie Gray, Alton Sterling, Philando Castile, Breonna Taylor, and George Floyd, among many other African Americans at the hands of police violence, appear quite distant from the geopolitical entity of China. But the resurfacing of the Tank Man imagery during the BLM protests brings to mind Bishnupriya Ghosh's argument that the circulation of "mass-media icons" like the Tank Man can "become essential to forging relations to that 'elsewhere' populated by those whose needs or resources affect the 'here' we perceive as 'our' locality."[118] The photo, indeed, is emblematic of the kind of relational space that Chimerican media help to create. In this sense, Kirkwood's portrayal of the present-day Tank Man as an environmental activist calling for state responsibility to make air breathable for Chinese citizens may be productively linked to the "I can't breathe" slogan of the BLM movement (see the conclusion). These last words uttered by Eric Garner and later George Floyd point to the long-standing effects of environmental racism in denying people of color in the United States and beyond (including those in China) the capacity to breathe. In the COVID-19 moment, they also remind us to foreground the act of breathing as a basis upon which to imagine an embodied form of citizenship, built upon an ecologically informed relational politics that defies the ideological othering of "rising" China.

Conclusion

Not long after I attended the performance of *Chimerica* at the Studio Theatre in Washington, DC, I received a mailer that featured a photo of Zhang Lin and the ghost of his wife, Liuli, gazing intently at a MacBook Pro computer. The heroism of the Tank Man back in 1989, as the play's ending reveals, was not quite as motivated by grandiose political ideals as by the personal grief over the death of Zhang Lin's wife and unborn child. Liuli continuously "haunts" present-day Zhang Lin, especially when he hesitates to embrace environmental activism—that is, using the computer to expose official corruption online. "Perceiving the lost subjects of history—the missing and lost ones and the blind fields they inhabit—" as cultural theorist Avery Gordon reminds us, "makes all the difference to any project trying to find the address of the present."[119] If Liuli's ghost functions as, in the words of a cast member, "a portal into another age,"[120] the material remnants of her life, contained in the shopping bags carried by Zhang Lin, may become like "apertures into" a political elsewhere that is yet to be configured and brought into being.[121]

The presence of the Apple computer in the mailer is also quite instructive. An artifact that bears the label "designed in California, assembled in China," it indexes the material processes of transpacific mediation that have made China a constant, if often elusive, presence in American media life. The inclusion of this artifact along with the characters played by two young Asian American actors in the mailer, therefore, resonates with the London production of *Chimerica* in generating the politically disorienting effect of Chimerican entanglements that is *affective*. Chimerican media, from the Tank Man to the Apple computer, not only make these entanglements visible but also activate them as forces that urge a rethinking of politics beyond the dichotomy of "American democracy" and "Chinese authoritarianism." This rethinking rests on the recognition of the Chinese state as a figure whose appearance exceeds image-based representation and whose agency is conjoined with transpacific mediation. "Rising" China, in other words, is best understood as a figural formation that disturbs the place-bound notion of national politics while being itself co-constituted with Chimerican media.

As the COVID-19 crisis has revealed more clearly, the rise of Trumpism in the United States has intensified both official anti-China rhetoric and widespread racism against people of color in the United States. In this context, the gendering of China in Kirkwood's play also invites us to consider the simultaneous embodiment and dehumanization of the nonhuman entity that is the Chinese state in Chimerican media. Arguably, the othering of China can be said to *inversely* mirror the stereotyping of black male bodies as hypermasculine and threatening. As I demonstrate in the remainder of the book, this racialization of the Chinese state works to preclude the kinds of political imagination that stem from the relational space conjured by Chimerican media. To probe into the uneven power relations that help shape this racialization, the economic entanglements of the two superpowers as they are manifested in Chimerican media is a good place to begin. I will turn critical attention to this mode of racialization, or what I call fiscal orientalism, in the next chapter.

CHAPTER 2

Economic Chimerica

Fiscal Orientalism and the Indebted Citizen

In July 2018, the Trump administration officially launched what a spokesperson from China's Ministry of Commerce called "the largest trade war in economic history to date."[1] Hyperbolic as it might sound, the scale of 25 percent US tariffs levied on $34 billion worth of Chinese imports was no doubt significant, if not unprecedented. In the eighteen months that followed, a $550 billion array of products, amounting to half of imports from China, became subject to US tariffs. The signing of a "phase 1" deal, on January 15, 2020, put a pause on the ongoing trade dispute, requiring Beijing to purchase an additional $200 billion worth of US imports between 2020 and 2021. In December 2020, President-elect Joe Biden also said in an interview that he would not immediately cancel the trade deal but would focus on "massive, government-led investments in American research and development, infrastructure and education to better compete with China."[2]

The US-China trade war has led to widespread speculation of "decoupling" between the world's two largest economies. Yet the language of "divorce" also sharpens the visibility of the "marriage" implied in economist Niall Ferguson's coinage of the word "Chimerica." In media coverage of the trade war, the two nations' economic interdependency has become more pronounced as businesses and consumers in America grapple with its implications. Some estimated that US households would have to pay over one thousand dollars extra on household items.[3] American companies big and small, including Apple, worried that the increased prices for their products would cut into their profits, as moving their manufacturing completely to other places like Vietnam and India was neither achievable nor desirable, at least in the immediate future.[4] Furthermore, rust-belt manufacturing continued to decline despite the rhetoric of "bringing jobs back," and US corporations such as Tesla and General Motors, incentivized by China's subsidies for electronic vehicles, actually expanded their investments in the Chinese market during the Trump era.[5]

What, then, prompted and legitimized the trade war with China if in reality it appears to yield little benefit to the American people? In this chapter, I return to the first decades of the twenty-first century, particularly the years after the 2008 financial crisis, to examine a specific mode in which "rising" China has appeared in a set of transpacific media that enact economic Chimerica. My focus is on a dominant rhetorical pattern that emerged in this period surrounding the Chinese ownership of America's national debt. I have come to call this pattern *fiscal orientalism*, a framework that heightens the agency of China while masking the uneven power relations that persist between the two superpowers. In the eyes of sociologist Ho-fung Hung, the economic entanglements of the two superpowers captured by the term "Chimerica" have been morphing into an intensifying "interimperial rivalry" since 2010.[6] As the rhetoric of delinking intensified in the long COVID-19 crisis, the kinds of interdependences characterized by economic Chimerica have now taken on more of a historical character, especially given the uncertain outlooks of US-China relations. Turning attention to the transpacific media that captured several key moments in the 2010s, after what Hung calls "the heyday of Chimerica,"[7] I hope to shed more critical light on the historically specific formation of the "China" figure in this recent past so as to parse out its ideological implications in shaping political visions in the United States and beyond.

The Post-2008 "China Panic"

Ridley Scott's *The Martian* (2015) is a science fiction film based on software engineer Andy Weir's best-selling novel released in 2011. Starring Matt Damon, the film opened on October 2, 2015, in the United States to critical acclaim. It went on to garner seven Oscar nominations and two Golden Globe awards and was widely voted one of the best films of the year. Set in 2035, the film narrates the rescue mission of Mark Watney, an astronaut who is stranded on Mars when a dust storm forces his crew to hastily depart the planet. Centrally featured in the story are Watney's "self-help" efforts as a botanist/mechanical engineer who manages, among other things, to cultivate potatoes on Mars. Yet in a key moment, after NASA's attempt to send a space probe fails due to insufficient safety inspections, China National Space Administration comes to the rescue by offering a classified booster named *Taiyang Shen* (which literally translates as "the Sun God," or Apollo) to deliver the supplies necessary to bring Watney back home. Plots like this have led comedian Stephen Colbert to suggest that Hollywood is now engaged in a "pandering" endeavor to obtain "a piece of that sweet and sour Renminbi [Mandarin name for the Chinese currency]" in the world's second-largest film market.[8]

Futuristic depictions of China have long permeated Euro-American science fiction works, in both literary and cinematic forms. But the presence of China in *The Martian* is noteworthy. While Scott has directed a wide range of films featuring diverse themes, one of his best-known works is the 1982 cyberpunk classic *Blade Runner*, a film invoked by David Morley and Kevin Robins, among others, as a representative text of "techno-orientalism."[9] Writing in the 1980s and 1990s, Morley and Robins discerned in Euro-America a form of anxiety triggered by the rise of Japan as a technological power. Popular and political narratives of the time became the means through which "a long tradition of racist fascination" was channeled into a specific "anti-Japanese feeling."[10]

In *The Martian*, China also appears as the provider of a crucial technical component, illustrating what literary scholar Christopher Fan has termed "techno-orientalism with Chinese characteristics."[11] While sharing many features with the "Japan Panic" in the 1980s, however, the manner in which China appears in this new "discursive site of Asian futurity,"[12] to use Asian Americanist Aimee Bahng's term, has come to exhibit unique characteristics of its own. This new form of Orientalism, which describes the specific mode in which China often appears in Chimerican media artifacts like *The Martian*, is what I have come to call *fiscal orientalism*.

While its emergence may be traced prior to the 2008 financial crisis, it is since then that fiscal orientalism has manifested itself with greater frequency and intensity in American media life. Prior to *The Martian*, a 2009 Super Bowl commercial sponsored by Defeat the Debt (part of the conservative think tank Employment Policies Institute), features a group of elementary students pledging their allegiance to "America's debt and to the Chinese government that lent us money." A map of China lingers on screen as the voice-over concludes the clip by telling viewers, "American taxpayers owe more than 500 million in interest payments every day to cover our government's debt. Much of that debt is owed to foreign governments."[13] The same rhetorical fixation can be found in a 2012 Super Bowl commercial aired in Michigan as part of the campaign of Pete Hoekstra, a Republican candidate who ran against Democrat Debbie Stabenow for a Senate seat. In this advertisement, much criticized as racist, an Asian woman bicycles past some rice paddies before stopping to thank "Senator Debbie Spend-it-Now" for offering jobs to China and strengthening its economy (in accented English).[14]

There is also the more widely seen "Chinese Professor" advertisement,[15] produced by Citizens Against Government Waste (CAGW).[16] Set in a high-tech classroom in 2030 Beijing, the spot begins with the professor posing the question "Why do great nations fall? The Ancient Greeks, the Roman Empire, the British Empire, and the United States of America." As the architectural landmarks of each "nation" flash across the screen, the professor responds, "They all made the same mistakes, turning back on the principles that made them great," before proceeding to offer reasons for the "fall" of America. "Enormous so-called stimulus spending, massive changes to health care, and government takeovers of private industries" are invoked as examples of America's attempt to "spend and tax itself out of a great recession." At the end of the clip, as the professor triumphantly declares "we owned most of their debt, so now they work for us," laughter erupts in an auditorium full of "Chinese youth."[17]

The notion that "the US owes China most of its debt" was blatantly misleading, since the Chinese government held no more than 10 percent of total US federal debt in 2010.[18] Yet as a frequently invoked issue by political candidates from both parties, the discourse successfully constructed China in the public imagination as a threatening foreign creditor. In a 2014 American Press Institute survey, more than half of the respondents, selected across the spectrum of political affiliations, were certain that "China owned at least half the US debt"; one participant thus voiced her concern: "I wouldn't want them to come here and be like, 'we're taking over your country because you owe us so much money.'"[19]

This (mis)perception of an oriental Other more powerful than the American Self is reminiscent of the "Japan Panic" that Morley and Robins discerned three decades ago. In 1985, Japan was the nation that rose to "a hegemonic position in the spheres of technology, manufacturing and finance."[20] It was also "the first non-white country to have inserted itself into modernity on its own terms," which defied the idea "that modernity can only be articulated through the forms the West has constructed."[21] Therefore, Japan's "rise" triggered a defense mechanism that is operative through an inverse "denial of co-evalness,"[22] whereby the West reimagined Japan "as the figure of empty and dehumanised technological power" that occupies a futuristic wasteland.[23] This is what Morley and Robins call "techno-orientalism," a style of representation that associates Japan with a hyper-technologized and yet dystopian future so as to delegitimize its present status as a leading nation of technological advancement.

If the "Japan Panic" was primarily configured in technological terms, the post-2008 "China Panic," appearing in cultural artifacts like *The Martian* and numerous campaign ads, has to some extent inherited this obsession. As Asian Americanists David Roh, Betsy Huang, and Greta Niu point out, technology has remained a narrative-framing device for a "rising" China, even though the nation is less known as an innovator of technologies than as a manufacturer of Western-invented technological products.[24] "If Japan is a screen on which the West has projected its technological fantasies," the dominant media representation of Chinese factory workers as dehumanized producers of electronics portrays the West as "being colonized, mechanized, and instrumentalized in its own pursuit of technological dominance."[25] This continuity helps to explain why elements of techno-orientalism are still prevalent in Hollywood films and media narratives that feature China or Chinese locations prominently, including the more recent Wuhan lab-leak theory during the coronavirus pandemic.[26]

However, between the techno-orientalist depictions of Japan then and China now, one can also discern more important distinctions. China's size, particularly its oft-noted "expanding middle-class" population, easily disturbs a facile equation between the two. The enormity of China invites an imagination of the nation as a vast market for Western-branded consumer goods, *in addition to* being a supplier of cheap and abundant labor for the production of these goods. The increasingly frequent inclusion of Chinese locales in Hollywood productions is, after all, also attributable to the studios' desire to maximize these films' profitability in the booming Chinese film market. This "dual image of China as both developing-world producers and first-world consumers," as Roh, Huang, and Niu suggest, "presents a representational challenge for the West."[27] The sleek high-tech auditorium and handheld touch-screen tablet featured in the "Chinese Professor" spot thus become one way in which such a representational dilemma is resolved. By showcasing the Chinese not just as producers but also as consumers of "technology supposedly rooted in US-based innovation," the advertisement works to "implicitly accuse China of stealing US intellectual property,"[28] something that has been repeatedly invoked in contemporary political campaigns.

Such a reading certainly befits China's long-standing notoriety as the world's knockoff mecca. But the acknowledgment of this difference between an "innovating" Japan and a "counterfeiting" China, among others, also necessitates a more critical look at mutations of what cultural studies scholar Dan Vukovich calls "a Sinological form of orientalism" in the twenty-first century.[29] Indeed, rather than subsuming the contemporary "China threat" into an analytical lens generated by the 1980s "Japan Panic," I call closer attention to the vastly different modes in which the two non-Western nation-states came to achieve their (presumed) global ascent. Scrutinizing these differences in political-economic terms also entails attending to significant changes in the cultural climate brought on by three decades of neoliberal globalization. This is why, I argue, the Chimerican media artifacts that were fixated upon "America's indebtedness to China" in the second decade of the new millennium demand a new critical category to account for their historical specificity.

I propose the category of fiscal orientalism to specifically reference postcolonial theorist Edward Said's famed term so as to highlight the racializing logic of these artifacts, as they perform important ideological work in perpetuating a historically specific form of *indebted* citizenship. At the same time, I also argue that the economic entanglement of the two superpowers that these media bring into visibility demands a rethinking of "rising" China as not just an object of orientalist representation but also an agent co-constituted amid transpacific processes. As such, a critical engagement with fiscal-orientalist media allows us to discern China as an agentive force that helps shape political visions, specifically by privileging certain understanding of the state over others.

Fiscal Orientalism

I have developed the term "fiscal orientalism" to refer to a new style of thought that has come to complement, not replace, techno-orientalism in representing a "Chinese future." The dictionary definition of "fiscal" tells us that it is an adjective denoting "of or relating to government revenue, esp. taxes" (*Oxford American Dictionaries*). Its Latin root is *fiscus*, which refers to "purse" or "treasury." In common-day usage, "fiscal" sometimes invokes that which is related to institutional financial matters in general, as in "fiscal year." But most often it is used to describe the financial behaviors of *the state*. One may recall the public panic over the "fiscal cliff" in the beginning of 2013, a term invoked in Kirkwood's play *Chimerica* (see chapter 1). It described the prospect of a minor recession induced by tax increases that would be too high and spending cuts that would be too extreme at once, which had to be prevented by last-minute legal measures.

Fiscal orientalism, therefore, can be defined as a mode of representing China that concentrates its gaze on the power contention between two nation-*states*—that is, between a "rising" Chinese creditor and a "declining" American debtor. To be sure, the frequent juxtaposition of these two superpowers in the contemporary US public sphere shares a degree of affinity with the techno-orientalist discourse centered on Japan. Both narratives involve a recasting of geopolitics (the politics of space) into a temporal framework—what the followers of Paul Virilio have come to call "chronopolitics" or the politics of time.[30] However, if techno-orientalism predicates itself on the logic of technological progress, which posits the Japanese Other as "a future that has transcended Western modernity,"[31] what has become operative in fiscal orientalism is a temporality predicated on America's *indebtedness* to China, the nation en route to become the next "No. 1." This distinction not only reveals the differences between the two "rising" stories of Japan and China, but it also reflects the impact of thirty years of neoliberal financialization that lie in between. Among other things, this is a period that has observed the rise of what literary scholar Rita Raley calls "Electronic Empires"—that is, deterritorialized and decentering "communication networks" that "are responsible for the circulation of finance and information."[32] These networks point to the merging of new media technologies and global, neoliberal capitalism. Techno-orientalism came at an earlier phase of this period, when the hegemonic status of Euro-American nation-states was contested ostensibly by Japan's rise as a vanguard of post-Fordist "Toyotism." Yet as Japanese media theorist Toshiya Ueno argues, techno-orientalism is also "the Orientalism of cybersociety and the information age, aimed at maintaining stable identity in a technological environment."[33] The real culprit for the "waning" of Western powers, or the nation-state as such, is arguably the ascending power of supranational informationalized networks and the kinds of transnational capital flows that they facilitate (as foreign direct investment, for example).

Extending but also steering away from the techno-fetishism embedded in techno-orientalism, fiscal orientalism more directly references the intensifying contestation between nation-state and (finance) capital.

It evokes the confluence of information technology and a post–Bretton Woods "new money imaginary," signaled above all by the expanded role of financial derivatives in the global market. This confluence has come to reconfigure "our experience of everyday temporal and spatial coordinates,"[34] creating a kind of relational space signaled by the neologism "Chimerica," as I've discussed in chapter 1. A fiscal-orientalist text such as the "Chinese Professor" spot, by figuring China as an agent, works to interpellate a historically specific kind of indebted citizen in the United States.

Characterizing this mode of interpellation is the distinct fusion of two sets of temporalities—the time of the Other and the time of debt. In the advertisement, besides the location marker of "Beijing, 2030" in the opening scene, the key moment that signifies "Chineseness" arrives when the "professor" smugly brings up the creditor-debtor relation between China and the United States. Accompanying his voice is a shot of the stage from the back of the auditorium, which displays a waving Chinese national flag appearing as a veil over the façade of the White House. On the side of the stage is a centrally displayed portrait of the Chinese communist leader Mao Zedong, sandwiched between two revolutionary-style posters typically seen in Maoist China (1949–1976).

The use of these iconic signs associated with Mao may very well reflect America's long-standing anxiety toward a "red China." What deserves more attention, though, is the manner in which this mentality toward a communist Other is recast in a framework of national indebtedness, poised to present severe consequences for America *in the future*. While the line delivered by the professor in Mandarin Chinese, "We are their biggest creditor," does not specify the time frame of this indebtedness, the English subtitle has displayed the verb "own" in its past tense. This word choice, combined with the "2030" time indicator at the clip's opening, invites viewers to ponder their viewing present as a moment already past. It indeed prepares them for the disembodied voice at the end of the spot: "You can change the future; you have to. Join Citizens Against Government Waste (CAGW) to stop the spending that is bankrupting America." The contact information for the video's sponsor, CAGW, is displayed against another shot of the auditorium, complete with the waving Chinese flag and imposing Maoist posters.

This attempt to "demonize" a Chinese future by invoking its Maoist-socialist past is perhaps more expected than surprising, given that the tendency to equate socialism with fascism and totalitarianism is part of a broader political discourse. It is therefore no coincidence that "Healthcare Debacle" is a prominently displayed slide in the professor's lecture as one of the key "mistakes" that led to America's "demise." The reference to "Obamacare" here is more than apparent. After all, the Republican candidate Mitt Romney, during the first presidential debate of the 2012 US national election, quite explicitly stated that "Obamacare" was on his list of programs to eliminate—that is, if it fails to pass the test, "Is the program so critical it's worth borrowing money from China to pay for it?"[35] Here and elsewhere in the Mitt Romney/Paul Ryan campaign, the link between *foreign* debt and *domestic* social programs was clearly amplified; while the former conflates debts held by both foreign governments and individual investors, the latter is configured via the long-standing trope of "welfare spending." In line with the Republican tirade against "big government," such a narrative often neglects to mention the sharp increase in military expenditures during the administration of George W. Bush.

At work, then, is a strategic mobilization of the national debt owed to the Chinese government as a means to delegitimize the US state's public spending on social welfare. The "Chinese Professor" advertisement has projected China in a future position that is equivalent to, if not more powerful than, the one occupied by America today. A reverse "denial of co-evalness," also operative in techno-orientalism, is hereby conjoined with a temporality of debt, albeit retroactively constructed. China cannot exist in the present, but a Chinese future that promises to "enslave" America, as indicated in the line "they (the US) now work for us (China)" in 2030—presents an unmistakable risk for the United States. The fixation of the Chinese Other in the future, therefore, works to obscure the *unpredictability* that is inherent in a temporality predicated on debt. It is in this way that (national) debt is rendered more than an "economic mechanism" but as "a security-state technique of government aimed at reducing the uncertainty of the behavior of the governed."[36] The Chinese future may still be avoided, as long as the citizenry take immediate action in the present—that is, to join in a movement to fight against "government waste," understood strictly as expenditures allocated for social welfare.

The specific invocation of Chinese socialism—as a distinct reference point in this and other narratives that criticize the US state's attempt to "spend and tax itself out of a great recession"—becomes especially ironic. For not only has China's post-Mao economic development drawn on the material and ideological legacy of the Mao era,[37] but the Chinese state has also continued to lay claims to socialism for purposes of self-legitimacy.[38] The role played by the post-socialist state in China's economic ascent, which departs significantly from those prescribed by the World Bank, is only one among many that distinguishes China's rise from that of Japan.

Certainly, China's sizable export-led growth may be seen as "a replication and extension" of the kind shared by Japan, among other East Asian countries.[39] But Japan during the Cold War, unlike China, was an ally of the United States and part of "a capitalist bulwark" against communist forces.[40] In addition, the 1970s deregulation of Japan's own capital market pioneered the kind of "financial engineering" that was later standardized in the West, which not only triggered the nation's 1980s economic boom but also led to its 1990s bust.[41] Also illustrative of Japan's economic dependency on the United States is its "massive investment in low-yield U.S. Treasury bonds," something that Ho-fung Hung has compared to "a tribute payment."[42] Perhaps for this reason, the Japanese state's own twentieth-century imperialist-expansionist history hardly, if ever, appears in techno-orientalist texts like *Blade Runner*. By contrast, the figure of the Chinese Communist Party-state has retained a constant presence in fiscal-orientalist discourses. A case in point is none other than the "Chinese aid" portrayed in *The Martian*.

In the film as in the novel,[43] the classified booster named *Taiyang Shen* is the key component of the timely assistance provided by China to bring Watney back to Earth. Guo Ming (played by the Hong Kong actor Eddy Ko Hung), the director of China National Space Administration, is featured in conversation with his subordinate Zhu Tao (played by the mainland actress Chen Shu) about the possibility to partake in the American rescue mission. He describes the project as a costly one, about which the State Council has long complained. Offering the booster to NASA would mean not only revealing a state secret but also foregoing the prospect of similar projects in the future. Concerned that "the American people may be sentimental, but their government is not," and believing that the US "State Department won't trade anything major for one man's life," Guo decides to "keep this among scientists," who are to "work out an agreement" and "present it to our governments as a fait accompli."[44] The plan, which requires the United States to return the favor by "putting a Chinese astronaut on Mars," would not only make China the one who has come to "rescue the Americans" but would also help "the world see China as equal to the U.S. in space."[45]

At first glance, the Chinese state's involvement here is rendered indirect at best, since it is scientists who have taken matters into their own hands. Yet the Chinese state's financial backing for the *Taiyang Shen* project, even if offered begrudgingly, is an essential component of the rescue plan. The mission highlights the role played by *Hermes*'s crewmembers, who are "willing to take risks to save lives" by collectively defying the order of NASA's director and returning to Mars to save Watney.[46] Their risk-taking courageousness stands in stark contrast with NASA and its Chinese counterpart. If the NASA official is depicted as overly concerned with the weighing of risks, Guo and Zhu's rationale for offering up *Taiyang Shen* is predicated on the calculation of the US *return on Chinese investment*. The debt that America incurs for bringing Watney back to his homeland can and must be repaid in the future by way of NASA's concession to boost China's national pride.

In this way, the input of the Chinese government provides an assuring fix for stabilizing a field of risks and uncertainty for the United States because it figures as a form of debtor-creditor relationship between the two nation-states. After all, in the words of the NASA director, the entire mission to save Watney is "a risky cowboy rescue."[47] China's aid ultimately enables the United States to complete a highly improbable task whose expenditure may be subject to public criticism were it not for the compensation of national reunification that would result from bringing Watney back to the homeland/the Earth/the United States. Indeed, Watney's safe return to the national community provides the grounds on which the US state's indebtedness to the Chinese government can be justified.

Of course, the allocation of vast public resources to save a white male character from adverse situations (and often in a foreign land) has been a long-standing trope in Hollywood. As Jenna Mullins writes, in addition to *The Martian*, Matt Damon alone has starred or appeared in several films within this genre, from *Saving Private Ryan* (1998) to *Interstellar* (2014).[48] Yet Watney's hyper-rational self-help efforts, exemplified by his meticulous calculation of food rations for survival on Mars, in many ways mirrors what cultural studies scholar Randy Martin calls the making of the "financial self."[49] As a stranded astronaut, Watney's character does not immediately resemble a welfare recipient. Nonetheless, it is telling that in one of his self-mocking moments, he describes himself as someone "indistinguishable from an unemployed guy for most of the day," since his primary daily activity involves watching seventies TV.[50] In this sense, the costly plan to rescue him becomes metonymic of the use of federal money to fund precisely those programs that are easily condemned as being of the "socialist" kind. The link between foreign aid and domestic social welfare is thus established in ways not unlike what is shown in the "Chinese Professor" video.

China's presence in *The Martian*, as Stephen Colbert suggests in his response to the film, is by no means unique, as similar kinds of Chinese "aid" are also discernible in previous productions like *2012* (2009) and *Gravity* (2013). Yet fiscal orientalism, if subtly manifested in *The Martian*, has made a more explicit appearance in Colbert's own version of "Pander Express." After commenting on the Chinese government's censorship (of imported films and Twitter, for example) and China's past achievements, Colbert praises the nation's "world-leading space programs," emphasizing that "your scientists currently discovered a black hole so large . . . yet it will still be easier to escape than America's debt to China." At the end of the skit, a "Chinese doctor" (who is also an astronaut) comes on stage to save Colbert from choking on "tingly lamb face salad" before telling the audience in Mandarin: "My name is the Future." The invocation of China as "the future" echoes Colbert's opening introduction of the film as "a sci-fi thriller that takes place in the near future where—and here's the twist—NASA has a budget."[51]

Given the fiscal uncertainties that have continuously troubled NASA, Colbert's parody strikes more than one chord. Itself a participant in the fiscal-orientalist discourse, "Pander Express" pokes fun at a widely shared obsession with a China-dominated future in American media life, equally discernible in Hollywood sci-fi thrillers and in political campaign spots. If the producers of "Chinese Professor" are quite blunt in making use of the "red scare" to call upon the indebted citizen-subject, Colbert has revealed a more complex form of othering in *The Martian*. That is, the depiction of China as a key aid to return an American astronaut to his homeland at once imagines the Chinese state as capable of rescuing NASA, if not the American government, from its perpetual fiscal crisis while projecting China as a lucrative market for US-originated media products (above all, those produced by Hollywood).

Emerging from these narratives are a set of Chimerican entanglements that mirror the conditions under which China has come to accumulate an unprecedented amount of US national debt. As Hung points out, "China's purchase of U.S. treasury bonds has become a compulsion" in part because China's trade surplus vis-à-vis the United States, which has risen drastically since China's 2001 accession to the World Trade Organization, resulted in a vast number of foreign reserves in the form of dollars.[52] Given that the dollar has retained a hegemonic status as an international currency even after the fall of Bretton Woods, it was in the interest of the Chinese government to use its dollar reserves to purchase US Treasury bonds. For not only did this holding promise "liquidity" and "stability of returns," but it also served "to secure the continuous increase in US demand for China's exports by helping to prevent a free-fall of the dollar, uncontrollable inflation, and an interest-rate hike in the United States."[53] China's ownership of US debt, rather than anticipating a China-dominated future, indeed encapsulated an economic symbiosis between China and America—or Chimerica as it was originally coined to mean (see chapter 1). Both the on-screen collaboration between the Chinese and US governments in *The Martian* and the off-screen interdependency between the Chinese market and Hollywood indexed by the film offer a glimpse into this symbiosis.[54]

At the same time, naming the relationship as one of symbiosis also belies other kinds of unequal power relations. To be sure, China has increasingly become a military contender with the United States, which distinguishes it from post–World War II Japan, a US protectorate. More recently, with the expansion of China's "One Belt, One Road" initiative, especially in the Global South, more attempts at internationalizing the Chinese currency renminbi have also become visible.[55] However, what is of particular interest here is how "the socioeconomic space of US-China interdependency," to use Christopher Fan's words, came to privilege a subject position marked by "a racialized mode of aspirational normativity" at a time when China's holding of US national debt in fact extended the subjugation of the Chinese economy to the hegemony of the dollar.[56] The particular mode in which this subject formation took shape in the aftermath of the 2008 financial crisis has thus necessitated the new category of fiscal orientalism. Such a category complements Fan's skillfully unpacked "techno-orientalism with Chinese characteristics" but is also poised to generate further insights into the conjoined workings of racialization and financialization.

Racializing Financialization

The mystifying effects of fiscal-orientalist narratives, which obscure the material conditions for the accumulation of US national debt and the power relation between China and America, are certainly not to be discounted. However, they also serve more than simply as vehicles of misinformation and indeed are better seen as constitutive of a generalized *spectacle* of *national debt.* In philosopher Guy Debord's provocative dictum, the spectacle is "not a supplement to the real world" but rather "the heart of the unrealism of the real society."[57] The dramatized representation of the Chinese state as a fearsome creditor of the US nation, however "unrealistic" it may be, is more usefully treated as a symptom of the very real constraints that *fictitious* capital has imposed on the sovereign state. As anthropologists Ed LiPuma and Benjamin Lee point out, the global financial markets, operating through "abstracted instruments of abstract power," are "too virtual to be visible" and do not constitute "an Other for the state or its citizens to act upon."[58] The racializing impulse in fiscal orientalism relies precisely on the otherness of China to lend legibility to the undecipherable accumulation of US national debt. It can thus be seen as stemming directly from the difficulty in formulating meaningful social responses to what Nancy Fraser calls "the political contradictions of financialized capitalism."[59]

One account that illustrates the link between this difficulty and the racialization that ensues comes from James Fallows, a longtime correspondent for *The Atlantic* who has written extensively on contemporary China as well as on Japan in the eighties and nineties. As he points out in response to the "Chinese Professor" video, the depiction of (post-) socialist China as a rising menacing power that threatens to overtake America's global status distorts the crucial fact that "stimulus spending" and "public intervention in major industries" are precisely part of China's "(successful) anti-recession policy."[60] Indeed, in November 2008, China's State Council announced a $586 billion stimulus package to strengthen the nation's infrastructure, in part to counter the impending impact of a global recession.[61] Nonetheless, Fallows has curiously endorsed the video "as a work of persuasion and motivation,"[62] despite the blatantly "unrealistic" portrayal of "the Chinese students" on screen. For him, the advertisement succeeds in deploying the threat of China as "a spur for us to do better," by highlighting that "the Americans erred by turning away from their own values."[63]

Fallows's endorsement of "American values" here in large part recycles his late twentieth-century treatise on "American exceptionalism" vis-à-vis a "rising" Japan. As literary scholar David Palumbo-Liu suggests, Fallows's 1989 book, *More Like Us: Making America Great Again*, was an unabashed celebration of "individualism" along with "the American spirit of spontaneous, creative, capitalistic mobility," which for him better adapts to the flexibility of global capitalism than Japanese culture.[64] While Fallows has now seemingly shifted his emphasis from the individual to the *state*, his acceptance of the "Chinese Professor" spot as a legitimate form of citizen mobilization bespeaks the ideological potency of fiscal orientalism. It prompts us to more closely analyze the ways in which fiscal orientalism obtains this potency through linking the time of the Other with the time of debt.

To do so, it is important to recognize that US national debt owed to the Chinese state, the central signifier of fiscal-orientalist narratives, is one of the "intertranslatable transnational forms" whose "metatemporally based dynamic of circulation" has destabilized the "secular time" on which the modern national imagination is based.[65] As LiPuma and Lee observe, the financial derivatives that enjoyed an explosion since the end of Bretton Woods have had the effect of "displacing critical determinants of local economic well-being to a temporality and space beyond the influence of the citizens and elected officials of each state."[66] This "debt economy," philosopher Maurizio Lazzarato suggests, has altered "time as decision-making, choice, and possibility" within the confine of the sovereign state.[67] The logic of racialization, as manifested in China-specific fiscal orientalism, aids precisely in offering an ideological fix for a crisis of the US state,[68] whose routine claim to liberal-democratic processes is perhaps more than ever failing to secure a national community imagined to occupy "homogeneous, empty time."[69]

Fallows, in other words, has resorted to a homogeneously imagined national body politic predicated on a temporality of return and revival, as shown in his emphasis on how America may "rise again" in another piece.[70] His sanctioning of the spot's fixation on China as a menacing future threat manifests a historically specific mode of "possessing the future in advance by objectivizing it."[71] That is, the othering of the Chinese creditor may be condoned on the grounds that it serves to reinvigorate the American nation's (always already superior) cultural values. Even though Fallows laments that the skills demonstrated in producing the spot were not used to educate the citizenry on "real budget and economic tradeoffs,"[72] he has allowed a form of cultural nationalism to overcome the need to enhance the public's understanding of the systemic accumulation of national debt. Fallows's response, then, becomes constitutive of a spectacle of national debt that bespeaks the "structure of feeling" specific to what cultural studies scholar Richard Dienst calls a "global regime of indebtedness."[73] This spectacle, in turn, precludes the possibility to engage national debt as "an apparatus to capture the collectivized potential wealth of a necessarily open-ended political community."[74]

Popular fiscal-orientalist texts like *The Martian*, as we have seen, help to perpetuate a similar kind of cultural nationalism in ways that impede alternative political imaginings of the state. Watney's homecoming is simultaneously prompted by America's desire for national unity and aided by a Chinese state seeking to contend with US national pride. But his survival is first and foremost hinged on his superb resilience as a midwestern white American, the default hero to uphold the nation's values. Such an imagination of the nation and its culture works to obscure the racializing logic that shores up fiscal orientalism. This logic can be more keenly discerned in another media controversy, which concerns a "Kid's Table" skit on ABC's *Jimmy Kimmel Live!*

The particular segment of "Kid's Table" aired on October 16, 2013, on the Disney-owned channel ABC, two weeks into the sixteen-day government shutdown that year. Kimmel, the host, opened by telling a group of five- and six-year-olds, "America owes China a lot of money, $1.3 trillion dollars," before asking, "How should we pay them back?" A blond-haired Caucasian boy mumbled in reply, "Shoot cannons all the way over and kill everyone in China." Kimmel reiterated and clarified the boy's message: "Kill everyone in China? OK, that's an interesting idea." He then turned to an African American boy, who suggested building a wall "so they can't get to us." "You are saying . . . a huge, 'Great' kind of a wall?" Kimmel responded. Moments later, Kimmel asked the whole group, "Should we allow the Chinese to live?" With the exception of the blond boy, all the kids said yes. When the discussion escalated into a cacophony of lines like "(if) we don't kill them," "they will kill us" and "we would all be killed," Kimmel concluded, "Well, this has been an interesting edition of Kid's Table—the *Lord of the Flies* edition," before calling for a "gummy break" and ending the segment.[75]

The reportedly "unscripted" comment, "kill everyone in China," offended quite a few viewers. It even led a group of self-identified Asian Americans to petition the White House for further investigation.[76] While not everyone agreed on whether the show was meant as a joke, the 105,111 individuals who signed the "We the People" petition appeared to have interpreted it as one that "promotes racial hatred."[77] Protesters gathered in front of ABC studios in San Francisco and Los Angeles, holding signs like "Fire Jimmy Kimmel, Save Children," "Racial Killing: No Joke," "To Love Not to Kill," and "Hate Speech Is Not Free Speech."[78] Some even portrayed Kimmel in a Hitler-style mustache next to a swastika.

Given the kinds of racial exclusion to which "Asians in America" have long been subject—from the 1882 Chinese Exclusion Act to the 1942 internment of Japanese Americans—there were ample reasons for the protesters to perceive this segment as a racist act, regardless of Kimmel's self-proclaimed attempt to poke fun at "childish politicians."[79] However, it is worth scrutinizing why the (intended) irony was rendered *illegible* within the representational apparatus of fiscal orientalism. For one thing, the multiethnic child participants, which consisted of one Caucasian boy, one Asian girl, one African American boy, and a Caucasian girl, were dressed in the adult attire of suits, a professional code that signified their on-screen status as public figures invited to deliberate on the possible solutions for the debt problem. But as children, they were also most likely *future* victims of the nation's debt. Therefore, it was only reasonable that they would become the bearers of responsibilities for mending that future. The time of the Other was again conjoined with the time of debt, in the figure of the (multiethnic) American child.

The "figural Child," as American studies scholar Lee Edelman argues, "embodies the citizen as an ideal, entitled to claim full rights to its future share in the nation's good, though always at the cost of limiting the rights 'real' citizens are allowed."[80] The properly "diversified" kids sitting at the table, in this sense, echoed the multiracial composition of schoolchildren featured in the "Defeat the Debt" advertisement. Highlighted at the end of that 2009 Super Bowl commercial was a dark-skinned girl with curly hair who rolled up her arms while speaking to the camera: "Debt stinks!"[81] The line clearly referenced public rather than private debt, but it also served as an eerie reminder that low-income African Americans and (Latino) immigrants were precisely among the populations most vulnerable to predatory subprime lending. The girl's racialized image and her disapproval of "debt" in the post-2008 moment therefore evoked the widespread accusation of such populations as "unqualified buyers" whose "overreaching" borrowing was to blame for causing the crisis.[82] Again, the emphasis on the Chinese creditor obscured the historical and structural exclusion of minority populations from credit and home ownership (in white neighborhoods especially),[83] as well as the neoliberal economy that further subjugated them to the vast web of financialized power relations.[84]

This racialization, predicated on an absent presence of "rising" China, arguably reappeared in Kimmel's "Kid's Table." The African American boy's invocation of the possibility of building a wall, for some, might be suggestive of the Berlin Wall or the anti-immigration discourse of erecting a wall along the Texas-Mexico border, as reenacted by President Trump. Yet Kimmel's rhetorical question, a "'great' kind of a wall," brought to mind the iconic Great Wall, one of the grandest architectural legacies of dynastic China. The reference to this landmark was reminiscent of orientalist portrayals of the millennium-old Chinese "civilization," which also operates through a denial of contemporaneity, by fixating the Other in times past. Incidentally, "Great Wall of Unknowns" was also the title of a 2004 piece by Robert Samuelson in the *Washington Post*, which described China as "a global goliath" that poses unforeseeable global impact in a future to come.[85] The same sentiment can be discerned in another China-related film starring Matt Damon in 2016, *The Great Wall*. A Chinese and American co-production, the film invited criticism even before its release (and subsequent flop at the box office) from Asian Americans regarding its "whitewashing"—that is, casting white actors like Damon as saviors in a film set in imperial China.[86] However, the plot of the film, which features (female) Chinese warriors and Europeans joining forces to fight against aliens, also centers on the latter's search for gunpowder, a technology that references China's more advanced state of development historically—arguably enacting yet again a form of techno-orientalism that deploys the past to project the future. Kimmel's response—"That'll never happen"—thus made manifest a latent anxiety perhaps shared by a significant segment of the US public that America may not be able to compete with "rising" China, because China is only "returning" to its glorious past as the world's greatest power.

Kimmel's unabashedly imperialist follow-up question—"Should we allow the Chinese to live?"—therefore can be read as mocking the tendency to reinsert America's national subjectivity through a violent domination over its oriental Other. The fact that the Caucasian boy was the only one among the four kids who responded no to this question is rather evocative of the racial hierarchy that persists in the American political sphere. Despite the celebrated election of the first black president in 2008 and the first black female vice president in 2020, as well as the attendant discourse touting the advent of a "postracial" society, the decision-making power within the nation remains undeniably tied to a white (male) privilege that continues to sanction racially motivated violence at home and abroad. The African American boy's wish to build a wall, a structure that can serve purposes of self-protection, also brings back the memory of repeated cases of (militarized) police brutality inflicted upon the African American community, which gave rise to the #BlackLivesMatter hashtag and movement in 2013 after the acquittal of George Zimmerman, who killed seventeen-year-old Trayvon Martin.

Kimmel chose to end the segment with an intertextual reference to *Lord of the Flies*, a young adult novel commonly assigned in US middle/ high schools and generally read as an allegory of men's all-too-easy descent from civilization to savagery. This reference, then, served as an anchor to the chaotic exchange of remarks like "we kill them" and "they kill us," which spoke pointedly to the kinds of systemic violence that had contributed to the accrual of US national debt over the past decade. Moreover, it brings to light the Chimerican entanglement that is obscured in fiscal orientalism's preoccupation with the two nation-states' creditor-debtor relationship. After all, if China is annihilated, America would lose a key buyer of its Treasury bonds.[87] Kimmel's response to the Caucasian boy's first comment, that "killing everyone in China" was "an interesting idea," was thus ambiguous at best.[88] On one level, using "cannons" to wipe out 1.6 billion people in the world's most populous country would appear to be a rather incredulous mission. Second, a nation-state that claims the only historical precedence of dropping not one but two atomic bombs on another (Asian) country—not unlikely due to "virulent racism," according to one Japanese critic[89]—certainly has the technical capacity to carry out this task.[90] On yet another level, one can argue that military expenses contribute to the accumulation of national debt to a much greater degree than the so-called stimulus spending invoked by advertisements like "Chinese Professor." The exchange between the Caucasian boy and Kimmel on "killing everyone in China," in a way, sharpened into the surface what is often suppressed in much fiscal-orientalist discussion about the linkage between state violence and national debt.[91]

The point of close reading Kimmel's segment here is not to blame the protesters for not "getting the joke" but rather to further discern what helped frame the discursive contours of this Chimerican media event—itself constitutive of the spectacle of national debt. Fiscal orientalism no doubt informed Kimmel and his production team's choice of the topic during a debt ceiling–induced government shutdown—a timing that inevitably played into the already widespread sentiment of national "weakening." But those who read the segment as propagating anti-China racism were also using "the language of the spectacular" in their protests.[92] After all, "China-bashing" rhetoric has long become part of the routine performance during political campaigns, as may be seen in the presidential election in 2020. This fixation on China had a radioactive effect on the public, who came to perceive the skit as enacting anti-China racism. Left out in this otherwise laudable antiracist struggle is a more critical inquiry into the systemic formation of the debt economy. Not only are this economy's racializing mechanisms less visible and more transpacific than the framing of *national* debt might suggest, but also the national space is itself experienced *differently* among various racialized subjects. The careful staging of the "Kid's Table" as representative of a multiethnic national body—signified visibly on screen by juice boxes with Star-Spangled Banners printed on them—points directly to this contested nature of the national imaginary.

Conclusion

The heyday of the proliferation of fiscal orientalist narratives centered on China's ownership of US national debt appears to have faded into the past. Yet the onset of a US-China trade war in 2018 reminded us that the transpacific media artifacts that I've examined here by no means exhaust the expanding fiscal-orientalist repertoire in contemporary America. Indeed, ongoing trade disputes that continued beyond the Trump administration make it quite necessary to turn more critical attention to this new genre of Yellow Peril discourse, which has merged with Sinophobia in intricate ways but demands a specific category of analysis. As I've suggested, such a racializing discourse centrally features the othering of the Chinese state and departs from the long-standing racialization of the Chinese people revealed in studies inspired by Edward Said. There is, therefore, a need to shift our analytical attention from an emphasis on "Chineseness"—understood as traits and characteristics of the Chinese people—to a focus on "rising" China as an agential force that is embodied and yet also objectified and dehumanized. The figural formation of the Chinese creditor speaks to the status of China less as a preformed object to be represented than a co-constituted subject with transpacific mediation.

As I have demonstrated in this chapter, this rethinking allows us to better discern the historically specific forces that have helped shape the formation of an indebted citizen-subjectivity in the era of neoliberal financialization. "To be indebted is to be fixated on the future," writes the award-winning writer and poet Cathy Park Hong in her 2020 best-selling book, *Minor Feelings: An Asian American Reckoning*.[93] For Hong, "The indebted Asian American is . . . the ideal neoliberal subject" because "the indebted Asian immigrant thinks they owe their life to America."[94] Contrasting this subject formation that is specifically Asian American,[95] what I have argued here is a broader but not unrelated formation of indebted citizenship predicated on the racialization of China as a menacing creditor. Fiscal orientalism, a rhetorical mode present in the "Kid's

Table," among numerous media artifacts, conjoins the temporalities of debt and otherness to augment the post-crisis spectacle of national debt in order to delegitimize the state as an agent for public good. Potentially impacted by this particular vision of the state are the lives of not just Asian Americans whose experiences defy the model minority myth but many other disadvantaged people of color as well. Nonetheless, that Kimmel's segment would trigger so many Asian Americans' antiracist protests is telling of the racializing logic at work in fiscal-orientalist narratives, even when the "China" figure may not appear in an embodied, representational form.

Yet calling out and protesting such racialization should not prevent us from further discerning the ideological work performed by this particular figuring of "rising" China. As I've suggested, fiscal-orientalist narratives, by pitting the Chinese and American states against each other, work to obscure economic Chimerica—a key dimension of the myriad transpacific entanglements that bound the two superpowers in the first two decades of the millennium. In the context of the trade war, the depiction of China as a contributor to unfair trade offered an excuse for the US state to display itself as an agent with more imaginary control over the national economy. Underlying these fiscal-orientalist narratives, again, is the "us versus them" framework—implied in none other than the "war" metaphor—which reifies the national distinction between China and the United States. This refusal to acknowledge relationality reflects precisely the operation of racial capitalism with regard to China (see the conclusion). The pervasive presence of these narratives, which continued well into the COVID-19 crisis that began in 2020, works to discourage alternative means of imagining the national community and the role of the state within it.

What, then, constitutes an example of these alternative forms of imagination? In the effort "to construct solidarity out of indebtedness,"[96] Richard Dienst has brought forth one such approach to radically rethink the relationship between state and society already bound by debt. He asks whether collective debts "express unmet social needs"—such as "housing, health care, and education"—that "should be understood as obligations that everyone owes to anyone, too important to be delegated to the calculations of a financial system indifferent to the common good" and therefore "can be recast as political demands."[97] To an extent, Dienst shares with Fallows the desire to call on the citizenry to reengage the state as an agent for public good. But he does so without sanctioning the kind of "foreign menace" that privileges a homogeneous, national body politic over the multiply heterogeneous citizen-subjects that occupy the *social* landscape.

At the end of *The Martian*, Watney ponders why it is worthwhile to spend so much money on his rescue. He comes to the realization that it is not just "progress, science, and the interplanetary future we've dreamed of for centuries" but, more importantly, that "every human being has a basic instinct to help each other out."[98] However romanticized this understanding may seem, it is suggestive that the multiple "technologies of the self" that Watney embodies are portrayed to have clear limits. It is ultimately with the help of others—the Chinese and American scientists and Watney's diverse group of teammates—that he is able to survive and return home. If the socialization of risk marks the making of the financial self, it also forms the basis on which "we can draw upon the intricacy of interaction that greatly opens up who and what we can be for one another."[99] Such a social vision appears to be crucial as China and America, among other nations, continue to battle the consequences of the pandemic, which has wreaked havoc on the global economy, disproportionally impacting communities of color in the United States and around the world. Indeed, this is the kind of vision that paves the way for alternative knowledge formations with regard to "rising" China and, in turn, help to conjure new political horizons.

CHAPTER 3

Cultural Chimerica

Imagining Chinese as a Global Language

A group of space-age outcasts roams on the rim of a postapocalyptic "verse," scavenging and selling illegal goods to willing buyers. They form the crew of *Serenity*, a spaceship of an outmoded "Firefly" class. Both the crew and the vessel they call their home look much less glamorous than their *Star Trek* counterparts. The year is 2517, and a corporate super government known as the Anglo-Sino Alliance has come to dominate the galaxy, having won the war against the rebel force not long before. The central planets under its direct rule feature high-tech architecture and transportation, while the outer rim appears grim and backward. Nevertheless, the *Serenity* crew unites around captain Malcolm Reynolds ("Mal"), a veteran of resistance movement. All crew members survive as a family, constantly evading the Alliance's surveillance and control. Most intriguingly, everyone seems to speak and understand Chinese, or at least some curse words or slang expressions in a mixture of Mandarin, Cantonese, and Hokkien.

Such is the premise of *Firefly*, a short-lived television show that first aired in 2003 on Fox. Created by Joss Whedon,[1] the space-Western series went on to acquire an impressive cult following via online streaming platforms like Netflix and Hulu. Its fandom even inspired a cinematic sequel by Universal Pictures in 2005 called *Serenity*. Among the first US sci-fi TV shows to feature a Chimerican future, *Firefly* continues to invite popular and critical attention. Its actors frequently make appearances at national and international Comic-Cons, and its fans find one another in on- and offline spaces alike.[2]

However, despite the creator's invocation of Sino-American relations in naming the "Anglo-Sino Alliance," the presence of "China" in the show is anything but explicit. Its plot and aesthetics are more immediately evocative of America's past, particularly the Civil War. The inspiration for the series, as Whedon recounts, came in part from *The Killer Angels*, a Pulitzer Prize–winning novel about the Battle of Gettysburg by Michael Shaara.[3] Not only does *Firefly*'s script include such Confederate references as "We Shall Rise Again," but its "twangy" theme song is also reminiscent of "a Civil War documentary."[4] In the words of Whedon himself, the point is for "viewers to equate the past, the present and the future" and "not to think of the future as that 'glowy thing that's distant and far away.'"[5]

For Whedon, there can be no mistake that China would assume a presence in this future of the United States. As he states in the special feature of the DVD for *Serenity*, "That these two cultures settled their differences and become one great superpower feels very very real . . . because that's what's going on right now. Powers and companies are merging into more and more powerful conglomerates."[6] Inspired by this amalgamation in economic terms, *Firefly* is an exemplary Chimerican media artifact that brings a *cultural* Chimerica into being. And Whedon has chosen, in part, to represent this cultural amalgamation *linguistically*.[7]

The imagination of Chinese as a prominent language for future global communication does not happen in *Firefly* alone.[8] In Lucy Kirkwood's play *Chimerica* (discussed in chapter 1), for example, an early scene set in 2012 shows Joe reuniting with Zhang Lin, now a teacher of "Crazy English" in Beijing, a language-training program with the intent "to make China stronger."[9] In his attempt to persuade Zhang Lin to go to America, Joe says, "Listen, you know how many Upper East Side assholes want their spawn speaking Mandarin? You could clean up."[10] Echoing the linguistic blending in *Firefly*, this exchange bespeaks the extent to which the two superpowers' cultural contention may very well take place in the linguistic realm—as the battle between English, the default global language of the present, and Chinese, the presumed lingua franca of the future.

In contemporary American media life, there is no shortage of examples that point to a desire to master Chinese skills as a means to prepare for a future world dominated by China. From Mark Zuckerberg to Arabella Kushner, from Sheldon in *The Big Bang Theory* to Dr. Temperance Brennan in *Bones*, Chinese learning is frequently displayed as a marker of intellectual prowess. Meanwhile, the Chinese government's establishment of the Mandarin-teaching Confucius Institutes (CIs) glob-ally, as part of its drive to strengthen its soft power, has triggered tre-mendous controversy in America, where the CI has the largest number of branches. Quite often, the anxiety stems from the perception that a foreign government is now *penetrating* the US higher education system, threatening to undermine its freedom of speech and academic inquiries, even though soft power is arguably something China has aspired to learn from the United States in the first place.

Amid this contention, *Firefly* is best seen as a Chimerican media artifact that construes "rising" China as a subject entangled with America in cul-tural terms. This chapter aims precisely to situate this artifact in a broader context of the beginning years of the twenty-first century, wherein vari-ous state and non-state actors have come to imagine Chinese as a global language of the future.[11] The discourses and practices mobilized by this imagination reveal different understandings of the relationship between language and culture. On the one hand, the performative display of Chinese fluency by what I call the "Chinese-speaking non-Chinese fig-ure" signals new forms and politics of racialization with regard to China, herein emerging as a cultural agent. On the other, the transpacific dis-courses and practices that construct Chinese as a lingua franca en route to challenge the global hegemony of English, which encompass both the buildup of CIs and artifacts like *Firefly*, invite us to consider the cultural entanglement of China and the United States as a basis for envisioning new forms of collectivity. The imaginary linguistic contention between Chinese and English, in other words, provides an opportunity to discern the complex relationships between language, culture, and (soft) power in ways that enable alternative visions of citizenship.

The Chinese-Speaking Non-Chinese

During President Donald Trump's first official China visit in Novem-ber 2017, his granddaughter Arabella Kushner became the real star on the Chinese web. When meeting with the Chinese president Xi Jinping and his wife, Trump proudly shared a clip from a tablet of Arabella donning a *qipao* (or *cheongsam* in Cantonese)—a garment symbolic of "Chineseness"—singing a number of Chinese songs as well as reciting the *Three Characters Classic* (三字经) and poems from the Tang dynasty. Peng Liyuan, the singer-turned-first-lady of China, immediately praised Arabella as "a small messenger of Sino-American friendship."[12] At the state banquet that followed, Arabella appeared on a giant LED screen to perform the number "Our Rice Field" (我们的田野), a nationally popular song readily recognizable by the guests. The next day, a spokeswoman from the Chinese Foreign Ministry called her performance a promising opening "to narrow the feelings and distance between the peoples of China and the United States."[13]

This, however, was not the first time that Arabella's Chinese-speaking skills had impressed the Chinese audience. Back in 2016 a video was taken of her reciting the famous poem "Sympathy for the Peasants" (悯农), and in 2017 a clip appeared of her singing a popular Chinese "New Year" song—both went viral on Chinese-language social media. Arabella was, however, not the first US public figure to showcase such dedication to Chinese learning. Mark Zuckerberg, the founder of Facebook, is known to have been studying the language for quite some time. Often accompanied by his wife, Priscilla Chan, who is of Chinese descent, Zuckerberg has made a habit of publicizing his passion for Chinese learning on his own Facebook page. In 2014, Zuckerberg held a thirty-minute conversation with a room of Tsinghua University students almost entirely in Chinese. During Chinese president Xi Jinping's 2015 visit to the annual US-China Internet Industry Forum in Seattle, Zuckerberg wrote on his Facebook page that he considered speaking with Xi in Chinese "a meaningful personal milestone."[14] In 2016, after the birth of their first child, Max, the Zuckerbergs posted a "Happy Lunar New Year from Priscilla, Max, and me!" video in Chinese on Facebook, garnering over 31 million views.

Both Arabella's and Zuckerberg's Chinese-speaking performances made it to China's state-run newspaper, *Guangming Daily*, which claimed that "Arabella's Chinese learning is a microcosm of the American public's enthusiasm in studying Chinese in recent years."[15] Also mentioned was the investor Jim Rogers's decision to move his entire family to Singapore, where his two daughters could study Mandarin Chinese alongside English.[16] Videos that feature one of Rogers's daughters speaking Chinese—in a manner strikingly akin to China Central Television newscasters—were also hits in China.

Calling this phenomenon a "Chinese fad [汉语热]," the Chinese official newspaper *Guangming Daily* cited the November 13, 2017, cover of *Time* magazine, which displayed "China Won" above its Chinese translation, "中国赢了." While the featured article with the title primarily focused on China's capacity to surpass the United States in terms of economic stability and political influence, the "unprecedented" bilingual cover, for *Guangming Daily*, served as evidence that the cultural influence of China has risen no less significantly.

The pronouncement of the Chinese official press was in fact not as grandiose as it may sound. Back in 2015, during Xi Jinping's US visit, President Barack Obama launched the "1 Million Strong" initiative to cultivate one million Mandarin learners in the United States by 2020. This amounted to no more than 2 percent of the "55 million students enrolled in US public and private primary and secondary schools"; in the words of Travis Tanner, head of the 100,000 Strong Foundation, "between 300 and 400 million Chinese students are learning English today, while only about 200,000 American students are studying Chinese," and therefore, "We must bridge that gap."[17]

The idea that Americans should "catch up" in Chinese learning is a telling sign of a widespread perception of China's rising world dominance in the foreseeable future (also discussed in chapter 2). As *Guangming Daily* suggests, the language was "seen by many American families as the most important skill" for their children. Rogers, for one, considered his daughters' Chinese-speaking skills the most valuable investment he had ever made. During speeches, he often encouraged people living in the West to let their children study Chinese, because "the 21st century belongs to China, whether we want it or not."[18]

If this perception informed the linguistic mixture in cult series like *Firefly*, it has also become more and more common in Hollywood films and popular TV shows. Since 2015, the Facebook page of a Beijing-based media company called Learn Chinese has shared a series of videos featuring Western celebrities (inexplicably) speaking Chinese in various popular media. One of them is titled "Learn Chinese with Foreign Celebrities," complete with a sarcastic Chinese tagline, "Watching Foreign Stars Showing (off) Chinese, Mesmerized." It features a clip of Hugh Jackman singing a Chinese pop song "Give Me a Kiss" (adapted from the 1953 English hit "Seven Lonely Days") on the *Conan* show.[19] Another video includes segments with actors from Bradley Cooper and Keanu Reeves to Angelina Jolie speaking Mandarin and Cantonese in various roles in Hollywood movies.[20] Yet another highlights Sheldon's attempts to study Chinese in the sitcom *The Big Bang Theory* (also hugely popular in China), which includes segments that accentuate his borderline autism.[21] Many of the videos are supplied with Chinese subtitles and dramatic on-screen texts like "How did you understand that?" to heighten their incomprehensibility.

These videos are archiving an emerging phenomenon in US media culture—what I call the rise of the Chinese-speaking non-Chinese. At the center of this phenomenon is a figure phenotypically not of Chinese descent—and often white—but presented as being able to speak Chinese competently if not fluently on screen. The "non-Chinese look" helps to differentiate the figure from Chinese speakers of Asian descent in the United States, whose minority status often leads to the loss of their primary or heritage language as they experience the pressure to assimilate to an English-dominant environment.[22] Despite the fact that this figure's spoken Chinese is often unintelligible to actual Chinese speakers—as indicated by those who created the videos shared by Learn Chinese—their linguistic competency is often conveyed through the expressions of their interlocutors. This feature also distinguishes them from the not uncommon representation of Asian characters as imperfect English or foreign-language (including Chinese) speakers, a trope that bespeaks the long-standing stereotyping of Asians as foreigners in the United States.

For instance, in the scene from *Limitless* (2011), Bradley Cooper's character, a former addict to an instant brain-enhancement drug, is shown in a Chinese restaurant ordering food in Cantonese. His pronunciation is so difficult to understand that the translators opted to use "???" in the subtitles. Yet not only does the Asian waiter appear to understand his orders, but his girlfriend also gives him a seemingly admiring look, to which he responds with a shrugging "What?" Likewise, in *The Day the Earth Stood Still*, Keanu Reeves, an alien sent to Earth to annihilate humanity, converses in what is presumed to be Mandarin with his contact—another alien who has adopted the look of a Chinese American—in a McDonald's restaurant. The conversation is so hard to decipher that a warning appears before the clip, as bolded on-screen texts in white against a black backdrop: "The following sequence is entirely in Chinese! Really! The Whole Thing! Entirely!" After playing the first few seconds, an intertitle says, "Forget it, just cut to the subtitles and don't bother guessing." When the clip starts up again, this time accompanied by the accurate Chinese subtitles, Reeves's lines are overlaid with the on-screen text, "Heavens, the aliens are speaking Chinese!"[23]

A similar mode of representing this Chinese-speaking non-Chinese figure can be traced in popular network TV shows like *Bones* and *House* as well as Netflix series like *House of Cards* (see chapter 4). In an episode of *Bones* titled "The Bone That Blew," for example, the brilliant anthropologist Dr. Temperance Brennan (aka "Bones") and FBI agent Seeley Booth visit the house of a rich businessman, where they find two children (brother and sister) conversing in Mandarin. Quoting his father, the boy tells Brennan that "China will run the planet in ten years" and that "it would be useful" to learn the language. "That's very smart," replies Brennan, who appears to perfectly understand the conversation in Chinese and acts as a translator between Booth and the two kids. She even knows the phrase "stupid inbred stack of meat," uttered by one of the children, even though it is not a recognizable idiom in China but more likely an intertextual reference to *Firefly* (episode 3, "Our Mrs. Reynolds").

Such demonstration of Chinese skills is by no means limited to fictional characters. Before the stardom of Mark Zuckerberg and Arabella Kushner, there was John Huntsman, the Republican governor of Utah and former US ambassador to China, who ran for president in 2011 and championed his ability to speak Mandarin Chinese. Even though his spoken Chinese is far from perfect, news outlets from NPR to the *New York Times* all came to describe him as "fluent in Chinese."[24] For example, in a television interview, Piers Morgan asked Huntsman to say something in Mandarin. Despite not knowing Chinese himself, he complimented the former ambassador for his "spectacularly good" Chinese.[25] According to Slate.com writer Geoffrey Sant, "none of the Beijing individuals" he spoke with "could understand this sentence even on repeated listens." Having surveyed a range of Huntsman's media appearances in China and the United States, Sant concluded that his Chinese was rather limited, which raised the question as to "why American media have been so eager to gush praise upon a skill it cannot evaluate."[26]

In other words, besides their predominant whiteness, the mode in which the Chinese-speaking non-Chinese figures appear in American media has a common feature. That is, even though their spoken Chinese is often incomprehensible, they are *made to appear* as being fluent in the language. Such a display of linguistic capacity is perhaps best described as *performative* in that the speakers' Chinese skills are constructed by way of the recognition of their interlocutors. As the Learn Chinese videos demonstrate, characters like those played by Bradley Cooper and Keanu Reeves are shown to be competent in Chinese via the approving gestures of those around them. The presence of these sideline characters, who are typically Asians playing roles that are one-liners, serves to reinforce the main characters' image of fluency regardless of the actual illegibility of their speech.[27]

This representation of the Chinese-speaking non-Chinese thus bespeaks an *inverse* kind of racialization through accent, as demonstrated by media scholars like Shilpa Davé and Jennifer Stoever. In Davé's study of "brown voices," accent operates "as a specific racializing trope for South Asian Americans"; it is "a means of representing race and particularly national origin beyond visual identification."[28] Likewise, Stoever discerns a "long historical entanglement between white supremacy and listening in the United States," what she calls the "sonic color line."[29] Whereas characters of color are racialized based on their voice and non-normative ways of speaking English, the white characters' *constructed* Chinese fluency presumes an English-speaking audience with little knowledge of the Chinese language. This ignores the fact that nearly three million residents in US households speak Chinese, making it the third most spoken language in the country after Spanish.[30]

Furthermore, if the othering of "brown voices" relies on a normative association between whiteness and proper accent, the Chinese skills performed by oftentimes white characters establish Chinese learning as a marker of prestige. It is linked to not only wealth and power, affording one the resources to learn such a demanding language, but also individual effort and talent, to which one's success is conventionally attributed. This is as true for Mark Zuckerberg and Arabella Kushner as it is for Dr. Brennan and Dr. House.

The Chinese-speaking non-Chinese phenomenon, just like the fiscal-orientalist narratives examined in chapter 2, bespeaks a mode of representation that is distinct to Chimerican media. In this mode, it is no longer the depiction of Chinese people as "Yellow Peril" that operates as a central trope. Rather, what motivates the desire to infuse white characters with Chinese speaking skills is the looming presence of an expanding Chinese state projected to overtake the United States in not just economic terms but cultural terms as well. China, in this sense, assumes the position of an imaginary Other more powerful than the American Self. As such, it cannot easily be "objectified" through direct visual representation. Rather, the containment of this Other requires a specific mode of listening that artificially erases accent as a sign of difference and subsumes it into a narrative of Chinese "fluency." It is this performative mode of listening that allows Piers Morgan to validate John Huntsman's Chinese as "spectacularly good" and President Trump to claim that Arabella Kushner is "fluent in Chinese," despite not knowing the language themselves.

What may be observed is a new mode of racialization that specifically corresponds to "rising" China, distinguishable from the othering of Chineseness more typically associated with an ethnicity. Instead, what has motivated this racialization is an imagination of China as an agential force. Chris Livaccari from the Asia Society, in an interview on the exponential growth of Chinese learning in the United States, observes, "If you look at the headlines over the last several years, it's clear that there is a perception among Americans that China is the place that is going to define our future."[31] Resonating with the CEO father's quote in *Bones*, comments like this are indicative of China's co-constituted presence in Chimerican media. That is, China is imagined as a subject, and as such, it exceeds the limit of orientalist representation, however prevalent the latter can still be, as may be observed in fiscal-orientalist narratives and seen most recently in journalistic reportage of "the Wuhan virus." It is this subject status that invites a new way of othering—that is, the reinsertion of a white speaking protagonist who can master the Chinese language and in so doing reclaim a position of superiority. Underlying this representational trope is none other than the desire to "Learn Chinese, Conquer the World."

More importantly, the status of China as a subject is not just imagined but also in many ways real. After all, the promotion of Chinese as a future lingua franca is not only a product of Euro-American media but also an active project on the part of the Chinese government, particularly through such entities as the Confucius Institutes. The fact that the China-based Learn Chinese website has archived and poked fun at the Chinese-speaking non-Chinese characters in American media is also telling of a situation wherein the object of representation no longer remains silent but is prepared to talk back. Emerging from these discourses and practices, therefore, is the figural formation of China as an agent whose subjectivity is thoroughly entangled with America. This entanglement, or what I have come to call "cultural Chimerica," is perhaps most clearly manifested in the Chinese state's adoption of the US-originated concept of soft power, which deserves more nuanced attention.

Language, Culture, and (Soft) Power

On some level a perceived relationship between language and culture informs the promotion and growing popularity of Chinese language learning globally. Often invoked among the proponents of Chinese learning is the belief that language is not just a tool for communication but a conveyer of culture. Zuckerberg, for one, cites "Learning Chinese helps me learn Chinese culture" as one of the three motivations for him to study Chinese.[32] Likewise, representatives of Confucius Institutes frequently speak of the organization's role in spreading "Chinese culture" in the world by teaching Chinese to foreigners. For example, Li Changchun, a member of the Standing Committee of the Politburo, described it as "a highlighted brand of Chinese culture internationally";[33] thus, it is "part of China's foreign propaganda strategy."[34]

Closely linked to the emphasis on the role of language in disseminating national culture is the discourse of soft power. For Joseph Nye, the Harvard political scientist who coined the term, soft power is "the ability to get what you want through attraction rather than coercion or payments."[35] Although the concept has been criticized for its ambiguity, China is one place where it has been embraced most enthusiastically, albeit in ways that are "complex and often contradictory."[36] Former party chief and president Hu Jintao, for instance, noted at the Central Foreign Affairs Leadership Group meeting on January 4, 2006, that "the increase of China's international status and influence depends both on hard power, such as the economy, science and technology, and defense, as well as on soft power, such as culture."[37] While this "hard versus soft" distinction follows Nye's formulation, it also corresponds to what communication scholar Jian Wang calls a "divided image" of China, "a divergence in perception between China as a polity and China as a society."[38] As Wang notes, "Chinese culture and tradition tend to be liked and admired by foreign publics, whereas its politics and governance are at a much lower standing."[39] The turn to "culture" as a means to enhance China's national "attraction" appears to be a logical step toward an aspired global power status.

The Chinese integration of soft power into its national policies often imagines the Chinese language as a force that shapes culture, which in turn allows the state to accrue power. This conception of the relationship between language, culture, and power is evident in an edited volume, *Language and Nation*, supported by the National Language and Literacy Working Committee and jointly published by the Commercial Press and the Communist Party History Publishing House. For the thirty experts who contributed to the collection, language is not just about soft power but hard power as well. Historically, China was once "a nation of strong language," but it is "by no means a linguistic power today"; therefore, "strengthening the nation linguistically . . . is an important part of realizing the Chinese Dream."[40]

Li Yuming, the department head of Language and Information Management at the Ministry of Education, also stresses the importance of building a "strong language." He argues that "a language's strength positively corresponds to the strength of the community to which it belongs." Since language is "the basis of culture, the symbol of a nation, and the core of 'soft national power,'" Li envisions that "Chinese can eventually play a bigger role in international linguistic life through a series of international communication measures," allowing China to "become not just an economic power, but also a linguistic power."[41]

Such a vision of Chinese as a "strong language" corresponds to the self-perception of China as a "great power" rising, on the one hand, and a long-standing mentality to catch up with the West, on the other. Although not always explicit, the comparison to English is not uncommon. After all, the rise of English from a relatively obscured status around 1600 to its global status today had much to do with the "old-brand British empire" and "newly prosperous USA."[42] While China's increasing global influence is widely observed, it has ranked only seventeenth on a list produced by the think tank Institute for Government, whose 2010 Soft Power Index highlights "international use of national language" as a cultural indicator of a nation's soft power, along others like "international reach of state-sponsored media" and 'number of winter and summer Olympic gold medals."[43] As communication scholar Terry Flew suggests, the list's Euro-American bias has put Britain, France, and the United States at the top while relegating China to "an unusually low position vis-à-vis not only major countries but also ones with less apparent claims to international influence."[44] The improvement of cultural ranking for the world's second-largest economy through language dissemination has understandably become a pressing task for the Chinese state.

Underlying China's quest for cultural soft power through language pedagogy, then, is a perceived hierarchy of power that persists between the West and "the rest." Here, the idea of the United States as an incumbent superpower looms large, in part because it is the culturally hegemonic position of America that gave birth to the "soft power" concept. The National Security Language Initiative launched by President George W. Bush in 2006, for instance, informs much of the discussion in Zhao's *Language and Nation.* Not only does the United States export the world's most influential cultural products, from TV shows to Hollywood films, but its post–World War II economic growth has propelled English into the global business lingua franca that it is today. Indeed, the relationship between English and America's rise to superpower status in the second half of the twentieth century demonstrates what linguist David Crystal calls "the closest of links between language dominance and economic, technological, and cultural power."[45]

This linkage between power and language appears to inform much of China's official vision regarding the role of Chinese in China's path toward a cultural superpower. Experts attending the 2015 Language

Strategy and National Security High-Level Forum invoked "America, France and Russia" as successful nations that recognized the role of language "in safeguarding national unity, defending national security, and expanding national influence," prompting them to elevate language to "the height of their (national) strategy."[46] As a nation that merely considers language as part of citizen education and an area of academic research, China has much catching up to do.[47]

The fact that the United States produces the bulk of English-language media output, for instance, is a significant source of concern. Wang Gengnian, head of China Radio International and member of the State Administration of Press, Publication, Radio, Film and Television (SAPPRFT), cites the import-export ratio of 4,000:24 in copyright trade with America in 2005 as a warning sign of the "cultural deficit" between China and the world. For Wang, without a more proactive expansion of Chinese culture abroad, China risks becoming "the target of cultural output, cultural penetration, cultural colonization, and cultural aggression of Western developed countries."[48]

The perception of China as potentially subject to Western and particularly US cultural "invasion" finds resonance in Chinese scholars' concern that English-language media may exert negative impact on China's national traditions. Some lament the immersion of youths "in the thoughts, culture, and values of foreign blockbusters with original soundtracks," which present threats to "the continuity of Chinese culture and national cultural security."[49] Others worry that the incorporation of more and more foreign words, especially English ones, into Mandarin may inhibit the future growth of Chinese, hence undermining the nation's "linguistic and literary sovereignty."[50]

The relationship between language and the information economy is also on the minds of experts like Li Yuming. For Li, while Chinese has the largest number of native speakers, it assumes a subordinate position in the cyberworld, in part because it is (US-originated) global firms that have pioneered the "research and development for Chinese-language information processing technologies"; therefore, the information sector is a key area of focus for "boosting the status of the Chinese language in cyberspace."[51]

Emerging from these discussions on language and culture is what may be called an *indigenization* of Nye's soft power concept, which adapts the idea to China-specific conditions. In Nye's framework, much of US soft power stems from the attraction of its ostensibly non-state sectors, particularly in the realm of popular culture. Hollywood is invoked as an example of a cultural voice that can sometimes be critical of US government actions, which Nye sees as the hallmark of a liberal society.[52] By contrast, China's official adoption of soft power has placed a much more explicit emphasis on the role of the state in the sphere of culture.

The establishment of Confucius Institutes in 2004 is perhaps the best example that demonstrates this closer linkage between culture and the Chinese state in terms of language pedagogy. In the words of Li Changchun, the CI is "an important achievement in culture going global and plays an important role in the improvement of cultural soft power."[53] The description of "cultural soft power" (*wenhua ruanshili*) not only positions the state as an actor in sponsoring entities like the CI but also envisions it as a beneficiary of the latter's global expansion.

To put this vision into practice, however, has proven to be quite challenging thus far. Indeed, the spread of CIs around the world and the controversy it has generated in the United States points to the multilayered ways in which the emergence of China's subjectivity is conditioned by America's global cultural hegemony. Just as Nye advocates a conception of culture as a type of "resource" for soft power, the relationship between English and America's superpower status has provided the Chinese state with very specific inspirations to turn language into an instrument of nation building through cultural means. But the extent to which the Chinese state's effort in accumulating cultural soft power can achieve its intended effects is influenced by factors not of China's own choosing. As literary scholar Lionel Jensen puts it, soft power initiatives "intended to mitigate a backlash against China's success . . . can still produce the very reactions they wish to avoid."[54] Reflective of this backlash is the increased tendency among Western observers to depict China's foreign policy as operative through "sharp power," a mode of global image projection characterized by information control and manipulation.[55] CIs are therefore worth analyzing as a case study that further illuminates the asymmetrical relations of power that are often masked by an imaginary Chimerican linguistic contention.

Confucius Institutes and Cultural/Linguistic Imperialism Reconsidered

At first glance, CIs appear to have no exact US counterparts. More often used as models for comparison are the British Council, France's Alliance Française, the Goethe-Institut of Germany, Spain's Instituto Servantes, Italy's Società Dante Alighieri, and the Japan Foundation. However, as Jensen points out, CIs "are the cornerstones of an ambitious international rebranding enterprise by the Chinese government built from a diplomatic strategy reminiscent of one employed effectively by the United States for many decades."[56] If understood as "public diplomacy through education," CIs are comparable to language exchange programs run by the US Information Agency (USIA)—an entity established in 1953 that took over the global network infrastructure set up by the Office of War Information (OWI) to promote an "idealized version of American culture" during the Cold War.[57] Since 1999 the State Department's Bureau of Educational and Cultural Affairs has absorbed USIA and oversees a number of related programs under the English For All initiative, including the English Language Fellow Program, the English Language Specialist Program, the Fulbright Foreign Language Teaching Assistant (FLTA), and the Peace Corps Volunteer/Response Volunteer Program.[58]

The CI's employment of volunteers as language teachers has been described as "Peace Corps–like."[59] But the comparison between the institute and its English-teaching equivalents set up by the US government is, with few exceptions, largely absent from public debates over CIs. This absence is likely due to two main characteristics that distinguish CIs from all other state-sponsored entities of language pedagogy. First, rather than independently operated, a CI is set up through the partnership between a Chinese university and a university in the host country, both connected to the Beijing headquarters. Second, prior to 2020, CIs were more directly administered by a state entity, formerly known as the Office of Chinese Language Council International, or the *Hanban*.[60] Originally overseen by the Ministry of Education, which has the mission "to plan, coordinate and direct the work of promoting the Chinese language in the world,"[61] the agency now refers to itself in English as the Council of the Confucius Institute Headquarters. In addition to university-based CIs, Hanban also partners with primary and secondary schools to set up Confucius Classrooms.

These distinguishing features combined have produced some cause for concern, as the Chinese state appears to have significant influence over the operation of CIs, which leads to the perception that a foreign government is now infiltrating the US higher education system. This perception, echoing the "othering" mode of fiscal orientalism (chapter 2), is evident in an April 2017 report released by the National Association of Scholars (NAS), titled *Outsourced to China: Confucius Institutes and Soft Power in American Higher Education*. Whereas the term "outsourced" evokes the economic anxiety toward China as a destination for US jobs, the report's cover features an imposing Confucius statue with a stern facial expression against the backdrop of a traditional Chinese pagoda overlaying the five stars of the Chinese national flag.[62] Simultaneously referenced are China's civilizational past and communist present. Both images work to construct China as a menacing power on the rise, however "softly" it may choose to present itself.

In reality, the English version of the "About Us" page of the CI website carefully avoids the language of "rising power," despite the official rhetoric of "peaceful rise." It describes itself as "a public institution affiliated with the Chinese Ministry of Education," one that "is committed to providing Chinese language and cultural teaching resources and services worldwide."[63] Emphasized is its goal of "meeting the demands of foreign Chinese learners and contributing to the development of multiculturalism and the building of a harmonious world."[64] The wording positions the institution—and by extension, the Chinese state—as responding to "foreign demands." The state, in this description, is offering a service to the world rather than being driven by an interest in advancing a particular set of political agenda.

At the same time, Chinese state officials have continuously referred to CIs as a diplomatic tool. In the words of Li Changchun, the CI is "an important achievement in culture going global and plays an important role in the improvement of cultural soft power."[65] More recently, in a 2018 speech at the second round of meeting of the Leading Group for comprehensively deepening the reform of the central government, Xi Jinping talked of "promoting the reform and development of the Confucius Institutes" as part of the development of the nation "as a socialist cultural superpower with Chinese characteristics."[66] It must serve the "great power diplomacy with Chinese characteristics" and is to become "an important force for Chinese and foreign humanities and cultural exchange."[67] For anthropologist Magnus Fiskesjö, who shared the news about this speech on the Modern Chinese Literature and Culture Listserv, the language here should dispel any belief that the CIs "are somehow innocent cultural entities, not direct instruments of the Chinese regime."[68] In his contribution to the edited volume *Yellow Perils: China Narratives in the Contemporary World*, Fiskesjö argues that "Party leaders are reviving the Confucius of the emperors—in the face of a near-total loss of faith in official Communism and Chinese State Marxism as a national religion, in a new social landscape that is heavily marked by the new class divides."[69] In this sense, the naming of the institutes after the ancient sage echoes political scientist Maria Repnikova's observation that "Chinese objectives behind soft power intermingle between external and domestic frontiers, with domestic publics being as much a target of soft power initiatives as international audiences."[70]

The instrumentalization of culture in China's CI project, then, lends itself to a critique in the US context precisely because it is, according to the NAS report, "a textbook example of a soft power initiative."[71] Citing Nye, NAS president Peter Wood explains in the preface to the report that this means CIs "attempt to persuade people towards a compliant attitude, rather than coerce conformity."[72] Based on an investigation of twelve CIs in New Jersey and New York, the report lists intellectual freedom, transparency, entanglement, and soft power as four troubling areas regarding CIs in the United States. Among them, "soft power" refers to the "positive" representations of China with an emphasis on "anodyne aspects of Chinese culture," which "avoid Chinese political history and human rights abuses, present Taiwan and Tibet as undisputed territories of China, and develop a generation of American students with selective knowledge of a major country."[73] This apparent attempt to influence American views toward China, according to the report, provides sufficient grounds for banning CIs completely in all US universities.

Perhaps not immediately recognizable from *Outsourced to China* is the fact that the NAS is a conservative organization that previously produced such dubious reports as *Sustainability: Higher Education's New Fundamentalism* (2015) and *Inside Divestment: The Illiberal Movement to Turn a Generation against Fossil Fuels* (2015). It is perhaps little surprise that it recommends Congress investigations into whether the CIs harm "American interests" or present "risks to national security" by potentially harboring espionage activities. Whereas Nye coined "soft power" to illustrate what he saw as a unique dimension of American power, the same idea, when associated with "one of America's international adversaries,"[74] becomes nothing less than a threat to US national security.

It is worth noting that the NAS report comes after the closing of two CIs, at the University of Chicago and Pennsylvania State University. The former is the home institution of one of CI's most vocal critics in the United States, the late renowned anthropologist Marshall Sahlins. In his short book *Confucius Institutes: Academic Malware*, Sahlins describes the organization as "a Chinese government agency inserted into an increasing number of universities and lower schools the world around, ostensibly with the reasonable and logical mission of teaching Chinese language and culture—and veritably with the practical mission of promoting the real political influence of the People's Republic."[75] Although implicit, critics like Sahlins are arguably rehearsing a case of "cultural imperialism," which has long been applied to criticism of the United States and only occasionally to that of China.[76] While the literature in critique of US cultural imperialism is vast, communication scholar Colin Sparks has usefully narrowed its definition as "the use of state power in the international cultural sphere."[77] It is with this presence of the Chinese state in a US higher-education environment that Sahlins and other critics of CIs have taken issue.

Perhaps more important, however, is the fact the neoliberal *weakening* of the US state has indeed provided the backdrop for such heightened anxiety toward China's "cultural invasion" in America. The majority of universities housing CIs are public rather than private universities.[78] These are institutions that have seen drastic withdrawal of governmental resources in the past several decades, as emphasized by the "numerous professors and administrators at universities with Confucius Institutes" interviewed in the NAS report.[79] Arguably, without this severe contraction of US state public spending,[80] the cultural and linguistic influence of China would not have appeared nearly as "imperialistic."

In the meantime, the "cultural imperialism" thesis has long been debunked for its lack of engagement with an "active audience," an erroneous description of "cultural invasion," and an inadequate understanding of the complex formation of national culture.[81] In this light, the anxiety toward China's cultural influence in the United States via CIs is also overstated at best. Even as Chinese officials imagine the state as a beneficiary of language-promoting initiatives like the CIs, the outcome of this quest for soft power through linguistic dissemination is far from certain. As anthropologist Jennifer Hubbert argues, "Policy objectives do not always equate with policy effects."[82] Indeed, "how policy targets understand the state depends as much, if not more, on the local audience's cultural practices and discourses as on the state's policy intentions."[83] As Hubbert's ethnographic account of a CI classroom on the US West Coast reveals, the intentional depoliticization of course materials with an emphasis on "cultural China" often has the opposite effect when it is interpreted as a result of governmental censorship of sensitive political contents. This has to do with the fact that "China is routinely imagined in the US public sphere as politically repressive and antagonistic to US interests."[84] Likewise, the imagination of China as a Communist state on the part of the parents of the CI students was also structured "not by Chinese culture but by U.S. culture and the ideologies of democracy that shaped their conceptions of Chinese state intentions and practices."[85] Echoing Hubbert's observation is international relations scholar Robert Albro, who suggests that criticisms of CIs "function to reinforce already frequently discussed and widely shared core values of US higher education"—namely, "academic freedom" and "integrity." "China's soft power strategy," rather than promoting diplomatic dialogues, "appears primarily to have provoked boundary-patrolling behaviour in the US public sphere."[86]

In other words, there is no necessary causal relationship between the increased global popularity of the Chinese language—whether instructed through CIs or otherwise—and China's cultural soft power. As historian Nianshen Song points out, just as the increased number of Russian learners during the Cold War and more people studying Arabic after September 11 in America does not reflect the rising soft power of the USSR and various countries in the Middle East, the increasing number of Chinese learners in the United States may in fact indicate "the expansion of American power."[87] Portraying China as an agent of cultural imperialism, as some critics of CIs have done, is premature at best.

This is not to say, however, that the Chinese state will unlikely benefit from language initiatives like CIs altogether. As communication scholar Randy Kluver argues, "The greater potential of the CI to enhance China's geopolitical influence power lies not in its constraint of political discussions, but rather in the potential to 'liberate' Chinese culture from its traditional geographical and linguistic boundaries, and to create a network of nodes, in which elements of Chinese culture (its philosophy, history, and literature, for example), enter the global network of cultural influence."[88] Similarly, as Hubbert notes, US students of CIs often wish to continue Chinese learning even though they may not want to study in China. Their "'desire' for Chinese may be understood as less a function of the CI program itself than a result of global economic forces in which Chinese offers a potential mechanism for empowerment in the domestic U.S. context."[89] Chinese language, then, is in some sense *detached* from the state so keen on instrumentalizing it as a means of promoting national culture globally. At the same time, the fact that students may indeed begin to perceive China as less than monolithic through their engagement with the CI instructors and programs also means that China may appear more "attractive" and less threatening. Since there is "a lack of cohesion among the various representatives and constituents of the state and between intent and implementation of state policy," CIs may indeed contribute to China's soft power—defined as national "attraction"—albeit not by enhancing its national unity but through "undermining perceptions of its uniformity and might."[90]

In this sense, the Chinese state vision of using language to strengthen its soft power may achieve its projected outcome not because language is a direct conveyer of culture but because the relationship between language and culture is *far less determinable*. In fact, initiatives like the CI, as Jensen argues, have sought to instrumentalize language to such an extent that they have taken on characteristics of the culture industry, in philosophers Theodor Adorno and Max Horkheimer's sense of the term.[91] Not only does the CI operate "like a business,"[92] but it has also adopted the imaginary of the brand as a way to promise "quality" and "returns" on investment.[93] What results is a standardized mass production akin to Hollywood films prone to the reproduction of sameness across its franchises.

China's emulation of American soft power through language pedagogy, in this way, more clearly manifests how China is influenced by the disciplinary power of the United States. In cultural critic Inderpal Grewal's words, "America" is best understood less "as an imperialist nation-state" than as "a nationalist discourse that produced many kinds of agency and diverse subjects."[94] In this sense, America's cultural imperialism does not so much work through "invasion" as through privileging particular ways of meaning making—that is, culture—over others. As I have argued elsewhere, one such privileged mode of meaning making works precisely through a branded imaginary that aims to turn culture into a resource for value production.[95] This is an imaginary that is closely associated with "America," whose disciplinary power stems much from Hollywood as a key agent of the global culture industry. As media scholar Aynne Kokas suggests, CIs are quite comparable to Disney English-language schools in Shanghai, which "drives brand awareness for Shanghai Disney Resort," part of the global franchise of Walt Disney.[96] Indeed, the CIs may well bespeak the hailing of the Chinese state as a subject by the imaginary of the brand—a cultural mechanism that is shored up by the US-led, globalizing intellectual property rights regime.

If the brand of Confucius ultimately is meant to augment the cultural unity of "brand China," it does so at the expense of recognizing, preserving, or revitalizing the cultural multiplicities within the nation, as may be seen in the privileging of official Mandarin over regional dialects in CIs' language programs. The disproportionate amount of money spent to "educate foreigners while so many children of the rural poor go unschooled" also warrants criticism.[97] "With only Confucius Institutes abroad but without any world-class universities domestically," argues Song, "no matter how much money is spent promoting one's national language and culture, it will only likely enhance others' soft power."[98] After all, when education inside China is in need of greater resource allocation, it can be quite difficult for the state to justify the overemphasis placed on promoting Chinese teaching in foreign locales.

Meanwhile, China is arguably still subject to what linguist Robert Phillipson calls "English linguistic imperialism," given the value associated with English among middle-class urban Chinese.[99] With slogans like "Conquer English to make China stronger," Li Yang, an English teacher known for promoting a shouting-aloud method of learning the language, has made himself a household name with "his campaign to turn China into a global hegemon through the mastery of English."[100] The status of English as a form of currency—"a privileged and pervasive mediator and measure of difference"—that anthropologist Vincente Rafael observes in Southeast Asia,[101] is keenly felt among many upwardly mobile or middle-class urban Chinese who highly value English education. In 2018 a Bollywood film with the title *Hindi Medium*, which depicts a middle-class obsession with children's English learning, became a hit in China, leading many to compare the situations in the two largest "emerging" economies. Before that, in 2013 a film directed by Peter Ho-Sun Chan from Hong Kong, *American Dreams in China*, became a hit for featuring an education enterprise akin to the real-life New Oriental Education and Technology Group, widely known for offering preparation classes for standardized English tests.[102] Phenomena like these, which bespeak the "structural and cultural inequalities between English and other languages,"[103] are indicative of the impact of "coloniality" in China despite its semicolonial past, which ostensibly differs from the history of India as a former colony of Britain.[104]

The Chinese state desire to accrue power by promoting Chinese, then, ultimately belies China's subjugation to the uneven power relations between the United States and China. The backlash against CIs in the US public sphere has failed to observe that this state practice is a product of the cultural impact of the US-originated discourse of soft power. It therefore shares with the rise of the Chinese-speaking non-Chinese figure in American popular culture the desire to contain a more powerful Other that is "rising" China. The projected cultural competition between the two superpowers privileges an instrumentalized relationship between language and culture in such a way as to obscure other alternatives. Yet one such alternative imaginary can be found in none other than the TV series *Firefly*, a media artifact that reconfigures the Chinese language as a productive force for meaning making—that is, as culture. This Chimerican artifact, indeed, projects a vision of community formation that has become increasingly difficult in neoliberal America, regardless of its ostensible multicultural aspirations.

Firefly Chinese: An Alternative Cultural Vision

Before delving into its many creative imaginings, it is important to acknowledge that *Firefly* as a popular show has invited much criticism for its orientalist depiction of a Chimerican future, and for good reasons. The sprinkling of anachronistic paraphernalia that signify Chineseness (or sometimes "Japaneseness") can be found throughout the show, from red lanterns and silk costumes to Chinese characters and ancient hairdos. Such a superficial display has led popular culture critic Leigh Adams Wright to argue that the show projects "'Asianness' . . . as a future fantasy and not as a contemporary reality."[105] Evocative of cultural theorist bell hooks's notion that the Other is "employed to add 'spice' to everyday life," with "bits of authentic culture recontextualized for a bored white mainstream's use,"[106] the show seemingly betrays a refusal to engage multiculturalism in the present.

Likewise, numerous fans and scholars have criticized the show's lack of meaningful Asian characters. In the words of Asian Americanist Douglas Ishii, for instance, *Firefly* projects an "Asian/American tomorrow" devoid of Asian people by mobilizing "palimpsest Orientalism, a techno-Oriental future laid onto a past-turning Oriental yesterday."[107] This is manifested through the orientalia that decorates the high-class citizens of the Alliance—a civilization defied by Mal, an "authentic" white masculine subject.

While criticisms like these are well grounded, they often insufficiently engage with the *linguistic* presence of Chinese in *Firefly* as a more consistent indication of China's world domination. In dialogue, the characters routinely switch from English to an untranslated mixture of Chinese dialects. Many of the words are swear words, while others are suggestive of intimacy between the characters—the dual presence of anger and attraction is perhaps symptomatic of the complex affective charge of Chimerican entanglements (see chapter 1).[108] The assumption, then, is that English has given way to Chinese as "the primary or expected language of communication."[109]

On some level, *Firefly* can indeed be denounced as part of the Chinese-speaking non-Chinese phenomenon in that the Chinese spoken is seldom comprehensible. As a native Mandarin speaker who is also fluent in Cantonese and several other dialects, when I first watched the show, I often had trouble deciphering the lines in Chinese. Only after repeated viewings, and with the help of the diligent translation done on such websites as browncoats.com and fireflyChinese.com, was I able to discern more of the Chinese conversations in the show. While some phrases may be based on Chinese spoken in Taiwan or elsewhere, many are not colloquial Chinese one would hear from native speakers in every-day situations, a case in point being the phrase "baboon's ass crack."[110] Yet the characters in the show all appear to understand one another perfectly. If the fluidity of their exchanges is meant to represent their bilingualism, it can also be argued that the portrayal of a group of non-Chinese capable of mastering the language in a Chimerican future again bespeaks the desire to contain "rising" China in the present.

Nevertheless, this reading, which aligns with the critique of the show's orientalist tendencies, does not account for the distinct vision for culture that it enacts. In *Firefly* one may discern a constant shifting of genre conventions and modes of identification that destabilizes any facile mapping of its narrative onto its intertextual referents, whether it's the nostalgia of Civil War or Orientalisms of various kinds: techno-, fiscal, or palimpsest. As art historian Rebecca Brown argues, because of the show's "shift in point of view from the empire to the periphery," its vision departs from that of other sci-fi shows like *Star Trek*, which manifests a modernist drive for discovery and conquest.[111] Instead, by highlighting the perspective of "a nomadic collection of disparate people who operate on the margins of society," it demonstrates that "while the war was lost and the empire prevails, difference has not been 'solved'" but is rather "multiplied and made messy."[112] Its multifarious and eclectic use of elements drawn from a wide range of Asian cultures therefore invites us "to see the potential within that messy *amalgam* instead of wishing for a cleaner, brighter, unified future."[113] In other words, the Chimerica that the show conjures warrants more nuanced scrutiny.

For one thing, the palpable presence of Orientalism in *Firefly* bespeaks the broader screen culture from which it emerges more so than it captures the show's many experimentations. As Ishii points out, "Palimpsestic Orientalisms are not a fiction to be proven false, but characterize the twenty-first-century anxieties of difference in the white supremacist culture from which Whedon writes; Asian American expression or presence alone cannot correct these interconnected racializations."[114] Certainly, the lack of explicit Chinese-ethnic presence within the *Serenity* crew—despite last names like "Tam" and the arguably Eurasian look of several main characters—proffers the idea that it is the (mix-raced) "American" independents who are fighting the "Sino" totalitarian regime. But to fully operationalize this racial divide, members of the Alliance could have featured a more "Chinese-looking" cast. This, however, is not the case. Instead, we see minor roles played by actors of Asian descent on the "rim," as indentured laborers (episode 7, "Jaynestown") and as "independent" prostitutes (episode 12, "Heart of Gold"), outside of the Alliance-dominant "core." Albeit as fleeting and seemingly inconsequential as those accompanying the Chinese-speaking non-Chinese main characters, their presence challenges a reading of *Firefly* that plainly affiliates whiteness with freedom and Chineseness with control.

It is also worth remembering that the show is set in a Chimerican future of 2517. In this context, the made-up phrases that are seemingly incomprehensible to contemporary native speakers can also be interpreted as an indication of the changing nature of language. After all, the "Chinese" spoken in 2517 will unlikely be exactly the same as it is known today. Just as "creolisation re-invents, re-localises, re-vernacularizes English,"[115] one can equally imagine multiple forms of "Chinese" spoken in 2517 that may not sound like any of its dialects today. The fact that "panda piss," or "*xiongmao miao*" ("Jaynestown") doesn't exist now doesn't mean it wouldn't exist in the future.

Moreover, the insertion of Chinese phrases is often meant to augment dramatic effects. As various recorded interviews with the *Firefly* cast reveal, the Chinese phrases are often directly translated from English ones. The process was likely quite difficult, given that, to my knowledge, no exact equivalent exists for phrases such as "baboon's ass crack."[116] But this is not necessarily a failure in translation. Rather, words like this are rarely central to the narrative. As Whedon himself says, "We only did phrases that we didn't need to know what they meant. Like if he shouts '*bizui*,' we know he says 'shut up!' and if he goes 'blah blah blah . . . ,' we know he's going 'oh my god I'm very surprised'"[117] The aim, therefore, is not to replicate contemporary Mandarin or Cantonese spoken by "real" Chinese people but rather to produce an affective intensity unmatched by their English equivalents.

The presence of Chinese in *Firefly* thus points to what linguist Alton L. Becker has called "languaging." Unlike language, which is "a system of rules or structures," languaging "combines shaping, storing, retrieving, and communicating knowledge into an open-ended process."[118] Such a context-specific communicative process is reflected in the ways the *Firefly* crew came to "learn" Chinese. Since the translated Chinese phrases are often much longer than their English counterparts, they also became more challenging for the actors to repeat and memorize. Although translator Jenny Lynn has supplied the actors with "simplified phonetic spellings and audiotapes," sometimes even opting for the Taiwanese pronunciation to make things easier, no Chinese speakers were on site to coach them.[119] The result is oftentimes pronunciations that diverge significantly from the recordings. But this learning process also highlights Chinese speech as a *performative* act that emerges from the co-constitution between the speaking subject and the linguistic medium—remediated through the nonhuman technology of cassette tapes—rather than a fixed and enclosed system of unchanging rules.

Furthermore, unlike the media commentators who unquestioningly celebrate the "Chinese fluency" of John Huntsman and the like, those on the *Firefly* crew appear to be quite aware of, even reflexive about, the imperfection in their training and pronunciation. As Jane Espenson, the writer for the episode "Shindig," mentions laughingly, "I bet there are a lot of people in China going 'What the hell are they saying?'"[120] The actress Jewel Staite, who plays the mechanic Kaylee, recalls, "It wasn't easy at all. Chinese is not exactly . . . you know . . . If it was French it would be fine but it was . . . a little difficult. . . . Most of the time none of us got the sound of it right anyway."[121] This sentiment is shared by Alan Tudyk, who plays "Wash" (the pilot) and openly expressed his resentment towards the Chinese-speaking part of the role. At a tenth-anniversary *Firefly* reunion panel, Tudyk even suggested that instead of translating everything from English, the writers should have chosen the best-sounding phrases from a set of Chinese curses—an idea seemingly unfathomable to coproducer Tim Minear.[122]

While the alternative mode of representing the Chinese speech that Tudyk suggested may indeed enhance the comprehensibility of the words spoken, it is precisely the constructed nature of the translated words from English that points to their performativity. The artificiality of these words is reminiscent of cultural theorist Rey Chow's understanding of languaging "as a type of prostheticization, whereupon even what feels like an inalienable interiority, such as the way one speaks, is . . . impermanent, detachable, and (ex)changeable."[123] Seen from this perspective, the laboriously rendered enunciation of Chinese words on the part of the *Firefly* cast is not meant to be an inferior imitation of the "real" but rather creations of an entirely different order. What is envisioned is a future development of Chinese not "as a linear, logical progression," as may be envisioned by officials in China intent on building a linguistic superpower.[124] Instead, the language is conveyed "as actual discourses that are dispersed and found in bits and pieces" whereby it "mutates and renovates itself."[125]

More importantly, this future Chinese is decidedly not a sign of individual power and privilege as it has been mobilized by the Chinese-speaking non-Chinese figure in contemporary American media life. As Whedon puts it, "The idea was your most basic white-trash person can speak Chinese. You're the person . . . with no education who . . . was the last person you'd expect speaks Chinese off the bat and it just gives it a lovely kind of lived in texture."[126] The point, as Brown suggests, is to "normalize" the language, not to exoticize it.[127] While some have speculated that the use of Chinese was meant to bypass censorship of swearing on television, Kevin Sullivan has counted a mere 45 percent of the Chinese expressions as curses.[128] Nonetheless, Adam Baldwin, the actor who plays "Jayne," has described the expressive freedom opened up by Chinese: "I did love the fact that you didn't have to 'bleep' anything out and you could actually say, you know, 'frog humping cat sucking pissant' in Chinese and not have to worry about the censors going 'oh you can't say 'shit.'" Here, the mechanism of censorship, more often known to be part of the Chinese regime than that of the United States, is defied by none other than the language of the authoritarian Other. The fact that cursing is more typically associated with the lower class further accentuates the show's appropriation of the language in ways that depart from the assumed linkages between Chinese learning and wealth and power, as manifested by Mark Zuckerberg and others. In fact, it may even mirror the hybridized linguistic space occupied by actual (working-class) Chinese immigrants in the United States whose experience resonates with that of other immigrant groups also engaged in language "mixing" in ways that defy mainstream standards and "purity."[129]

Chinese in *Firefly* in some ways takes on features of what literary scholar Shuh-mei Shih calls "the Sinophone," which does not denote "Chinese-speaking" as much as it references a "family" of Sinitic languages, one that is "polyphonic and multilingual."[130] For Shih, Sinophone invites critical investigation into Sinitic cultural productions in places that have endured previous or ongoing colonial occupation by the Chinese empire, such as Xinjiang and Tibet. A similar sense of revolt against Chinese linguistic imperialism certainly finds resonance in the practices of languaging in *Firefly*. Upon closer examination, however, the series presents a more complex vision of cultural Chimerica that challenges the simplistic equation of China with the status of a colonizer and the *Serenity* crew as postcolonial linguistic subjects.

Taken at face value, the series appears to be an emblem of the neo-liberal triumph of individualism vis-à-vis a totalitarian state, the latter reminiscent of the long-standing "Red China" scare in US media culture. The background story of the Alliance and the principal characters' struggles against it, for instance, have inspired viewers to interpret the series as a libertarian manifesto,[131] as "frontier narratives" that champion individual liberty,[132] and as evidence of Whedon's "commitment to Lockean ideals of government,"[133] to name a few. The theme of freedom, as noted by almost every critic, is certainly manifest in the first verses of the series' theme song:

> Take my love, take my land
> Take me where I cannot stand
> I don't care, I'm still free
> You can't take the sky from me.

Lyrics like this are reasonably associated with the character Mal, often admired for his "unquenchable thirst for freedom" and unabashed statements like "That's what governments are for, getting in your way" ("Pilot").[134] To some extent, the *Firefly* franchise as a whole does seem to pit freedom-loving individuals against state control, a struggle that culminates at the end of *Serenity* in a celebration of "free speech," when the crew succeeds in broadcasting the previously classified information about the origins of Reavers to the "verse." Reavers, as the film reveals, are monstrous by-products from state-sponsored experimentation in behavior-modifying drugs. These drugs' pacifying effect on the majority of their subjects, as one critic tellingly interprets, is "a horrific metaphor for the diminution of man's ambition under the corrosive influence of socialism."[135]

Nonetheless, interpretations of this kind are perhaps more illustrative of the pervasive presence of fiscal orientalism (chapter 2) with regard to China than they are reflective of the show's artistic vision. For one thing, the *Firefly* franchise does not present enough evidence that the authoritarian character of the state is chiefly attributable to the "Sino" portion of the Alliance. Whedon's own explanation also presents a more nuanced scenario:

> Mal's politics are very reactionary and "Big government is bad" and "Don't interfere with my life." . . . And sometimes he's wrong—

because sometimes the Alliance is America, this beautiful shining light of democracy. But sometimes the Alliance is America in Vietnam: we have a lot of petty politics, we are way out of our league and we have no right to control these people. And yet! Sometimes the Alliance is America in Nazi Germany. And Mal can't see that, because he was a Vietnamese.[136]

Here, Whedon makes no mention of China or socialism. Instead, he references the contradictory nature of US hegemony, using its imperialist war in Vietnam and its role in anti-Nazi struggles during World War II as examples. The description of Mal as "a Vietnamese" is particularly telling because it destabilizes the identity of the protagonist solely based on his phenotypical whiteness. As River, the genius sister of Simon Tam, tells the audience, "Mal" means "Bad" in Latin (episode 1, "The Train Job"). In sound, it arguably also resembles that of an Anglicized pronunciation of "Mao." These connotations are in line with the depiction of Mal as an antiestablishment, rebellious, and charismatic figure who takes on the persona of a hero against imperialism—whether Chinese, American, or Chimerican—even a revolutionary leader of the Third World.

Seen from this perspective, the Chinese speech in *Firefly* is less suggestive of Sinophonic hegemony than subversive of the linguistic imperialism of English. As linguist Susan Mandala points out, the show's representation of codeswitching and use of Chinese more generally can be compared to textual strategies observable in postcolonial writing;[137] on the one hand, they challenge "the status of standard English as the primary (or most valued) form of communication (abrogation)"; on the other, they engage "varieties of the language . . . that arise from within local communities of speakers (appropriation)."[138] The "grammatically perverse but semantically rich" Chinese creolized in the show therefore signifies resistance more so than it reflects dominance.[139] It is better seen as a practice taken up by the disenfranchised to formulate bonds within communities that defy the power of the Anglo-Sino regime.

Interestingly, the community formation via Chinese dialogues in *Firefly* also finds resonance in its fandom. "After only a few episodes had aired," Sullivan reports, "fans in online communities were begging for weekly translations, and Mandarin-speaking fans would try to provide them. Translation debates sometimes followed."[140] The website Firefly Chinese (https://fireflychinese.com), created by Asian American media scholar Jason Q. Ng, is exemplary in providing a platform to inform non-Chinese-speaking audiences with the meanings of numerous untranslated Chinese terms in the show. The distinct Chinese slangs from the show have also found its way into "fan art, fan fiction, song parodies (filk) and role-playing games" as well as fan gatherings, even prompting some usage "in daily life," such as "getting away with swearing at work or in front of children."[141] These generative effects of *Firefly* have in some sense brought into reality its producer Jane Espenson's half-joking remark that she "would like to think that we educated the world by teaching them a little bit of Mandarin."[142]

Such meaning-making practices of building communities through language, both on screen and online, point to a vision for culture that departs significantly from the one motivating the linguistic performance among American elites or the buildup of Confucius Institutes backed by the Chinese state. Here, Chinese is not instrumentalized as a means to accumulate personal prestige or state power. Rather, it becomes a means to establish bonds within a marginalized community on screen, which in turn prompts devoted fans to appropriate the language into an in-group code of communication. This alternative vision of community formation thus resonates with those offered in speculative fictions, or what Asian Americanist Aimee Bahng calls "migrant futures." Emerging here is an understanding of Chinese as a form of meaning making for the "under-commons" over and against the neoliberal fantasy of value extraction.[143] Defying the speculative ideology of financial globalization that manifests itself in fiscal-orientalist framing of Chinese futures, this vision presented by a pioneering Chimerican media artifact is illustrative of the politically disorienting effects of "rising" China that are also affective in forming communities of meanings through inter-personal bonds.

Conclusion

The imagination of Chinese as a lingua franca of the future continues to manifest itself in an expanding repertoire of Chimerican media that bring a cultural Chimerica into visibility. Engaging with the transpacific discourses and practices that construct Chinese as a global language allows us to probe into the cultural entanglement of the two "superpowers" in the first two decades of the twenty-first century. Both the workings of and responses to the Confucius Institutes in America and the localization of US-originated soft power discourse in China are indicative of America's pervasive global cultural hegemony. Yet the increasingly felt presence of China in America has also prompted the media phenomenon of the Chinese-speaking non-Chinese in the United States, operative through a different racializing logic than the stereotypical represen-tation of Chinese people on screen.[144]

In many ways, both the branding efforts of China's Confucius Insti-tutes and numerous elite Americans' wish to equip themselves and their offspring with the linguistic currency of Chinese are prompted by the desire to secure a future increasingly plagued by risks.[145] These risks can take the form of America's perceived cultural "invasion" among Chinese government officials or the prospect of a Communist China–dominated world order in the eyes of American parents, students, politicians, and entrepreneurs. Such an instrumentalization of language may be linkable to the neoliberal ethos of privatization that has not only internalized individual self-help as a primary means to secure one's future, linguisti-cally or otherwise, but also induced the budget cuts for language educa-tion in US public schools, thus creating the condition for them to more readily accept the financial influx from China's Confucius Institutes.

Set against the backdrop of this Chimerican cultural entanglement in the beginning years of the millennium, *Firefly* presents an imaginative attempt to deconstruct the monopolistic reign of English in America. The appropriation of Chinese in *Firefly* as a meaning-making practice that is perpetually "on the move" reminds us that "the future remains profoundly unknowable and unpredictable."[146] Such an indeterminist vision of the future clearly distinguishes itself from finance capitalism's tendency to colonize the future through speculative instruments. The linguistic crossing taken up by *Firefly*'s cast and fandom provides a vision for community formation that both reflects and challenges the deficit of collectivity under neoliberal globalization. Its playful mistranslation, which may be read as a fictional "mutant offspring" of Chinese,[147] points to a future wherein Chinese is mobilized less as a form of instrumental-ized cultural capital than as a meaning-making practice that cultivates communities of protest, struggle, and survival.

"Language is a virus," says historian Daniel Immerwahr, connecting the lingua franca status of English to America's rise to global hegemony after World War II.[148] "Global English," he argues, "isn't really, in the end, the product of a few big decisions made in Washington or London" but rather "the product of a billion or so smaller ones made all around the world."[149] Linguistic hegemony, much like the globalized discourse of soft power, perpetuates itself through establishing the standards to which others must conform. As the case of the Confucius Institutes tell-ingly suggests, China is far from being in a position to set the terms for cultural negotiation with the incumbent superpower. Despite the value

CHAPTER 4

Political Chimerica

House of Cards *and/in China*

American TV shows (known as *meiju* in Mandarin) have had a presence in China since the 1980s. But their risen popularity in recent decades is largely attributable to online video streaming enabled by broadband internet. Thanks to numerous illicit video-streaming sites, *Prison Break* and *The Big Bang Theory*, among others, have become urban Chinese viewers' favorite programs. In Euro-American journalistic accounts, the popularity of these shows is often staged as a battle between fans and the party-state. For Evan Osnos, a journalist best known for his writings in the *New Yorker*, the "self-described 'netizens'" who volunteered to trans-late and upload a popular series like *Prison Break* online "inhabit what that name implies: an ever-more autonomous online nation that sets its own laws about what is acceptable."[1] Discontent with the domestic and South Korean offerings on state-run channels such as China Central Television, these "netizens" have collectively contributed to the spread of these shows despite the lack of official government approval.[2]

In 2013, when the Netflix-produced political drama *House of Cards* (hereafter *HoC*) became a hit in China, part of the surprise lay in its legitimate mode of distribution. Sohu, one of China's largest internet service providers, purchased the exclusive rights to screen the series in the country on February 16, 2013. Within ten days after its release on March 2, it shot up the chart of the most-watched American TV shows on the site.[3] Season 2, which features a prominent Chinese presence by way of a corrupt Chinese Communist Party insider, attracted eight times as many Chinese viewers as the first one.[4] Sohu's decision to put on the season at the same time as its US release also contributed to this growth in viewership, as it "left no time for pirate sites."[5]

Ma Ke, the senior executive of audiovisual copyrights acquisition at Sohu, first learned about *HoC* at a presentation in the United States in May 2012.[6] When the first season came out in the United States on February 1, 2013, right before China's Spring Festival break, Ma initially thought it was "too high-end" for the market. As members of the senior staff at Sohu reportedly claimed, "they loved watching it themselves" but "their wives couldn't stand it."[7] However, Ma soon noticed the show had generated waves of discussion on Sina Weibo (one of the largest social media platforms in China), even prompting subtitling groups (*zimuzu*) to provide numerous pirated versions. This popular demand quickly prompted Sohu to purchase the show.[8]

The experience of watching *HoC* on the Chinese web, for CNN's Steven Jiang, was nothing less than "surreal"; after all, the State Administration of Press, Publication, Radio, Film and Television (SAPPRFT) has often censored American and British television content that negatively portray China.[9] Yet not only did *HoC* persist online, unperturbed, but it also attracted the attention of high-ranking officials in Beijing. Among its fans was Wang Qishan, the head of the anticorruption committee, who reportedly urged his subordinates to watch the series. Even President Xi Jinping made a joke in reference to the show during his 2015 US visit, claiming that his anticorruption campaign, unlike *House of Cards*, "was aimed squarely at stamping out graft and not purging political rivals."[10]

The Chinese popularity of *HoC*, then, defies the "fans versus the state" narratives that typify journalistic accounts regarding the presence of American TV in China. A closer look into its producer, Netflix, and its making, distribution, and reception also raises important questions about the relationship between media and politics beyond the territorial confines of the nation-state. Like Osnos, media scholar Mareike Jenner has argued that Netflix's mode of operation reflects a fragmented political landscape quite unlike the era of national television.[11] Further compounding the *HoC* phenomenon is the rising role of the Chinese state in shaping global media and politics, which has become a constant source of anxiety within the United States, as may be observed in recent controversies regarding Chinese investment in Hollywood.[12] *HoC* therefore provides an opportunity to discern the *political entanglement* of the two superpowers. By making this political Chimerica visible, *HoC* and its transpacific reception disrupt the common ideological positioning of

China as a racialized political Other, a framing common in journalistic accounts of Chinese censorship.

My study of *HoC* and its engagement with China highlights the workings of transpacific media in enacting a relational space. This space can be discerned through the multifaceted ways in which *HoC* is received in China and how China manifests itself in *HoC*. The emergence of Netflix as a distinctively globalizing data-driven media platform with a keen interest in entering the Chinese market has informed the production, distribution, and reception of *House of Cards* in ways that reflect "rising" China as an agent co-constituted with transpacific media. The political Chimerica manifested in this co-constitution, just like the economic and cultural entanglements to which it is closely linked (see chapters 2 and 3), illuminates media as an environment in which politics take place. Recognizing this political entanglement, then, invites us to pay closer attention to the depoliticizing tendencies across the Pacific in an era of algorithmic media, thus opening a path to imagining new forms of politics.

House of Cards in China

Originally a 1990s BBC trilogy with the same name, the story of *HoC* came from Michael Dobbs's best-selling novel. A former member of the British Conservative Party in the 1980s, Dobbs once worked as Margaret Thatcher's chief of staff, an experience that no doubt informed his writing. The American version, as the first product of Netflix's original content creation, was part of the company's attempt to construct itself as a participant in "high culture" that offers quality drama.[13] In 2013 this self-branding effort led to two Emmys following fourteen nominations, making it the first online drama series to win the awards. The first two episodes of Season 2 were screened at the Berlinale Film Festival in 2014, further bespeaking Netflix's intent to nurture a high-profile brand identity.

The "high quality" image of the show cultivated by Netflix attracted Charles Zhang, the CEO of Sohu, who was looking to upgrade the company's online streaming status. His attempt to target a quality drama at a high-end market appeared to be quite successful. Sohu's audience survey indicated that government employees and Beijing residents made up the bulk of the 24.5 million Chinese viewers for season 1.[14] This profile reflected the demographics of the Chinese audience for American TV shows in general. Averaging 19–40 years old, 80 percent of them had at least two years of college education, and they seldom watched domestic shows.[15] On February 14, 2014, like many of their US counterparts, these young white-collar workers in China reportedly planned to "go home early after work" so that they could spend the Valentine's Day evening binging the new season.[16]

For many Chinese fans, the main attraction of *HoC* was its unabashed representation of political reality in America. Such was the view of Zhao Lin, an author affiliated with the CCP's anticorruption campaign. In an article on the website International Anticorruption Outlook, Zhao used *American Gangster* and *HoC* to comment on the often "hidden" corruption problem in the United States and other Western developed nations. He believed that such legally sanctioned corruption practices as campaign donations and lobbying had been endemic in these countries, and they accompanied the export of Western democracy to the developing world.[17]

Zhao's piece caught the attention of Western journalists because it provided easy proof that the CCP might well be using the show as educational material that illuminates the perils of US democracy. For the *New York Times*, Zhao's account omitted the discussion of the portrayal of Chinese corruption in season 2, likely because topics like this were unthinkable for Chinese television.[18] Numerous Chinese viewers appeared to concur with this perception of the state as a routine censor of media content. As a CEO of a Chinese investing firm put it, "Only one of [the two countries] can make and screen this type of TV show."[19]

On the other hand, American politics as depicted on screen also reminded Chinese audience of politics in China. This can be best illustrated in the frequent mention of "mirror" in the plentiful reviews published online and in print. One such review came from Bai Ping, an editor-at-large at *China Daily*, who drew attention to *HoC*'s "relevance to the present Chinese reality." For Bai, "*House of Cards* holds up a mirror to Chinese officials on how human weaknesses such as greed and self-centeredness can send them over the cliff, especially when they have unchecked power."[20] Likewise, Dong Chunling, a researcher at the Chinese Academy of Modern International Relations, suggests that even though the show was filled with "negative energy," it nonetheless retained "the laudable spirit of critique and reflection"; therefore, it served "as a mirror—the one who knows others is wise, the one who knows the self is shrewd."[21]

Comments like these suggest that Chinese viewers had no trouble connecting the American drama to "China's own official corruption problems."[22] Indeed, many of them even came to call the show "*Legends of Empress Zhen* in the White House," seeing it as an American version of a popular court drama set in Imperial China, one (among many) that features the competitions among courtesans as they strive to become the most powerful in the palace.[23] For participants in an online comparison of the two, these shows shared much in common in how they depicted *gongdou* (宫斗), or "palace infighting," referring to power struggles in high places.[24] Yet again, some viewers pondered why there weren't any shows about politics in China quite like *HoC*, whose Chinese equivalents were typically set in dynastic pasts rather than in the present.[25]

Underlying these narratives, then, are two competing assumptions regarding Chinese and American politics. First, *HoC* is seen as a show that reflects *real* politics, whether in China or America. From this perspective, there is at least a level of *sameness* between the two political systems. Second, *HoC* is regarded as an American media product about American politics that does not have a contemporary Chinese counterpart. In this view, the Chinese and American political systems remain fundamentally *different*, and the key marker of difference is none other than the possibility of an audiovisual artifact to *represent* political reality free from state interference.

A closer look at the show and the Chinese responses to it reveals that neither of these assumptions can be substantiated. For one thing, the idea that China does not and cannot have its own *HoC* ignores the fact that (anti-)corruption dramas were among the most prominent genres on Chinese television between the mid-1990s and mid-2000s. As media scholar Ruoyun Bai recounts, even after 2004, when the state issued a ban on such topics on prime-time television, corruption has been "reincarnated" in a variety of shows that "provided a different spin" on the issue in ways that appealed to urban youths.[26] In 2017 one such repackaged drama of high production value, *In the Name of the People* (*Renmin de Mingyi*), became the hottest trending TV show on Chinese social media. It featured the highest-ever-ranked corrupt official on screen—that is, at the subnational (or *fuguoji*) level. While fictional, its storyline clearly indexed the case of Zhou Yongkang, the former security chief convicted of bribery and other crimes in 2015. Before it aired, *China Daily* had claimed the show was "poised to challenge the popularity of the US hit *House of Cards*."[27] China Global Television Network (CGTN), the global branch of the state-run China Central Television (CCTV), even featured a discussion program "Why Is the Chinese 'House of Cards' So Popular?" on April 16, 2017, to talk about how the show came to be viewed as "one of the most daring and realistic Chinese TV dramas ever."[28]

Still, for some viewers, *In the Name of the People* shared with *HoC* a sense of unrealism, as it portrays several CCP members as "flawless."[29] While fans of *HoC* across the Pacific cited the numerous real-world events it references as evidence of *HoC*'s more truthful connection to political reality, many of them also took note of its far-fetched plotlines. For instance, former US president Bill Clinton reportedly told Kevin Spacey, "[Ninety-nine] percent of what you do on that show is real. The 1 percent you get wrong is you could never get an education bill passed that fast."[30] The *Washington Post* even went so far as to suggest that "*House of Cards* is the worst show about American politics," as it misleadingly portrays, among other things, Frank and Claire Underwood as the "only . . . smart people in Washington," with no rivalry of equal ambition and intellect.[31] Echoing this is Chinese critic Dong Chunling, who noted that *HoC* overexaggerated the power of Underwood and painted the president as unrealistically weak, contrasting the actual power of the presidency.[32]

Understandably, for many Chinese viewers, the most vexing aspect of *HoC*'s realist claims is its representation—or rather, *mis*representation—of China. As communication scholar Weiyu Zhang's study of a thread on the Chinese online forum Baidu Tieba (Baidu Post Bar) shows, "the authenticity of the depiction of China in the show" was a constant topic for discussion. Fans invoked such details as a map of China sans Taiwan as illustrative of the show's intent "to distort reality in order to make China a villain or a political tool to distract Americans' attention from their internal conflicts."[33] But a more focal point of debate, judging from media reportage and social media commentaries, was the portrayal of Xander Feng, the Chinese businessman at the center of a series of corruption scandals that unfolded in season 2.[34]

Some viewers read Feng's character, who routinely engages in "bribery, murder, and back channeling," as a form of "China smearing (*hei Zhongguo* 黑中国)." Others, such as the well-known film critic Raymond Zhou, believed that *HoC* is more critical of the US political system than of the Chinese one, as "Feng is but one person from China."[35] Interestingly, an interview with Terry Chen depicted the Canadian-born actor who played Feng as someone "not too familiar with Chinese politics" and who couldn't even name the chairman and president of China. Rather than seeing himself as a problematic embodiment of China, Chen seemed more concerned with the long-standing "stereotyping of the Chinese people" and the "many challenges faced by people of color" in Hollywood.[36]

Perhaps echoing Chen's comment, a number of viewers in China and the Chinese diaspora saw Feng as a refreshing update to Chinese stereotypes on screen—a reflection of the rising significance of China in shaping US and indeed the world's affairs.[37] As film scholar Ying Zhu pointed out, "This is the first time ever that a major U.S. production has put China at the center of its narrative, granting real power to a Chinese character."[38] Kenneth Lin, an Asian American Netflix staff writer, explicitly linked Feng's character—"a fairly new arrival to the world stage"—to the "economic miracle" of China, which "has taken decades to evolve."[39]

The connection between Feng and "China" in *HoC*, however, warrants closer scrutiny. On the one hand, viewers were divided on the "believability" of the plotline that involves Feng's corruption,[40] which challenges the realism of the show. On the other hand, Feng's presence was, for most viewers, informed by China's rise, at least economically if not also politically, which appears to reinforce *HoC*'s claim to reality. While Feng is a character that departs from orientalist depictions of Chineseness, a more careful reading of Feng and "China" in the second season reveals that ultimately the show enacts a condition under which China can no longer be merely represented as an object but is an emergent actor whose political agency is intricately entangled with that of America.

Rising China in *House of Cards*

The fifth episode of season 2 ("Chapter 18") begins with an unconventional sex scene. A man with hands tied and face wrapped in plastic is receiving oral sex from a blond woman and a blond man. As he climaxes, the woman pulls off his plastic mask, revealing the face of Xander Feng. Later described as a telecom tycoon, Feng is a corrupt official with close ties to the CCP. With an estimated asset of $50 billion, he is even richer than his American business partner Raymond Tusk, an old friend and mentor of President Walker's. In his next appearance, Feng perfects his tie in front of a mirror when his aid informs him that it is time to depart (for a meeting with Underwood). "Ten thousand," Feng instructs his subordinate, clearly referring to the bundle of money being handed over to the white couple, who immediately stop dressing themselves to start counting.

We also learn that Feng's father "fought side-by-side with Mao" and died in the Chinese Revolution. In his first private meeting with (then) Vice President Underwood, Feng tells him in impeccable English: "I keep Western hours; my midnight is your midnight."[41] He demands that the United States not drop the currency manipulation suit filed against China at the World Trade Organization. "Free-floating currency is inevitable," says Feng, presenting himself as a reformer against the more conservative members of the Standing Committee. Underwood, translating Feng's request as driven by profit motives, manipulates the situation to distance President Walker from Tusk. As the plotline develops in the season, Feng turns out to be central in Tusk's political contribution scheme; he brings Chinese visitors to the Adohi Gaming Casino owned by the Native American tribal leader Daniel Lanagin in Kansas City. The revenue they generate is then donated to a Democratic Super Pac. The act therefore constitutes an illegal form of foreign contribution that renders President Walker impeachable.

Walker's subsequent resignation leads to the consummation of Underwood's quest for the presidency. The ending of the season echoes Underwood's well-circulated quote in a previous episode, when he was inaugurated as the vice president: "One heartbeat away from the presidency and not a single vote cast in my name. Democracy is so overrated."[42] Once Underwood takes office, he asks to speak with China's President Qian—pronounced throughout the episode as the Anglicized "Kiang" rather than in standard Mandarin—on the phone. Feng's asylum, granted earlier during the investigation of Walker, is rescinded in Underwood's move to end the trade war with China.

More than a few viewers in the United States came to read Feng's sexualized entrance as an allegory of China's troubled rise on the world stage.[43] As gender and sexuality scholars Bee Vang and Louisa Schein point out, Feng acts in a form of "gender transgression" that, not unlike other sexually perverted Asian men in numerous popular texts, "arguably synergizes with the panic spurred by the wildness of China's unconventional capitalism, its lawlessness metaphorized by the violation of the gender binary."[44] Importantly, Feng's character departs from the feminized stereotypes ascribed to Asian *American* men in that "this Asian's deviance is expressed through extravagant sexual purchase, an ironic upending of the trope of the western male consuming the Asian female sex worker or bride";[45] therefore, the scene of Feng paying the couple with whom he engages in erotic asphyxiation illustrates "the hysteria of Western countries about China's rising buying power."[46] This financial reward in exchange of perverted sex indeed foreshadows the money-laundering scheme—foreign/Chinese money as an illegal form of political contribution—that is to become the central driving plot throughout the season.

Building on Vang and Schein's reading, the figure of Feng may be usefully seen to embody the co-constituted agency of "rising" China within transpacific mediation. In many ways, the plotline of money-laundering reenacts the "Chinese money scandal" prior to the 1996 presidential election in the United States, when the Democratic National Committee was accused of accepting illegal campaign contributions coming from Red China. In the media responses to this "Chinese money scandal," literary scholar David Palumbo-Liu discerns a "rehash of Cold War rhetoric" that depicts Asian financial invasion as a threat to national security.[47] This rhetoric obscures "how the vulnerability to such 'infiltration' was created by the American political system, or to the fact that such 'Chinese interests' as there may be are often the same as American corporate interests."[48] The formation of this economic *and* political entanglement is referenced in *HoC* through the alliance between Feng and Tusk, even accentuated by Tusk's proper Mandarin pronunciation of "Feng" vis-à-vis Underwood's and Walker's "Fang." The kind of "respatialization" that Palumbo-Liu identifies as bringing China "closer" to US politics is only intensified in the twenty-first century, after three more decades of neoliberal globalization.[49] Indeed, the series of events that Feng's role sets in motion in *HoC* can be seen to enact the relational space of Chimerica as a milieu in which the figure of China assumes a troubled presence, at once *masculine* in terms of its financial invasiveness and *deviant* in its political perversion. As such, Feng may be seen as less a direct representation of China than an allegory of its entanglement with America through transpacific mediation.

This is not to say that Orientalism does not help frame Feng's appearance in *HoC*. For example, the only scene in which Feng appears in his native land is set in his garden estate in Beijing, where Feng greets Doug Stamper, the negotiator sent by Underwood. The scene was shot in the Yurong tourist resort in Lijiang, Yunnan. Its traditional setting struck some Chinese viewers as "inauthentic," since wealthy Chinese often prefer Western-style mansions to Chinese-style architecture.[50] In addition, Feng not only serves Stamper Chinese soup and houses him in a chamber with traditional Chinese decor complete with a dragon sculpture, but he also sends him two young women—whom he describes as "beautiful things"—in silk nightgowns at night, whose service Stamper subsequently rejects. Given the presence of these orientalist tropes, it would seem like despite the writers' efforts to include "realistic" Chinese elements, *HoC* has still catered to the fantasy of Western audiences by exoticizing Feng's residency,[51] if not also eroticizing the "Chinese" experience he intends to provide for his American guest.

However, understanding these orientalist depictions of Feng as a direct personification of "rising" China would be rather inadequate.

After all, the plotline of season 2 also prominently displays the *disjuncture* between Feng's Chinese identity and the geopolitical entity of China. Feng's close connection to the party does not prevent him from fleeing China due to corruption charges. He later becomes a stateless subject, first seeking refuge in Dubai and then in the United States. His political asylum is eventually revoked amid the trade war between the United States and China. He is sent back to his homeland, where the death penalty awaits him. In this turn of events, it is the Chinese state that emerges as a subject whose agency is conveyed through a series of actions that are closely linked with those of the US state.

This political entanglement manifests itself most clearly in the following three-way phone exchange with Tusk and President Walker, after Chinese delegates storm out of a Joint Commission on Commerce and Trade, having refused to discuss cyber warfare:

UNDERWOOD: And I can tell you firsthand that we are dealing with a regime that is not being forthright and will seize upon the faintest whiff of trepidation. This is a test to see how far they can push us before we break. Do not play their game. End the talks.

TUSK: We can't overreact here.

UNDERWOOD: Well, they walked away from the Joint Commission. We can walk away from the summit.

TUSK: The economic fallout would be catastrophic. The market would—

UNDERWOOD: Or we can just kowtow and submit to the new reigning superpower.

WALKER: Don't be hyperbolic, Frank.

UNDERWOOD: Well, we are dealing with one quarter of the world's population.

TUSK: Mr. President, you would be making a disastrous mistake.

UNDERWOOD: Where are your allegiances, Raymond? With Xander Feng or to the United—

TUSK: Don't you dare question me about—

WALKER: All right. Silence.[52]

Here, the invocation of China as "the new reigning superpower," though deemed "hyperbolic," is shored up, if sarcastically, by the size of the country's population and its potency to engender a market fallout. Later in the same episode, President Walker, despite Tusk's attempt to persuade him into an apology after the breakdown of the Joint Commission talks, acts on Underwood's suggestion to proceed with a show of strength. Yet this apparent display of prowess causes China to retaliate, resulting in the trade talk deadlock that in turn constrains the actions of the United States. Here, rather than appearing as two nation-states with clearly demarcated boundaries, China and America engage in what feminist philosopher Karen Barad calls an "intra-action."[53] On the surface, the two governments may appear as actors in contention with each other. But the transpacific market that enmeshes both economies has come to delimit the efficacy of their political actions. This economic-political entanglement has revealed itself quite prominently in the contradictory results of the Trump-era trade war in 2019 (see chapter 2).

Importantly, the emergence of "rising" China as a co-constituted agent with transpacific mediation is not only manifested representationally, as demonstrated in the close reading above. Its presence is also enacted *infrastructurally*, given that the show's producer, Netflix, is a media company keen on entering the Chinese market. Reed Hastings, the CEO and cofounder of Netflix, during his keynote at the 2016 Consumer Electronics Show in Las Vegas, informed the audience, "The Netflix service has gone live in nearly every country of the world but China—where we also hope to be in the future."[54] Even though countries like Iran, North Korea, Syria, and Crimea were also not yet "Netflixed" due to US trade sanctions, China was the only one invoked during Hastings's launching of a self-proclaimed "global TV network."[55] *HoC*, touted as the show that gave birth to the now routine practice of binge watching, was prominently featured during the switch-on. The chief content officer, Ted Sarandos, speaking against the backdrop of an enlarged portrait of *HoC*'s cast, highlighted the real-time release of *HoC*'s entire first season as "a shocker of an opening statement," which offered "a compelling universal drama" for "millions of people around the world to enjoy how and when they wanted it."[56] If the plotline of season 2 discursively enacts the political intra-action between China and America, the material practices of Netflix's global expansion are also symptomatic of a media environment that has enmeshed the politics of the two "superpowers" in the era of big data. A further investigation into these practices, then, is crucial in aiding us to rethink the meanings of politics as online streaming extends a relational space beyond nation-specific confines.

Rethinking Politics and Algorithmic Media

Netflix as a company and a platform, according to media scholar Roman Lobato, "does not fit particularly well with the scalar vocabulary of national/transnational/global on which the field of media studies has traditionally relied."[57] It is better described as a form of "algorithmic media," which communication scholar Taina Bucher defines as "media whose core function depends on algorithmic operations."[58] Characterizing a mode of value creation that has been termed "surveillance capitalism,"[59] "platform capitalism,"[60] "data capitalism,"[61] or "data colonialism,"[62] the company's operation predicates itself on the extraction of behavioral data. Netflix is known to be tracking "30 million behaviors" daily, including "stopping, rewinding, fast-forwarding and pausing," along with "four million ratings provided by subscribers" and "three million search requests" generated by users.[63] Mohammad Sabah, senior data scientist for Netflix, first shared this information at the Hadoop Summit in 2012. He announced that "75 percent of users select movies based on the company's recommendations, and Netflix wants to make that number even higher."[64] To do so means retaining, among other things, device information, geolocation data, types of media consumed during various times, third-party (e.g., Nielsen) metadata, and social media commentaries.

The making and marketing of *HoC* clearly reflected Netflix's status as a paradigmatic form of algorithmic media. Upon its 2013 release, the series was immediately celebrated as "a cornerstone for data-driven programming, the idea that successful business decisions are driven by big data analytics."[65] Kevin Spacey and David Fincher were chosen as the star and director, for instance, based on close analysis of user preferences, since data suggested that fans of Spacey and Fincher were also likely followers of the 1992 BBC original. Netflix purchased the BBC miniseries for $100 million, outbidding HBO and AMC.[66] As media scholar Ed Finn suggests, not only did this make *HoC* the "most expensive drama on television (or 'Internet TV')," [67] but also its creators enjoyed unprecedented artistic freedom, as Netflix committed to two thirteen-episode seasons from the outset, a decision informed by the company's complete confidence in its "algorithmic calculus."[68] Moreover, rather than releasing one trailer that fit all market segments, Netflix produced as many as ten variations that targeted different viewers.[69] "Fans of Mr. Spacey saw trailers featuring him," reports David Carr in the *New York Times*, "women watching 'Thelma and Louise' saw trailers featuring the show's female characters and serious film buffs saw trailers that reflected Mr. Fincher's touch."[70] How users interact with the platform and "the patterns emerging from it," in other words, "are turned into a means of production."[71]

To be sure, algorithms do not guarantee popularity. Netflix certainly also resorted to conventional marketing tactics while exploring new ones. Its trailers, for example, can be seen in movie theaters months before the seasonal release. In addition, the refusal to disclose its viewership data allowed the company to claim every new show as the most popular without having to face any challenge of disputes. This "power of illusion," for *Fast Company* writer Nicole Laporte, "is something that Netflix has learned . . . from Hollywood itself."[72]

The marketing lesson that *HoC* has taken from Hollywood brings to mind philosopher Jean Baudrillard's well-known critique of America's simulated politics, attested to by such entities as Disneyland, Los Angeles, and the first appearance of reality TV. As he famously puts it, "Disneyland is presented as imaginary in order to make us believe that the rest is real, whereas all of Los Angeles and the America that surrounds it are no longer real, but belong to the hyperreal order and to the order of simulation."[73] From this perspective, *HoC* may be seen as simply another rendition of real politics as simulation. Netflix's aggressive advertising campaign in Washington, DC, quite vividly enacts this hyperreality of politics. In February 2016, a month before the release of season 4, forty-five ads featuring Frank Underwood next to the slogan "A Push in the Right Direction" appeared in the metro stations of the capital city, accompanied by two hundred ads with the tagline "Putting America Back on Track." In the midst of a heated race centrally focused on the (unexpected) rise of Donald Trump, it was only reasonable that the *Washington Post* found this four-week-long campaign "creepy."[74] To top it off, the trailer for season 5 appeared on Twitter on none other than January 20, 2017, when President Donald Trump was inaugurated into office. It featured the show's stock image of an upside-down American flag along with the tagline, "We Make the Terror," a cliffhanger by the Underwoods at the end of the previous season. Strategies like these blurred the boundary between *HoC* and real-world politics to such an extent that the latter would become indistinguishable from its representation, enacting Baudrillard's assessment of politics in the postmodern era.

At the same time, the rise of Netflix as a big-data-driven platform arguably signals a new relationship between media and political reality. For one thing, as media scholar Sarah Arnold argues, "The Netflix model's method of knowledge production reduces humans to digital traces or events."[75] This approach departs from conventional modes of measuring audiences, which generate knowledge about viewers' practices through their own responses. Instead, "the data mined by Netflix is not used to infer anything about the human agent interacting with the service" but only "finds correlations between profiles and data interactions."[76] The platform therefore displays "radical indifference" toward the human experiences that help shape viewing behavior.[77] As a result, users are stripped of the agency to lend meanings to their actions and even instructed to take on algorithmically construed identities through Netflix's recommendation system.

In this way, Netflix enacts what data scholar Antoinette Rouvroy calls an "algorithmic production of 'reality,'"[78] which presents profound political implications. At work is a form of "data behaviourism" in knowledge production, which operates through an "algorithmic logic" that "spares human actors the burden and responsibility to transcribe, interpret and evaluate the events of world."[79] Rouvroy extends this analysis to an account of "algorithmic governmentality," which contrasts with neoliberalism in that it "does not produce any kind of subject" and instead "bypasses consciousness and reflexivity, and operates on the mode of alerts and reflexes."[80]

Rouvroy's account initially seems less applicable in the surprise Chinese popularity of *HoC*. For one thing, Netflix viewers located in China do not immediately contribute to the data pool mined by the company in producing the show, given that they have previously gained access to American TV largely through unofficial channels. Moreover, the subtitling groups that informally helped to spread the show did not personally encounter the targeted ads directed at their US counterparts due to their restricted access to Netflix, though an oft-referenced tweet about *HoC* from President Obama indicated that the show's fame in the United States might have played a role. The Chinese market, it would appear, exceeds the algorithmic calculation of Netflix as a media producer. However, this is not to say that Netflix's use of big data in producing *HoC* has gone unnoticed in the Chinese media coverage of its popularity. In fact, many Chinese commentators seem to be more impressed by the magic charm of big data to predict the future than by the workings of liberal democracy to elect a president.[81] For those eager to replicate *HoC*'s commercial success, a popularly selected show seems more important than a system of governance that derives its legitimacy from electoral votes.

This fetishization of big data emanating from the United States but no less palpable in the Chinese context brings to mind what political theorist Jodi Dean refers to as the "fantasy" of participation under communicative capitalism, wherein "technology covers over our impotence and supports a vision of ourselves as active political participants."[82] It also bespeaks Rouvroy's observation that algorithmic governmentality does not (necessarily) entail the production of neoliberal subjects as such but may indeed preempt the making of political actors. Such an emptying out of political subjectivity echoes media scholar Ed Finn's analysis of *HoC*, whose "aesthetic of abstraction" is manifested, among other things, in the show's opening credits, set in Washington, DC. The sequence features no humans but only their "physical and cultural traces," the same way that Netflix processes its user data.[83]

If China is seemingly outside of Netflix's algorithmic machinery, it has nonetheless served as a data point of sorts for the creators of *HoC*. Thwarted in its ambition to successfully penetrate the lucrative Chinese online streaming market, Netflix had tried to incorporate "China" into the making of *HoC*. According to writer Kenneth Lin, the creative team, headed by Beau Willimon, had already decided to highlight China prior to his arrival; for Lin, this is understandable because "'House of Cards' is an exploration of power at the highest levels. Today, you can't tell that story without considering China."[84] To achieve this goal, the team consulted Lu Xiaobo, a political science professor at Columbia University (Willimon's alma mater) on major issues in US-China relations. Upon the release of season 2, Lu noticed that some of the political issues covered in the show had surfaced after 2013, indicating the continuous updating of material on the part of the scriptwriters.[85] Much like the allegorized political Chimerica in that season, it would appear that "rising" China is an actor co-constituted in the cultural machine that has produced *HoC*. This co-constitution, in turn, contributes to the Chinese popularity of the show, despite the absence of Chinese viewers in the Netflix data pool.

The incorporation of China in *HoC* and its ensuring Chinese reception, therefore, enact a transpacific communicative space that extends beyond national territories. It is through the making of this space that the algorithmically construed media artifact of *HoC* invites us to reflect on the changing relationship between politics and media. In the US context, as literary scholar Joe Conway argues, the show *HoC* exemplifies a new genre of "political satire vérité," one that adopts an aesthetic of "apparently real."[86] This aesthetic, characteristic of what cultural critic Alan Kirby calls "digimodernism," boasts a kind of "overly credulous authenticity."[87] By highlighting individual characters' "managerial competence despite a fundamentally flawed system," shows like *HoC* promote "the depoliticized political grammar of populism" even as they profess to display the inner workings of democratic government without corporate media distortion.[88] The rise of this genre thus signals "the end of politics" in conjunction with "the end of television," since "the same online technologies that have so drastically reorganized the television industry" have also offered consumers an illusory "command" over content creation.[89]

The election of Donald Trump as the forty-fifth president of the United States perhaps most vividly demonstrates this relationship between real politics and the "apparently real" media aesthetic. In this election, as media scholar Lynne Joyrich argues, media has not "failed" the public, as some journalists suggest; rather, the process "operated fully through a media logic," what she calls "the 'reality televisualization' of political formations."[90] By that, Joyrich is referring to "a kind of televisual epistemology and a televisual affect intertwined, a meshing of modes of thinking and modes of feeling" that "has become the 'medium' in which our politics now exist."[91] Therefore, it makes little sense to say that politics is something outside of media to be represented in an artifact like *HoC*. Instead, the show, from its data-driven inception and production to marketing and reception, is integral to the media environment in which politics takes place.

It is in this media environment, enacted through the transpacific circulation of *HoC*, that the political entanglement between China and America is brought into greater visibility. It is worth noting that so many Chinese viewers see no difference between the politics in *HoC* and Chinese imperial court dramas like *Legends*. This comparison rests on a shared understanding of a media artifact not as a direct instrument of representation but as a stage on which politics is *performed*. In fact, it is through the *detachment* of representation from the real historical context (i.e., America) that gave rise to it that Chinese viewers have come to identify with the political struggles in *Legends* and *HoC*. This identification in turn stems from the material circumstances in which they find themselves. As one viewer notes in an article titled "Probing Politics in *House of Cards*," "The reason I like *House of Cards* is because I find in it the resonance of work-place struggles."[92] This is a view shared by those participants in the online discussion who watch the show to learn about useful means for career advancement. Politics, for them, has less to do with the formal procedures of liberal democracy and is more about individual survival in a competitive environment. Such an understanding, as Conway suggests, is precisely what the series proffers—"a wholly depoliticized version of politics" in which "government is simply a symbolic arena for a family's private ambitions."[93] To be sure, this depoliticizing tendency is by no means unique to *HoC* but can be said to characterize many other mass media artifacts that profess to invite critical reflections on politics. However, *HoC* is nonetheless symptomatic of the ways in which this depoliticized politics has become part of a globalizing algorithmic culture. Such depoliticization has arguably come to dissolve the geopolitical boundaries between China and America, an amalgamation that is not only indexed in the second season of *HoC* but also enacted in its reception in China.

One way in which this depoliticization manifests itself is through the "fansubbing," or fan-subtitling, of *HoC* among Chinese viewers, which had propelled its popularity prior to its official distribution via Sohu. At first glance, such activities seem to suggest an attempt to subvert normative assumptions about politics within China. Some of the subtitling groups, for instance, have called upon themselves to provide background information on screen (on the meaning of "whip," among other things) to illuminate the workings of America's procedural democracy in ways that may differ from China's state-level politics. However, as a more critical viewer points out, echoing Conway, such attention to "the reality of details" on the part of the creator and audience alike only serves to "subvert the reality of history," as it obscures real historical struggles.[94] Moreover, contrary to the kind of "netizen-against-the-state" activism described by journalists like Osnos regarding the online distribution of American shows, the Chinese fansubbing of sensitive political messages in the second season of *HoC* actually "services the objectives of the current administration by reinforcing its anti-corruption message and the legitimacy of the regime, thus fulfilling the function of official propaganda."[95]

In this sense, rather than claiming that *HoC* "represents" political reality, it may be more appropriate to say that it enacts the representational crisis that has come to entangle China and America alike. This is a crisis that extends what cultural theorist Wang Hui calls the "(global) decline of representation in contemporary politics," brought on by the "large-scale expansion of the media" and the subsequent "contraction of the public sphere."[96] "In China," Wang observes, "though the media may appear to be controlled by politics, the political sphere has, in fact, been gradually colonized by the media."[97] In this reversal of the liberal critique of the CCP's censorship, Wang suggests that "the media and the Party" have become "two entangled interests" that "are organically linked, each maneuvering for their own gain in order to replace and obscure free speech and political debate among the citizenry."[98] The Chinese audience's reading of *HoC* as a lesson of self-improvement or a regime-affirming text rather than an aspiration for genuine democratic politics is more than indicative of this depoliticized media environment.

Although Wang is referring to the commercialization of Chinese/global media that renders citizens' political engagement difficult, the idea that media is colonizing politics strongly resonates with what media scholars Nick Couldry and Ulises A. Mejias have termed "data colonialism." For Couldry and Mejias, data has become "the interlocking force of capitalism and colonialism,"[99] as the appropriation of human life for corporate profit "damages the minimal integrity of the self as a space of self-relation."[100] Netflix's datafication of user behavior appears to exemplify this sanctification of data as "the force of information processing or algorithmic power" that presumably "know[s] human life better than life can know itself."[101] It was also under this data colonial regime that the company Cambridge Analytica was able to extract Facebook users' data without their knowledge and targeted them with political ads of misinformation, a practice understood to have contributed to Brexit and to Trump's victory in the US presidential election in 2016.[102]

The linkages between algorithmic media and politics also became more pronounced in the last seasons of *HoC* while casting a shadow over the 2020 US election. As political scientist Maria Repnikova notes, despite the prevailing tendency in media and journalism studies to contrast China's authoritarianism with Western liberal democracy such as that of the United States, "There are important points of convergence in media practices."[103] Just as "intensifying government surveillance" is present in both countries, "journalists can be co-opted in the government apparatus regardless of the political system," such that the "distinctions in media control and media oversight" are better viewed as "different shades of grey, as opposed to opposing absolutes engrained in authoritarian or democratic systems."[104] In this context, it is perhaps more urgent than ever to further investigate media as what cultural studies scholar Clare Birchall calls "complex information-communication environments" that produce diverging political effects, rather than merely treating them as instruments of representation.[105] The transpacific communicative space that *HoC* opens up has allowed us an opportunity to more carefully rethink this relationship between media and politics, which forms the basis for reimagining what politics can mean and become.

Conclusion

The popularity of *HoC* is certainly not exclusive to China. Vladimir Putin, the president of Russia, was reportedly a big fan of the show as well, even urging his defense minister to see it as an unfiltered documentation of

American reality.[106] Indeed, the presence of Russia in the seasons that followed and the media frenzy surrounding the Russian influence in the 2016 US election warrant a separate but perhaps not unrelated analysis regarding the relationship between algorithmic media and politics. Yet even as Russia seemingly dominated the headlines of cyber threat to the United States during the Trump administration, the Senate Select Committee on Intelligence released a report on January 29, 2019, identifying China as "the most active strategic competitor responsible for cyber espionage against the US Government, corporations, and allies," one who "is improving its cyber-attack capabilities and altering information online, shaping Chinese views and potentially the views of US citizens."[107] This othering of China as an agent infiltrating American politics also arguably informed the Trump administration's attempt to ban the Chinese platforms of WeChat and TikTok in the midst of the COVID-19 pandemic for fear of their extraction of US personal data to serve the political interests of the Chinese state.[108]

Meanwhile, Western critics of datafication have also turned to China as a point of reference. Business professor Shoshana Zuboff, for instance, has devoted a section titled "The China Syndrome" in her influential book, *The Age of Surveillance Capitalism*, highlighting China's social credit system, among other technological instruments, as a dystopian vision for liberal democracy unless the latter awakens to the perils of surveillance capitalism.[109] Likewise, for Couldry and Mejias, data colonialism has "at least two poles of power in what, until now, we have called the West and in China."[110] For them, "The drive to appropriate data is fueling China as much as, if not more than, it is the west," and therefore, "it makes no sense to read data colonialism as exclusively a Western project."[111]

To be sure, these arguments insightfully point to a kind of political convergence that has rendered "the orders of 'liberal' democracies and 'authoritarian' societies . . . increasingly indistinguishable," given the continuous dispossession of human life under data colonialism.[112] But they also fall short in taking note of the relation between media and politics that the Chimerican artifact of *HoC* has invited us to contemplate. Arguably, the focal attention to the Chinese state's censoring power, as also manifested in the journalistic coverage of *HoC*'s reception in China, is part of the racializing tendency among Western observers to depict the "authoritarian" character of the Chinese state in opposition to liberal democracy. This figure of China as a censor, much like the construction of China as a creditor in fiscal-orientalist narratives (chapter 2), obscures the depoliticization under communicative capitalism that has entangled the two "poles" of data colonialism. The uneven relation of power between America and China that has helped shape this racialization, then, limits our ability to imagine politics otherwise under the conditions of algorithmic media.

Certainly the role of the Chinese state in shoring up corporate practices of datafication in China and elsewhere is not to be discounted. But *HoC* has also helped us to better recognize "rising" China as a co-constituted agent with transpacific mediation. This recognition invites us to reconsider the dominant ideological framing of China as a political Other and shifts critical attention to the entanglement of politics with a media environment increasingly permeated by artificial intelligence. Media, as my analysis of *HoC* and its transpacific circulation has shown, does not stand outside of politics but is the practice and environment in which it takes place. This understanding also prompts us to expand the notion of politics beyond the electoral realm—that is, as Politics—to encompass "ways of world-making," or what Bucher calls "the practices and capacities entailed in ordering and arranging different ways of being in the world."[113] From this perspective, the political entanglement of the two superpowers as manifested in the production, narrative, and reception of *HoC* also encourages a rethinking of politics as the making and enactment of reality in a media environment permeated by algorithms. As anthropologist Annemarie Mol suggests, "Reality does not precede the mundane practices in which we interact with it, but is rather shaped within these practices."[114] If algorithms are best understood to be "interwoven in the social fabric of the contemporary media landscape,"[115] so too may the figure of China be grasped as a disorienting force to shape politics as it partakes in bringing into being the relational space of transpacific media. In the concluding chapter that follows, I will further reflect on this political disorientation that "China" activates by turning closer attention to the transpacific environment that encompasses both China and America ecologically.

Ecological Chimerica

Breath, Racialization, and Relational Politics

On January 23, 2020, the city of Wuhan in Hubei Province went into lockdown to prevent the spread of COVID-19. Its 11 million people began sixty days of quarantine life. Fang Fang, a writer born and raised in Wuhan, kept a record of her and her fellow city dwellers' experience under lockdown. On March 12, one day before the situation in the United States elevated into a state of national emergency, Fang Fang related the following comment by a reader of her *Wuhan Diary: Dispatches from a Quarantined City*; her writing, the reader said, had served as "a breathing valve to save us from our boredom." Moved by this comment, Fang Fang realized "as I myself struggle to breathe, I have also been helping others to breathe."[1] The act of breathing together, albeit denied by the virus in a quarantined city, was seemingly made possible again in the relational space enacted by Fang Fang's online diaries.

A few months later, on May 25, 2020, George Floyd, an African American man who had lost his job due to COVID-19, used a counterfeit twenty-dollar bill to purchase a pack of cigarettes at a corner store in Minneapolis. Upon receiving a 911 call from the store clerks, four Minneapolis police officers arrived at the scene. Floyd, citing claustrophobia, resisted getting into the police car. But despite the fact that Floyd displayed no attempt at violence, the officers pinned him to the ground. One of them, as shown on witness videos taken by mobile phones, placed his knee on Floyd's neck for a total of nine minutes and twenty-nine seconds.[2] During this time, Floyd was heard saying "I can't breathe" sixteen times before losing consciousness. He was soon pronounced dead in a nearby hospital.[3]

Wuhan and Minneapolis were among the many distant places that were connected by the global pandemic in 2020. The gravity of Floyd's death at the hands of police is in no way commensurate with the experience of "boredom" of those under lockdown in Wuhan. Nonetheless, Fang Fang's diaries allowed many people living within and beyond her city to witness firsthand a profound tragedy taking place in China (through media platforms such as WeChat). A virus that caused the death of thousands within Wuhan soon reached millions around the world, disproportionately infecting black and brown populations in the United States. Just as the pandemic has engendered a newfound affinity between far-flung locales, these events in China and America were brought into closer proximity through transpacific media, whether in the form of online diaries written in Chinese and quickly translated, published, and studied in English,[4] or via the capturing of Floyd's death on smartphones assembled by Chinese workers before inspiring protests in the United States and elsewhere. Together, these events provide an opportunity to think more deeply about how breathing, the life-sustaining act, might connect many people from both sides of the Pacific—minorities in the United States, the workers in China, and others beyond the imaginary and geographical confines of Chimerica.

Floyd was not the first to enunciate "I can't breathe" in a moment of racial violence. They were also the last words of Eric Garner, another victim of structural racism who suffered from asthma and died of police brutality. The phrase has become a well-known slogan in the Black Lives Matter movement, appearing on protest signs, T-shirts, and other cultural artifacts. Its visibility during the mass protests triggered by Floyd's death accentuates the idea that "breathing—that essential act of life . . . is often constrained or denied to people of color in US cities today."[5] The long-standing and well-documented history of environmental racism has provided ample evidence of the disproportionate distribution of air pollution and other environmental hazards among multiple communities of color in America.[6]

Under conditions of neoliberal globalization since the 1970s, the environmental consequences of economic development have become unevenly distributed transnationally. For people living in China, among other parts of the developing world, the difficulty of breathing has long been a very real problem. In 2013, for instance, Beijing, along with over thirty other Chinese cities, suffered a severe episode of smog. The

Air Quality Index used by the US Embassy in Beijing, whose toxicity level normally ranges from 0 to 500, gave a "jaw-dropping" reading of 755, and the whole city "looked like an airport smokers' lounge."[7] China's air pollution was reportedly "killing about 4,000 people" per day, "accounting for one in six premature deaths."[8] It was perhaps not surprising that the pandemic-induced economic slowdown in 2020 led to cleaner air in major Chinese cities, leading some to speculate that more deaths could have resulted from air pollution than from COVID-19.[9]

"We all breathe the same air. We all cherish our children's future. And we are all mortal"; President John F. Kennedy's 1963 speech had a distinctive focus on "the right to breathe air as nature provided it, the right of future generations to a healthy existence."[10] These words arguably take on new meanings in the twenty-first century, when increasingly polluted Chinese air travels in greater intensity across the Pacific back to the West Coast of the United States, forming what scientists call "a 'ribbon' covering the entire Pacific Ocean basin bent back and forth."[11] "Nation-state divisions," amid this transpacific movement of polluted air, "shifted into an uncomfortable meteorological kinship," to borrow a phrase from anthropologist Jerry Zee.[12]

"Breathing together, sharing fate" (*tong huxi, gong mingyun*) is a slogan not unfamiliar among the Chinese viewers of a viral documentary from 2015 called *Under the Dome*.[13] Taking the title from an American TV show, author, reporter, and TV anchor Chai Jing produced the film to explain the origins of PM2.5, a core pollutant in China's smog, so as to call on citizens to take up the responsibility to fight air pollution. Yet despite the video's inspiring message, its focus on the role of consumers to adapt their behavior and engage in individualized forms of activism failed to consider the structural linkages between China's smog and the country's status as the "world's factory." Moreover, the transpacific media coverage that celebrated the video's speedy and viral spread via cell phones and internet platforms reflected a fetishization of digital media that does not sufficiently consider media technologies' contributing role in the problem of air pollution. What this coverage obscures, as I have argued elsewhere, is an alternative dialogue about the materiality of media production, from mineral extraction and workers' health hazards to the continual generation of e-waste under the corporatized regime of planned obsolescence.[14]

A similar kind of erasure can be discerned in Euro-American journalistic depictions of China's smog. In these narratives, Chinese residents are often seen wearing face masks—much like the images of everyday life under SARS and COVID-19—as a way to survive the "airmageddon."[15] Anthropologist Ralph Litzinger and I have argued that such a mode of depicting China "as a polluting and polluted Other slowly destroying the planet" suffers from what we call "Yellow Eco-peril."[16] This kind of othering renders China as "a distant object to be represented" and does not fully account for China's role as "a subject shaping the material conditions that make this representation possible."[17]

The ideological conditions that render invisible China's material presence have prompted me to rethink "rising" China as both a subject co-constituted with, and an object represented in, Chimerican media. In many ways, Chimerican media are not unlike the air that crosses the Pacific to bring China and America into an eco-unity. These media artifacts may take the form of contents, technologies, platforms, or infrastructures, and many of them analyzed in this book indeed originate from America. But just like the polluted air that comes from China also has American "roots" and returns to America, the mediation processes that help to produce these media stem from the Pacific as a contact zone. Therefore, as transpacific media, they form an ecosystem—or an environment, as I have discussed in chapter 4—in which politics takes place.

My core argument has been that while Chimerican media make visible the numerous entanglements of the two superpowers, the ideological framing of the Chinese state as a racialized Other has eclipsed the possibility to engage these entanglements as a basis for imagining politics anew. This dominant way in which China assumes its presence in American media life became even more pronounced during the COVID-19 crisis in conjunction with the 2020 US presidential election, during which the "China virus" and "the radical, socialist left" were easily conflated as the key targets of attack for primarily but not exclusively rightwing politicians.[18] The racialized figure of China gives shape and form to a foreign menace against which "Americans" can presumably be united. Whether Democrat or Republican, liberal or conservative, politicians continue to feel the need to take a strong stance toward China as an "anti-thesis" for US democracy so that the latter can be defended even and especially when it is clearly in crisis.[19] The challenge remains as to how one may better envision a relational politics that acknowledges the multifarious and interconnected Chimerican entanglements,[20] at once economic, cultural, political, and *ecological*.

A Politics of Relationality

As I argued in chapter 1, a relational politics takes into account the role of media in creating a communicative space that disturbs the conventional ties between politics and place. Chimerica is one such space conjured in Chimerican media that offers contradictory accounts of China and in turn competing visions for the state and citizenship in America. International relations scholar Stephanie Fishel points out that the state is not to be taken as a given but instead "has to be made real; it is invisible until it is performed . . . until it is made visible through metaphor."[21] Despite the long-standing metaphor of the body politic in referencing the nation-state, however, the body and its materiality have received limited attention in theorizations of citizenship and the state. Turning to the microbial environment in which the human body coexists and is in constant interaction with microorganisms, Fishel urges us to rethink the human body as "a community, not only a container."[22] The new metaphor of "bodies politic,"[23] then, emerges from this re-conception to complicate "the 'personhood' of the state" and paves the way for imagining a global politics based on relationality.[24]

My insistence on using racialization in referencing the figure of China in America is inspired by the connection that Fishel has drawn between "biological and political communities."[25] The racialization of the Chinese state, as featured in the rhetoric of "China virus" discussed in the introduction to this book, at once relies on the personification of China as an agent and works to objectify—that is, dehumanize—this embodiment. Framing the presence of China in this way helps to distinguish the subject-object status of this figure from long-standing orientalist representations. As the making of Chimerican media has revealed, China is better seen not as a static object but as a co-constituted agent in America's media life. This perspective enables a more nuanced understanding of Sinophobia and its ramifications beyond the specific forms of anti-Asian racism in the United States. As I've argued throughout the chapters, the prevailing tendency in Chimerican media to other "rising" China has consequences for the multiethnic members of the United States as a "bodies politic." As such, a racialized Chinese state can also be usefully connected to the critique of racial capitalism in global contexts, for which China has been an understudied locale.

The globalized production, consumption, and recycling of media technologies in the twenty-first century arguably reflect a continuation of racial capitalism within the new regime of data colonialism (chapter 4).

The well-documented outsourcing of "800" customer service calls from English-speaking Euro-America to India,[26] a former colony of Britain, and the content moderation of Facebook and other platforms by workers in the Philippines,[27] a former colony of the United States, provide immediate examples of the mapping of colonial pasts onto the digital present. The working of this racialized digital capitalism is also present in Africa, where "digital slavery" persists in places like the Democratic Republic of the Congo in the enslavement of workers in cobalt mining, a precondition for the batteries that power our digital devices.[28]

Modern China's relation to historical (Western) colonialism is certainly complex, given that the nation has never been fully colonized despite the imperialist territorial encroachment in places like Hong Kong and Macau. The "Beijing consensus" that propelled the country toward a drastic path of GDP growth in defiance of the neoliberal order dictated by the Washington Consensus also distinguishes China from societies that are more explicitly postcolonial (e.g., Latin America) or post-Communist (e.g., Eastern Europe). Nevertheless, the fact that China can today be (erroneously) perceived as the United States's first "great power competitor that is not Caucasian" is telling of the persisting presence of "racial sensibility" in American nationalism.[29] As I have shown in chapter 2, the techno-orientalist discourse associated with Japan, the first nonwhite nation to become an economic powerhouse on par with the United States, is refashioned in wide-ranging media accounts as fiscal orientalism in the era of "rising" China. What this racializing discourse masks is the uneven economic and financial power relations to which the Chinese state has been subject, despite its seemingly ascending role in the global arena.

Still, the framework of fiscal orientalism, as I have shown in subsequent chapters, does not sufficiently account for the agency of the Chinese state in shaping global media culture. This agency is perhaps more clearly manifested in the establishment of the Confucius Institutes worldwide in the interest of advancing Chinese soft power, a state practice faced with much pushback from US universities (chapter 3). It also surfaces in the US controversy over the potential banning of such globally popular apps as TikTok and WeChat owned by Chinese companies, even though their alleged data-collecting practices share much in common with those carried out by Netflix (chapter 4). Yet in each of these cases, I have discerned an ideological tendency to depict "rising" China as an authoritarian state that is fundamentally distinct from a democratic America. This sentiment displays a refusal to consider the multifarious imbrication of the two superpowers as a basis for generating political alternatives.

The kind of relational politics that I propose challenges precisely this dichotomous framing of "us" versus "them," a separation that I insist is a symptom of racial capitalism. Ethnic studies scholar Jodi Melamed, following geographer Ruth Gilmore, has urged us to think of "racial capitalism as a technology of *antirelationality*."[30] Building on Gilmore's definition of racism as "the state-sanctioned and/or extra-legal production and exploitation of group-differentiated vulnerabilities to premature death," Melamed invites us to attend to its operation "*in distinct yet densely interconnected political geographies*."[31] The "partition" of these geographies, as Gilmore suggests elsewhere, "exists and develops according to its capacity to control who can relate and under what terms."[32] The perennial charge by politicians that rapacious China "steals" American jobs, among other accusations, showcases the capacity of racial capitalism in mobilizing national-territorial divides as a means to "truncate relationality for capital accumulation."[33] What is diminished is the potential for workers from both sides of the Pacific to connect with one another on the basis of their shared uneven relation with transnational capital whose border-crossing movement is sanctioned by both American and Chinese states.

Indeed, the exploitation of Chinese workers in the manufacturing of global electronics offers perhaps the clearest enactment of coloniality—that is, the presence of colonial power relations without actual colonization—in the context of China (see the introduction). Writing about the conditions of workers at the Taiwan-owned Foxconn factory in Shenzhen, one of the world's largest suppliers for Apple and other global technology conglomerates, communication scholar Jack Linchuan Qiu reminds us that "even in the twenty-first century, we are still haunted by the specter of slavery, morphing from physical place to cyberspace."[34] The transatlantic slave trade and "the transpacific US-China duo of 'Chimerica'" now constituting the "new epicenter" of the "world system," despite their vast differences, have more in common than they are different.[35] In this sense, Chimerican media can be seen as producing an important segment of what Couldry and Mejias call the "new geographies of the Cloud Empire" under data colonialism.[36]

Slavery, as cultural studies scholar Christina Sharpe writes in *In the Wake*, is often "imagined as a singular event even as it changed over time and even as its duration expands into supposed emancipation and beyond." Challenging this conception, Sharpe asks us to consider slavery instead as "a singularity—a weather event or phenomenon likely to occur around a particular time, or date, or set of circumstances."[37] By conceptualizing antiblackness as a "climate" that produces the weather of slavery, Sharpe draws attention to an "ecology" of racialization, one that carefully engages the entanglement of bodies and environment. This attention to embodiment presents an opening for envisioning new paths toward global justice. As environmental studies scholars Lindsey Dillon and Julie Sze point out, "Anti-racist struggles have always been struggles about life-sustaining environments, at least as 'the environment' is defined by the environmental justice movement as the place where we 'live, work, and play.'"[38] The Atlantic Ocean, the backdrop for Sharpe's treatise, is an environment that, as performance studies scholar Sean Metzger shows in *The Chinese Atlantic*, also entangles China, race, and the Chinese diaspora in intricate ways.[39] Just as Metzger aims to bridge the epistemological distinction between the Pacific and the Atlantic as oceanic frames, the conception of Chimerican media as a form of transpacific media allows us to connect nineteenth-century slavery to twenty-first-century data colonialism, enabling us to grapple with the ecology of racialization. It is within this ecology that the materiality of the Pacific Ocean, much like the polluted air that crosses it and is slowly causing its acidification, can be better engaged as a media environment for envisioning a new kind of politics that attends to relationality.

Disorientation through Transpacific Media

"The ocean is fundamental as a means of communication," writes cultural studies scholar Elspeth Probyn; it "is a lively and fluid medium that connects the human and the more-than-human."[40] As the body of water that links China and America, the Pacific Ocean has long enabled the movement of people, goods, information, air, and much more between these nation-states. But it can also serve as what media studies scholar Melody Jue terms "a 'disorientation device' for theory and philosophy, a milieu that denatures our normative habits of orienting to the (terrestrial) world through language."[41]

In this book, I have deployed the concept of disorientation to disrupt our normative assumptions about politics. Engaging with Sara Ahmed's *Queer Phenomenology*, I have argued in the introduction that disorienting politics has a dual meaning. On the one hand, it describes the racializing discourse surrounding the Chinese state that renders Chinese/Asian bodies out of place within the US nation-state. On the other hand, it proposes a way of thinking about media, place, and space that shifts the "ground" for politics, from the place of the nation—the site of Politics—to the space of transpacific media, where place-based Politics and deterritorialized politics intersect. The Pacific, then, is a privileged site that enables this disorientation of politics. After all, the ocean, or what Jue calls "the blue lungs of the planet," always "interacts with the atmosphere as a single fluid system."[42] By challenging our terrestrial bias that takes breathing for granted, the embodied mode of breathing underwater inspires us to foreground the conditions of breathing as a basis for forming a relational politics—a politics that engages the "complex ecology of air that moves between atmosphere, ocean, and self, an interface that is about the interpenetration of selves and the world."[43] Breathing, in other words, would ground our bodies in relation to the atmospheric and the oceanic; it points to a vision of politics as a form of relational world making, a way to reorient bodies to the environment.

As I conclude this book, many of us living in the United States are finally regaining the ability to "breathe each other's air" again,[44] even with the lingering threat of COVID-19 still present. "Thinking about the materiality of air and the densities of our many human entanglements in airy matters," anthropologist Tim Choy tells us, "means attending to the solidifying and melting edges between people, regions, and events."[45] The unevenly experienced tragedy of the pandemic has reminded us that, globally, people of color have long endured unequal access to the capacity to breathe. The vaccine for COVID cannot provide sufficient prevention for what writer Jamieson Webster calls the multiple "asphyxiating forms of oppression" that have made it difficult, even impossible, for people of color across the Pacific to engage in the basic bodily act of breathing.[46]

Breath, then, can be grasped as "a geographical site of political struggle and resistance to unsustainable socioenvironmental conditions,"[47] both in the United States and beyond. Eric Garner, George Floyd, and many more are members of communities of color in the United States who have long suffered from higher rates of asthma, a condition "inseparable from histories of racism, urban planning, and industrial and military waste."[48] These enactments of environmental racism in America are linkable to the widespread black lung disease, or pneumoconiosis, among Chinese workers,[49] especially those employed in deep earth mining and polishing factories for sleek digital gadgets.[50] To be sure, the racial injustices that surround the deaths of African Americans like Garner and Floyd cannot be comfortably equated to the experiences of suffering among the residents of Wuhan reading Fang Fang's diary or the victims of air pollution in China. Compounding this are the growing tensions of racialization within China's own "bodies politic," as revealed in recent coverage of Xinjiang's mass detention centers that target Uyghurs and other ethnic minorities. As critical race scholar David Theo Goldberg argues, however, there is tremendous value in deploying "relationality" as a methodology to study the ways in which the iterations of racialization across different geopolitical locales interact with one another.[51] Indeed, anthropologist Darren Byler has shown that the CCP's "preventive policing system" in Xinjiang "was built on models of counterinsurgency that emerged from the United States, Israel, and Europe, but adapted to 'Chinese characteristics' . . . that came from China's Maoist past."[52] A relational politics, then, propels us to recognize and probe deeper into the interconnected nature of these instances of "relational racism" without losing sight of the local specificity of each iteration.[53]

To unpack the connections between incommensurable injustices, in other words, does not mean to reduce the seemingly disparate experiences into false equivalences. Rather, it means a kind of continuous grappling with the relations between the universal and the particular. In this regard, paying closer attention to the materiality of air points toward a way to turn the incommensurable into opportunities for building relationality. As Choy reminds us, "If bodies are an intimate location of effects and agencies, air is the substance that bathes and ties the scales of body, region, and globe together, and that subsequently enables personal and political claims to be scaled up, to global environmental politics, and down, to the politics of health."[54] The COVID-19 pandemic has perhaps more than ever illuminated this capacity of air to collapse the global and the local. After all, the airborne virus seemingly has no regard for boundaries of any kind, whether bodily or national; yet its impact has manifested so differently in various contexts, disproportionately inflicting itself upon ethnic minorities in the United States through interactions with preexisting structural inequalities. Among other things, it has further alerted us to the importance of attending to "the many means, practices, experiences, weather events, and economic relations that co-implicate us at different points as 'breathers.'"[55]

The State of/for Breathing

We have seen the aspiration to engage in such "human-atmospheric relations" in Lucy Kirkwood's play *Chimerica* through the action of Zhang Lin (chapter 1).[56] There, the Tank-Man-turned-environmental-activist urges his fellow citizens to hold the state accountable as an agent to make air breathable (again) for the nation's inhabitants. Echoing this fictional character is the young Chinese environmental activist Howey Ou (Ou Hongyi), known for the tagline: "You can develop vaccines for COVID19 but there is no vaccine for climate emergency."[57] If the pandemic, as anthropologist Bruno Latour says, is a dress rehearsal for the unfolding crisis that is climate change,[58] the COVID moment has made it more urgent to ground our notions of (global) citizenship in the shared practice of breathing.

Seeing the pandemic as "the spectacular expression of the planetary impasse in which humanity finds itself today," philosopher Achille Mbembe suggests, "it is a matter of no less than reconstructing a habitable Earth to give all of us the breath of life."[59] The question remains as to how a relational politics may inform the joint roles played by the world's two superpowers—also the world's two greatest waste generators and emitters of greenhouse gases—in tackling these planetary challenges.[60] Political scientist Robyn Eckersley has put forth the vision of a "green state" to imagine the state as "an ecological steward and facilitator of transboundary democracy rather than a selfish actor jealously protecting its territory and ignoring or discounting the needs of foreign lands."[61] This vision of "ecological democracy," predicated on an ecological critique of liberal democracy, offers an appealing alternative to what American studies scholar Julie Sze calls "eco-authoritarianism."[62] "Within the United States," Sze argues, "our greatest ecological desire is to fixate on China as the focal point of the vast majority of global pollution and thus displace our own responsibility for global environmental damage."[63] This "eco-desire" coincides with many US environmentalists' projected "fantasy of China as the 'go-to' place where great green things happen on a vast governmental scale."[64]

Echoing Sze, in the Chinese context, environmental scholars Yifei Li and Judith Shapiro have also used "coercive environmentalism, state-led environmentalism, authoritarian environmentalism or eco-authoritarianism" to describe a top-down, technocratic mode of environmental governance.[65] "Counterintuitively," they argue, "the success of state-led environmentalism hinges not on a strong state, but on mechanisms that place state power in check."[66] Indeed, it is through "mutually agreed upon coercion," achieved via the government's working with a multitude of "non-state actors," that China's efforts toward building an "ecological civilization" have been most effective.[67]

Li and Shapiro's call for citizens to partake in efforts aimed at "greening the state," then, urges us to disrupt the false dichotomy between authoritarianism and liberal democracy often operative in the racializing discourse of "rising" China examined in this book. From 2017 to 2020, the White House, under a president who had once blamed China for creating the "hoax" of global warming, initiated drastic rollbacks of environmental regulation at home and withdrawal from global commitment like the Paris Climate Accords to combating climate change.[68] Even with the Biden administration's directives from day one to rejoin the Paris agreement and restore necessary environmental policies, it would take years to undo the damage, barring potential profit-driven oppositions.[69] As many have observed, the decline of the American government's role in global environmental initiatives has given the Chinese state under Xi Jinping the opportunity to emerge as a leader in tackling planetary challenges. Among other things, the grandiose infrastructural development project of the "One Belt, One Road," or "Belt and Road Initiative," announced in 2013, has purportedly sought to export green technocracy to Southeast Asia, Latin America, and Africa while generating waves of protests and critiques in Euro-American media along the lines of ecological destruction and social injustices.[70] Neither China nor the United States, therefore, has yet set a model for a green state that engages politics as a form of relational world making.

The global pandemic of COVID-19 has pushed us to rethink breathing as not simply an individual right to be taken for granted but an aspiration that demands collective striving. At this conjuncture, it seems crucially important to further engage media scholar John Durham Peters's call to rethink the environment as media across the Pacific so as to imagine what a truly green state might look like and what role citizens might play as part of a "bodies politic" in producing that green state.[71] The fire-breathing and elusive figure of chimera that Chimerica brings to mind is perhaps again instructive for challenging our terrestrial notions of breath and disorienting our place-bound assumptions of politics.[72]

Coda: The Materiality of Chimerican Media

On November 24, 2022, two years after the mass BLM protests in the United States and around the world triggered by George Floyd's death, a fire broke out in a quarantined apartment building in Urumqi, the capital of Xinjiang.[73] The *New York Times*, referencing local authorities, cited "inhaled toxic fumes" as the immediate cause for the ten people killed and nine others injured.[74] In the days that followed, hundreds of thousands of people in various Chinese cities took to the streets to express their outrage against the government's by then unreasonably strict zero-COVID policy. In place since the beginning of the pandemic, the policy involved routine testing, extended quarantines, and repeated lockdowns. Shanghai, the megacity and global trade hub of 26 million residents, for instance, endured such extreme measures in 2022, which upended the widely shared support for the Wuhan lockdown back in 2020. Again, it was the denial of breath in Xinjiang and elsewhere that instigated the mass protests, lending a new layer of meaning to the "I can't breathe" slogan popularized by the BLM movement.[75]

Just as Floyd's death was caught on cell phone cameras before becoming viral online, a video showing the Xinjiang fire with residents screaming for help from inside the building spread widely on social media both within and outside China. Overseas Chinese held vigils mourning the deaths of the victims across US cities and university campuses, often in conjunction with protests organized by college students originally from the mainland. Given such activation of a population known for widespread depoliticization in the past decades (chapter 4), it wasn't long before observers started comparing the movement to Tiananmen Square in 1989, the backdrop for the Tank Man photo.[76] After all, a precursor for the November movement was what some refer to as the "Bridge Man" incident on October 13, 2022, right before the 20th National Congress of the CCP when Xi Jinping secured his third term as the president of China.[77] That day, one protester disguised as a construction worker put two banners on Sitong Bridge in Beijing, one of which displayed the words: "We want to eat, not do coronavirus tests; reform, not the Cultural Revolution. We want freedom, not lockdowns; elections, not rulers. We want dignity, not lies. Be citizens, not enslaved people."[78] While both the protester and the banners were immediately taken away, the images of the slogans quickly circulated beyond the censored realm of Chinese social media, inspiring "copycat protests" in 350 campuses globally.[79]

Smartphones, the medium highlighted by communication scholar Alissa Richardson as central to a new form of "Black witnessing" in the twenty-first century,[80] again became a key force that galvanized transnational publics into actions. In an image showing the Sitong Bridge slogan in a *Washington Post* report of the event, one masked pedestrian is shown in the front holding up a camera phone and pointing it at the slogan.[81] Student protesters were also reportedly "airdropping flyers to strangers in public places" before organizing more in-person events through Telegram,[82] an alternative social media platform to which numerous WeChat groups moved during this time to evade state censorship.

There has been, therefore, a considerable shift in the processes of transpacific mediation between the Tank Man of 1989 and the "Bridge Man" of 2022. No longer is the white American journalist (embodied in Joe's character in the play *Chimerica*) occupying a privileged position to capture a lone protester fighting state power at Tiananmen Square, the place central to Politics in its state-bound form. Rather, it is smartphone-users-turned-witnesses situated in multiple locations who took it upon themselves to document the events unfolding in front of them before feeding footage to American (and globally dominant) legacy media such as the *New York Times*.

At first sight, the demand of these deterritorialized Chinese protests was not immediately comparable to that of BLM, a global movement that has transformed itself in different places beyond the specific struggle against police brutality in America. But the mode in which citizens in both China and America have sought "to improve their societies through their own actions," to use sociologist Bin Xu's words, points to "a high degree of similarity in civic engagement in both countries."[83] Importantly, these seemingly incommensurable experiences are intricately connected through the materiality of mobile phones as a form of Chimerican media.

Prior to the fire in Urumqi, in October 2022, workers at a Foxconn factory in Zhengzhou (Hunan Province) walked out of the plant where they had been put under a "closed-loop system" of production of iPhones and other Apple products. As labor scholar and activist Eli Friedman notes, the closed-loop system was first implemented in the United States in 2020 by the National Basketball Association; with players housed in a so-called bubble with entries permitted for supplies but not other personnel, the goal was "to ensure that the season and the finals could proceed."[84] Deployed in the 2022 Winter Olympics in Beijing, the system was later extended to workplaces throughout China, including "666 companies" identified as "key to the functioning of Shanghai's economy," Tesla among them. As Foxconn sped up the production to prepare for the holiday season in the West, it also began implementing the system but failed to ensure workers' health and well-being when cases broke out in the facility, which employs two hundred thousand people. Even though the workers ostensibly had the choice to opt in, the situation was akin to one of "forced labor." As video footage has shown, "when workers were leaving, they weren't walking out the front door comfortably but jumping over fences or finding gaps in the fences and running through,"[85] lending vivid imageries to Qiu's notion of "iSlaves."

While less frequently invoked as the direct inspiration for the translocal uprising in various Chinese cities later, the Zhengzhou workers' collective escape was also captured by smartphones and circulated on Chinese social media before appearing in global news outlets. Without "a centralized leadership," the workers "almost certainly were sharing information about where to escape. Once they got out, there was information about where they might find transportation or access to food."[86] Though they might not be using the same high-end smartphones they had literally put their bodies on the line to produce, the communication device of the smartphone became a key instrument for "deterritorializing" their resistance, in this case in terms of both their physically breaking through the fences and extending the messages about exits to others. Moreover, their action highlights the fact that although the Chinese state was the primary target of the subsequent protests, the adoption of the closed-loop system is one in which "America's most valuable corporations" such as Apple and Tesla "are implicated."[87]

The smartphone, then, may be seen as a material embodiment of Chimerican entanglements that offers disorienting potential to challenge the antirelationality of racial capitalism. The label "Designed in California, Assembled in China" on the back of iPhones among other communication devices consumed in the United States serves as a daily reminder of the presence of "China" in American media life. To highlight the role of this technology in social movements on both sides of the Pacific is not to fall into the euphoria of technological determinism but to foreground the historically specific ways in which marginalized groups in China and America can indeed be brought into a relationality that is often obscured by the national frames for Politics. As participants in the BLM protests after Floyd's death and the Chinese resistance against zero-COVID policy observed, both movements were marked by transnational, cross-class, and multiethnic characteristics.[88] Bringing them together through the Chimerican media artifact that is the smartphone, in this sense, can help us conjure a vision of relational politics that entwines place-bound Politics with the space of dissensus opened up by transpacific communication.[89]

One example of this vision based on relationality can be seen in what is now referred to as the "blank paper" meme, or "#A4Revolution," when protesters in China "held blank sheets of white paper in a symbol of tacit defiance."[90] According to one resident in Shanghai referenced by the

New York Times, "The purpose of the papers initially was to signal to the police that those gathered were going to mourn those lost while saying nothing. But as more people gathered, the feelings of grief and frustration morphed into broader calls for government accountability."[91] Demonstrators cited both the Soviet Union and the 2020 Hong Kong protests as sources of inspiration.[92] Commenting on the meaning of the blank paper, one Beijing-based protester said, "We are the voiceless, but we are also powerful."[93] Many users of various social media platforms changed their profile pictures into those of blank papers, mirroring the black squares adopted by those who joined the Blackout Tuesday initiative in support of BLM.[94] Herein lies another point of comparison between the "blank paper" movement and the 1989 Tiananmen demonstrations. As sociologist Andrew Barry suggests, the latter "demonstrate a political collectivity not by expressing an identity which pre-exists the action, but by forging an association marked by difference."[95] Initially triggered by a fire, the "blank paper" and related memes, to use John Durham Peters's words, "tear through the Internet like prairie fires" in defiance of the censoring "firewalls" of the Chinese government, via none other than the touchscreen devices that are lit from within and "fulfill a certain fantasy of touching flame."[96]

My point in invoking such memes is not to romanticize the efficacy of these movements but to engage them as opportunities to rethink citizenship in the transpacific context. After all, neither the BLM nor the "blank paper" protests could be said to have significantly overturned injustices in their respective contexts in profound, empirically verifiable ways, despite the fact that the murderers of Floyd were indeed found guilty and China ended its zero-COVID policy shortly after the uprising in 2022. While I've turned to the *New York Times* to reference protesters' quotes and actions, I also couldn't help but wonder if the desire to report on the movement so thoroughly was informed by an impulse to interpret it as an "anti-state" one, which is arguably different from "holding the state accountable," as we have seen in Zhang Lin's environmental activism (chapter 1). As interdisciplinary scholars Christian Sorace and Nicholas Loubere point out, even though "some protester demands are clearly driven by broader political grievances—for instance, calls for Xi and the CCP to step down," they were by no means "demanding the nihilistic necro-politics of the United States and other Western countries," nor were they "asking for complete state abdication to allow the virus to decimate the population."[97] Given "that student protesters (as they did in 1989)" were "singing *The Internationale*," it would seem "that socialist values are not the monopoly of nominally socialist regimes."[98] Indeed, a reading of the protests as a fight for "freedom against the authoritarian state," reminiscent of the journalistic accounts of Chinese reception of American shows (chapter 4), abstracts freedom out of contexts and, as such, obscures alternative political imaginations.

Echoing Sorace and Loubere's attempt to break through the US-China binaries that inform an ideological othering of China, what I wish to draw attention to is the *relationality* indexed by the "blank paper" that is in some ways comparable to the "future Chinese" spoken in the Chimerican media of *Firefly* (chapter 3).[99] Much like "rising" China in American media life, the absent presence of the paper devoid of immediate meanings signals the disorienting effects of the fire-breathing chimera/Chimerica. Traversing the place of the streets and the space of the internet, the potency of such a shared "code" in movements like these offers a glimpse into what politics might look like when citizens become active participants in the "bodies politic" and collectively seek new openings of breathing for themselves and for others. Air, the invisible form of elemental media that is required for producing fire (and whose smokey contamination can be viscerally felt when a fire breaks out even in far-flung locales), has metonymically, even poetically, manifested itself in the relational sign of the "blank paper."

The first two decades of the twenty-first century, the period I have focused on in this book, are slowly fading into memory, perhaps already getting too "old" for media scholars of the present and yet still too "new" for historians of the future. Chimerican entanglements also extend beyond the immediate geopolitical tensions between the United States and the PRC and may indeed find different expressions in other sites in the Pacific that deserve critical attention on their own.[100] What I have hoped to achieve is a critical cut of the transpacific mediation that congeals the fluid entanglements of the two superpowers into objects of contemplation, as Chimerican media. Much like the transpacific air that brings China and America into an uncomfortable embrace, these media may continue to provide us with generative resources to envision a relational approach to politics that more deeply connects people, places, and the environment.

Notes

INTRODUCTION

1. The exact origin of the virus remains disputed, though scientists have found evidence suggesting that the outbreak may have begun elsewhere and much earlier than November 2019, when the first case was confirmed in Wuhan. See Hannah Osborne, "Coronavirus Outbreak May Have Started as Early as September, Scientists Say," *Newsweek*, April 17, 2020, https://www.newsweek.com/coronavirus-outbreak-september-not-wuhan-1498566/

2. Javier C. Hernández and Austin Ramzy, "China Confirms New Coronavirus Spreads from Humans to Humans," *New York Times*, January 20, 2020, sec. World, https://www.nytimes.com/2020/01/20/world/asia/coronavirus-china-symptoms.html/

3. Arguably, the Chinese term *fengcheng* (sealing the city) does not have the same connotation as the English word "lockdown," the latter more often associated with "stern prison control, state mandates and active shooter protocols" in the United States. See "Covid Tech & China," ESC Routes, https://esc.umich.edu/covid-tech-china/

4. See, for example, Donald Trump, "Donald J. Trump on Twitter: 'The United States Will Be Powerfully Supporting Those Industries, Like Airlines and Others, That Are Particularly Affected by the Chinese Virus. We Will Be Stronger Than Ever Before!,'" *Twitter*, March 16, 2020.

5. Carl Zimmer, "Most New York Coronavirus Cases Came from Europe, Genomes Show," *New York Times*, April 8, 2020, sec. Science, https://www.nytimes.com/2020/04/08/science/new-york-coronavirus-cases-europe-genomes.html/

6. Jabin Botsford, "Close-Up of President @realDonaldTrump Notes Is Seen Where He Crossed out 'Corona' and Replaced It with 'Chinese' Virus as He Speaks with His Coronavirus Task Force Today at the White House. #trump #trumpnotes," *Twitter*, March 19, 2020, https://twitter.com/jabinbotsford/status/1240701140141879298/

7. David Frum, "The Coronavirus Is Demonstrating the Value of Globalization," *The Atlantic*, March 27, 2020, https://www.theatlantic.com/ideas/archive/2020/03/dont-abandon-globalizationmake-it-better/608872/

8. Caitlin Yoshiko Kandil, "Asian Americans Report over 650 Racist Acts over Last Week, New Data Says," NBC News, March 26, 2020, https://www.nbcnews.com/news/asian-america/asian-americans-report-nearly-500-racist-acts-over-last-week-n1169821/

9. Marion Smith, "Blame the Chinese Communist Party for the Coronavirus Crisis," *USA Today*, April 5, 2020, https://www.usatoday.com/story/opinion/2020/04/05/blame-chinese-communist-party-coronavirus-crisis-column/2940486001/

10. Nick Wadhams and Jennifer Jacobs, "China Concealed Extent of Virus Outbreak, US Intelligence Says," Bloomberg.com, April 1, 2020, https://www.bloomberg.com/news/articles/2020-04-01/china-concealed-extent-of-virus-outbreak-u-s-intelligence-says/

11. James Gorman, "With Virus Origins Still Obscure, W.H.O. and Critics Look to Next Steps," *New York Times*, April 7, 2021, sec. Health, https://www.nytimes.com/2021/04/07/health/coronavirus-lab-leak-who.html/

12. Fox News, "The Wuhan Institute of Virology: The Mysterious Lab Where US Officials Believe the Coronavirus Started," April 16, 2020, https://www.foxnews.com/health/the-wuhan-institute-of-virology-the-mysterious-chinese-lab-where-us-officials-believe-the-coronavirus-pandemic-may-have-begun/

13. Throughout the book, I use "China" as a shorthand for the PRC as a geopolitical entity.

14. While I use "party-state" to refer to the Chinese state as it is often depicted in anglophone media narratives, I by no means subscribe to the reductive understanding of the Chinese state as a monolithic entity. Rather, I hope this study draws attention to the ways in which this understanding of the Chinese state as a powerful actor *emerges* through these narratives.

15. Karen Michelle Barad, *Meeting the Universe Halfway: Quantum Physics and the Entanglement of Matter and Meaning* (Durham: Duke University Press, 2007), ix.

16. While my focus is on the American context, I recognize that this othering of China is not exclusive to views stemming from the United States alone. See Ivan Franceschini and Nicholas Loubere, *Global China as Method* (Cambridge: Cambridge University Press, 2022), 1.

17. See, for example Alice Miranda Ollstein, "Politico-Harvard Poll: Most Americans Believe Covid Leaked from Lab," Politico, July 9, 2021, https://www.politico.com/news/2021/07/09/poll-covid-wuhan-lab-leak-498847/. One precedent of such narratives, of course, was the mystifying anglophone coverage of the 2003 SARS global epidemic, which also began in China. See Belinda Kong, "Recovering First Patients," *Boundary* 2 (blog), August 27, 2020, https://www.boundary2.org/2020/08/belinda-kong-recovering-first-patients/

18. Jocelyn Kaiser, "Federal Watchdog Finds Problems with NIH Oversight of Grant Funding Bat Virus Research in China," *Science*, January 25, 2023, https://www.science.org/content/article/federal-watchdog-finds-problems-nih-oversight-grant-funding-bat-virus-research-china

19. My use of the term "absent presence" is primarily informed by film and

media studies. I thank Cara Wallis for pointing out that communication scholars are more familiar with its use in describing the impact of mobile phones on sociality. See, for example, Kenneth J. Gergen, "The Challenge of Absent Presence," in *Perpetual Contact: Mobile Communication, Private Talk, Public Performance*, ed. James E. Katz and Mark Aakhus (Cambridge: Cambridge University Press, 2002), 227–41, https://doi.org/10.1017/CBO9780511489471.018/

20. HuffPost Entertainment, "Donald Trump Says 'China,'" YouTube, 2015. https://www.youtube.com/watch?v=RDrfE9I8_hs/

21. Niall Ferguson and Moritz Schularick, "'Chimerica' and the Global Asset Market Boom," *International Finance* 10, no. 3 (December 27, 2007): 215–39, https://doi.org/10.1111/j.1468-2362.2007.00210.x/

22. Aware that "America" encompasses not only the United States but the hemisphere of the Americas, in this book I retain the common colloquial usage of "America" to refer to the US nation-state so as to better attend to the historical conditions that helped shape the coinage of "Chimerica."

23. James Palmer, "Winter Olympics: Eileen Gu and the Chimerican Dream," *Foreign Policy*, February 9, 2022, https://foreignpolicy.com/2022/02/09/eileen-gu-china-winter-olympics-chimerica/

24. John Branch, "Eileen Gu Is Trying to Soar over the Geopolitical Divide," *New York Times*, February 3, 2022, sec. Sports, https://www.nytimes.com/2022/02/03/sports/olympics/eileen-gu-china-freeski.html/

25. For a more in-depth analysis of the Eileen Gu phenomenon at the intersection of neoliberal feminism, cosmopolitanism, and Chinese nationalism, see Chelsea Wenzhu Xu, "The Making of 'China's' First Skiing Princess: Neo-Liberal Feminism and Nationalism in Eileen Gu's Online Presence during the 2022 Winter Olympics," July 11, 2023, https://doi.org/10.1386/eapc_00103_1. I recall when Gu's story broke, many of my friends with whom I share the background of having grown up in the PRC and come to the United States for graduate school chimed in on the Chinese social media platform WeChat. Just as we occupy the media space of Chimerica via the app on our smartphones, our offspring also share the (often quite privileged) experience of growing up between the two countries. At a moment of heightened geopolitical tensions, many of us felt the need to insert a critical voice in the American public sphere to conjure a different kind of "Chimerican Dream," one that speaks more truthfully to these lived and deeply felt experiences of Sino-US entanglement.

26. For example, it is also the title of Anita Felicelli's 2019 novel about a South-Asian American lawyer's encounter with a lemur that escaped from a mural and expressed its wish to return to Madagascar. While the novel invokes "chimera," there is no discussion of Chimerica in Ferguson's sense of the term.

27. Donna Haraway, "A Cyborg Manifesto," in *The Cultural Studies Reader*, ed. Simon During, 2nd ed. (London: Routledge, 1999), 272. For a critical discussion of Haraway's problematic invocation of Asian women workers in this formulation, which she revisits in later works, see, for example, Jeffrey A. Ow, "The Revenge of the Yellow Faced Terminator: The Rape of Digital Geishas and the Colonization of Cyber Coolies in 3D Realms' Shadow Warrior," in *Asian America. Net: Ethnicity, Nationalism, and Cyberspace*, ed. Rachel C. Lee and Sau-Ling Cynthia Wong, 249–66 (New York: Routledge, 2003); Alison Kafer, *Feminist, Queer, Crip* (Bloomington: Indiana University Press, 2013); Julia R. DeCook, "A [White]

Cyborg's Manifesto: The Overwhelmingly Western Ideology Driving Techno-feminist Theory," *Media, Culture & Society* 43, no. 6 (September 2021): 1158–67, https://doi.org/10.1177/0163443720957891/

28. Richard Jean So, *Transpacific Community: America, China, and the Rise and Fall of a Cultural Network* (New York: Columbia University Press, 2016), xiv.

29. Mark Deuze, *Media Life* (Cambridge, UK: Polity, 2012), x–xi.

30. Caetlin Benson-Allott, *The Stuff of Spectatorship: Material Cultures of Film and Television* (Oakland: University of California Press, 2021), 1–6.

31. For a discussion of the rise of this place-specific label, see Diana Budds, "The Fascinating History of 'Designed in California,'" *Fast Company*, June 14, 2017, https://www.fastcompany.com/90129351/the-history-of-designed-in-california/

32. Jennifer Gabrys, *Digital Rubbish: A Natural History of Electronics* (Ann Arbor: University of Michigan Press, 2011).

33. While the waste import ban may be seen as "part of China's trade war arsenal of weapons, tightening and loosening according to the temperature of US trade relations," domestic recycling has become more systematized through state subsidy since the ban. Yifei Li and Judith Shapiro, *China Goes Green: Coercive Environmentalism for a Troubled Planet* (Cambridge, UK: Polity, 2020), 140–41.

34. Benson-Allott, *Stuff of Spectatorship*, 14.

35. Viet Thanh Nguyen and Janet Alison Hoskins, "Introduction: Transpacific Studies: Critical Perspectives on an Emerging Field," in *Transpacific Studies: Framing an Emerging Field*, ed. Janet Alison Hoskins and Viet Thanh Nguyen (Honolulu: University of Hawaii Press, 2014), 2.

36. Lily Wong, *Transpacific Attachments: Sex Work, Media Networks, and Affective Histories of Chineseness* (New York: Columbia University Press, 2018), 14.

37. Monica DeHart, *Transpacific Developments* (Ithaca: Cornell University Press, 2021), 21.

38. Tina Chen, "(The) Transpacific Turns," in *Oxford Research Encyclopedia of Literature* (Oxford: Oxford University Press, January 30, 2020), 5, https://doi.org/10.1093/acrefore/9780190201098.013.782/. Chen's point also echoes the epistemological remapping in Brian Russell Roberts and Michelle Ann Stephens, "Introduction: Archipelagic American Studies: Decontinentalizing the Study of American Culture," in *Archipelagic American Studies*, ed. Brian Russell Roberts and Michelle Ann Stephens, 1–54 (Durham: Duke University Press, 2017).

39. Belinda Kong, "Pandemic as Method," *Prism* 16, no. 2 (October 1, 2019): 370, https://doi.org/10.1215/25783491-7978531. I further discuss this nonhuman characterization of China in Fan Yang, "Learning from Lana: Netflix's *Too Hot to Handle*, COVID-19, and the Human-Nonhuman Entanglement in Contemporary Technoculture," *Cultural Studies*, March 10, 2021, 1–11, https://doi.org/10.1080/09502386.2021.1898036/

40. Chen, "Transpacific Turns," 3.

41. I have therefore opted to use the phrase "'rising' China" or simply "China" in quotation marks to refer specifically to this figure, which encompasses the simultaneously imaginary and material presence of the Chinese state in American media life.

42. Mel Chen, *Animacies: Biopolitics, Racial Mattering, and Queer Affect* (Durham: Duke University Press, 2012), 7. I thank Lily Wong for reminding me of this connection.

43. Stefanie R. Fishel, *The Microbial State: Global Thriving and the Body Politic* (Minneapolis: University of Minnesota Press, 2017).

44. I thank one of the anonymous reviewers for pointing this out.

45. The fact that in both the PRC and the United States, the leader has always been male bespeaks the masculine undertone of the "rising" formulation. While a more thorough examination of this gendered dimension of the (Chinese) state is beyond the scope of this study, I do touch more on this in chapter 1.

46. Mid-April Designs, "China Lied People Died, Coronavirus Shirts, Covid Shirt, Trump 2020, MAGA Shirts, Trump Coronavirus Navy," Amazon, April 20, 2020, https://www.amazon.com/China-People-coronavius-Shirts-coronavirus /dp/B087C7FXJL

47. See, for example, Steven Lee Myers, "Facing New Outbreaks, China Places over 22 Million on Lockdown," *New York Times*, January 13, 2021, sec. World, https://www.nytimes.com/2021/01/13/world/asia/china-covid-lockdown .html/

48. Gordon H. Chang, "Chinese Americans and China: A Fraught and Complicated Relationship by Gordon H. Chang," *US-China Perception Monitor* (blog), July 18, 2019, https://uscnpm.org/2019/07/18/chinese-americans-china-fraug ht-complicated-relationship/

49. Kimberly Kay Hoang, "How the History of Spas and Sex Work Fits into the Conversation about the Atlanta Shootings," Vox, March 18, 2021, https://www .vox.com/first-person/22338462/atlanta-shooting-georgia-spa-asian-american/

50. Juan Alberto Ruiz Casado, "It Is Not Sheer Racism against 'Asians-Americans,' but Sinophobia due to a Dehumanizing Anti-China Narrative—The Invisible Armada," *The Invisible Armada* (blog), March 20, 2021, https://invisibl earmada.web.nctu.edu.tw/2021/03/20/it-is-not-racism-against-asians-americans -but-sinophobia-due-to-a-dehumanizing-anti-china-narrative/

51. For a thorough discussion of race and racialization in global-historical contexts, including East Asia and Asian America, see Martin Orkin and Alexa Alice Joubin, *Race*, The New Critical Idiom (New York: Routledge, 2019).

52. Perhaps it is not entirely a coincidence that a 2022 novel by Taiwanese American author Elaine Hsieh Chou, which touches on themes such as "Yellow Peril 2.0," is also named *Disorientation*. The novel is currently being adapted into a film.

53. Edward W. Said, *Orientalism* (New York: Vintage Books, 1979), 2.

54. See the critique in, among others, Anne Anlin Cheng, *Ornamentalism* (New York: Oxford University Press, 2019).

55. Daniel Vukovich, *China and Orientalism: Western Knowledge Production and the PRC* (Abingdon, Oxon, UK: Routledge, 2012), 5.

56. Daniel F. Vukovich, *Illiberal China—The Ideological Challenge of the People's Republic of China* (New York: Palgrave Macmillan, 2018), 200.

57. Ching Kwan Lee, *The Specter of Global China: Politics, Labor, and Foreign Investment in Africa* (Chicago: University of Chicago Press, 2018), xiv.

58. CNBC Television, "President Donald Trump: Calling It the 'Chinese Virus' Is Not Racist at All, It Comes from China," March 18, 2020, YouTube, https://www.youtube.com/watch?v=dl78PQGJpiI/

59. "President Donald Trump: Calling It the 'Chinese Virus' Is Not Racist at All."

60. James S. Brady Press Briefing Room, "Remarks by President Trump, Vice

President Pence, and Members of the Coronavirus Task Force in Press Briefing," White House, March 23, 2020, https://trumpwhitehouse.archives.gov/briefings -statements/remarks-president-trump-vice-president-pence-members-coronavir us-task-force-press-briefing-9/

61. That the five-hour PBS documentary *Asian Americans* premiered during the COVID-19 pandemic, on May 11, 2020, is a case in point.

62. Ho-fung Hung, "Holding Beijing Accountable for the Coronavirus Is Not Racist," *Journal of Political Risk* 8, no. 3 (March 17, 2020), https://www.jpolrisk .com/holding-beijing-accountable-for-the-coronavirus-is-not-racist/

63. Michael Martina and Trevor Hunnicutt, "Biden Says Trump Failed to Hold China Accountable on Coronavirus," *Reuters*, April 17, 2020, https://www .reuters.com/article/us-usa-election-china-idUSKBN21Z3DZ/

64. Hung, "Holding Beijing Accountable."

65. "Trump Blames China for Acting Too Late in Coordinating U.S. Corona-virus Response," *The Onion*, May 4, 2020, https://www.theonion.com/trump-bla mes-china-for-acting-too-late-in-coordinating-1843243502/

66. Katherine Eban, "As Trump Administration Debated Travel Restrictions, Thousands Streamed in from China," *Reuters*, April 5, 2020, https://www.reuters .com/article/us-health-coronavirus-nsc-idUSKBN21N0EJ/

67. George Packer, "We Are Living in a Failed State," *The Atlantic*, April 20, 2020, https://www.theatlantic.com/magazine/archive/2020/06/underlying-co nditions/610261/

68. Catherine Liu, "Inequality, Technocracy, and National Healthcare: Taiwan and COVID-19," in *The Pandemic: Perspectives on Asia*, ed. Vinayak Chaturvedi, Asia Shorts (New York: Columbia University Press, 2020), 113, https://www.asian studies.org/wp-content/uploads/Chapter-8-Liu.pdf/

69. Michael Levenson, "Scale of China's Wuhan Shutdown Is Believed to Be without Precedent," *New York Times*, January 22, 2020, sec. World, https://www.ny times.com/2020/01/22/world/asia/coronavirus-quarantines-history.html/

70. Priscilla Wald, *Contagious: Cultures, Carriers, and the Outbreak Narrative* (Durham: Duke University Press, 2008), 33.

71. Lisa Lowe, *The Intimacies of Four Continents* (Durham: Duke University Press, 2015).

72. It is revealing that back in January 2020, Wilbur Ross, the US secretary of commerce, commented that the outbreak could "help to accelerate the return of jobs to North America," displaying no empathy for the coronavirus victims in China. Simon Jack, "Trump Official: Coronavirus Could Boost US Jobs," *BBC News*, January 31, 2020, sec. Business, https://www.bbc.com/news/business-5127 6323/

73. Yến Lê Espiritu, Lisa Lowe, and Lisa Yoneyama, "Transpacific Entangle-ments," in *Flashpoints for Asian American Studies*, ed. Cathy Schlund-Vials (New York: Fordham University Press, 2017), 183.

74. See, for example, Jacques Rancière, *The Politics of Aesthetics: The Distribu-tion of the Sensible* (London: Continuum, 2006).

75. Terhi Rantanen, *The Media and Globalization* (London: Sage, 2005); Man-uel Castells, *The Information Age: Economy, Society, and Culture*, vol. 1 (Oxford: Blackwell, 1996).

76. Arjun Appadurai, *Modernity at Large: Cultural Dimensions of Globalization*, vol. 1: *Public Worlds* (Minneapolis: University of Minnesota Press, 1996).

77. Fan Yang, *Faked in China: Nation Branding, Counterfeit Culture, and Globalization*, Framing the Global (Bloomington: Indiana University Press, 2016).

78. Benedict R. O'G. Anderson, *Imagined Communities: Reflections on the Origin and Spread of Nationalism*, rev. and extended ed. (London: Verso, 1991).

79. Deuze, *Media Life*, 15.

80. At one point, President Trump's contraction of the coronavirus during the 2020 presidential campaign led to the accusation that China had attempted an "assassination." See Emily Ferguson, "China Accused of Attempted Assassination after Trump Catches Covid—Not Coincidental," *Express*, October 4, 2020, https://www.express.co.uk/news/world/1343389/donald-trump-latest-news-chi na-assassination-attempt-trump-health-update-deanna-lorraine/

81. Andrew Barry, *Political Machines: Governing a Technological Society* (London: Athlone Press, 2001), 7. Barry's distinction between "politics" and "the political" to some extent parallels my differentiation of "Politics" from "politics."

82. Kent A. Ono and Joy Yang Jiao, "China in the US Imaginary: Tibet, the Olympics, and the 2008 Earthquake," *Communication and Critical/Cultural Studies* 5, no. 4 (December 1, 2008): 409, https://doi.org/10.1080/1479142080241 6168

83. See, for example, Chih-Ming Wang and Yu-Fang Cho, "Introduction: The Chinese Factor and American Studies, Here and Now," *American Quarterly* 69, no. 3 (September 19, 2017): 443–63.

84. So, *Transpacific Community*, xxii.

85. Chen, "Transpacific Turns," 2, 12.

86. This understanding of the Pacific resonates with Roberts and Stephens's notion of "archipelago," which "serves to mediate the phenomenology of humans' cultural relation to the solid and liquid materiality of geography." See Roberts and Stephens, "Introduction: Archipelagic American Studies," 7.

87. Sara Ahmed, *Queer Phenomenology: Orientations, Objects, Others* (Durham: Duke University Press, 2006), 114.

88. Ahmed, *Queer Phenomenology*, 118.

89. Ahmed, *Queer Phenomenology*, 160.

90. The concept of "relationality" as it connects with Chinese thought has been attentively taken up in international relations. But my use of the term "relational" is more akin to the "relational way of being" in "Indigenous ontology and epistemology." See Yaqing Qin, *A Relational Theory of World Politics* (New York: Cambridge University Press, 2018); Shawn Wilson, *Research Is Ceremony: Indigenous Research Methods* (Black Point, N.S: Fernwood, 2008), 80.

91. Nguyen and Hoskins, "Introduction: Transpacific Studies," 2.

92. Biao Xiang, "The Pacific Paradox: The Chinese State in Transpacific Interactions," in *Transpacific Studies: Framing an Emerging Field*, ed. Janet Alison Hoskins and Viet Thanh Nguyen (Honolulu: University of Hawaii Press, 2014), 87.

93. Xiang, "Pacific Paradox," 89.

94. Yunte Huang, *Transpacific Imaginations: History, Literature, Counterpoetics* (Cambridge, MA: Harvard University Press, 2008), 6.

95. Xiang, "Pacific Paradox," 88.

96. I thank an anonymous reviewer for pointing this out.

97. Chen, "Transpacific Turns."

98. Kuan-Hsing Chen, *Asia as Method: Toward Deimperialization* (Durham: Duke University Press, 2010), 200.

99. Ivan Franceschini and Nicholas Loubere, *Global China as Method* (Cambridge: Cambridge University Press, 2022), 6, https://www.cambridge.org/core/elements/global-china-as-method/E384D0A1545B1DBC554C878C3012011D/

100. Arif Dirlik, *Complicities: The People's Republic of China in Global Capitalism* (Chicago: Prickly Paradigm Press, 2017).

101. Ho-fung Hung, *Clash of Empires: From "Chimerica" to the "New Cold War"* (Cambridge: Cambridge University Press, 2022), 24.

102. Lowe, *Intimacies of Four Continents*, 149–50.

103. Lowe, *Intimacies of Four Continents*, 150.

104. More recent scholarship on this matter includes Yinghong Cheng, *Discourses of Race and Rising China* (New York: Palgrave Macmillan, 2019); Frank Dikötter, *The Discourse of Race in Modern China* (Oxford: Oxford University Press, 2015).

105. Robeson Frazier, *The East Is Black: Cold War China in the Black Radical Imagination* (Durham: Duke University Press, 2015).

106. For an engaged discussion of the limits and possibilities of this alterity in the Chinese context, see Vukovich, *Illiberal China*.

107. While the predominant image of the Chinese workers is that of the factory labor toiling in "the World's Factory," it is also important to note that the number of workers in the service sector, such as couriers as part of the platform economy, is also growing rapidly in China.

108. Isabella Weber, "Could the US and Chinese Economies Really 'Decouple'?," *The Guardian*, September 11, 2020, sec. Opinion, http://www.theguardian.com/commentisfree/2020/sep/11/us-china-global-economy-donald-trump/

109. Kate Brown, "The Pandemic Is Not a Natural Disaster," *The New Yorker*, April 13, 2020, https://www.newyorker.com/culture/annals-of-inquiry/the-pandemic-is-not-a-natural-disaster/

110. So, *Transpacific Community*, 217.

CHAPTER 1

1. Several pictures of the staging can be viewed at Almeida Theatre, https://almeidatheatre.files.wordpress.com/2013/09/chimerica-3-by-es-devlin.jpg

2. See a thorough discussion of these terms in Terhi Rantanen, *The Media and Globalization* (London: Sage, 2005).

3. Lucy Kirkwood, *Chimerica*, rev. ed. (London: Nick Hern Books, 2013), 7. Niall Ferguson, *The Ascent of Money: A Financial History of the World* (New York: Penguin Press, 2008).

4. Kirkwood, *Chimerica*, 12.

5. Interestingly, Niall Ferguson has created a documentary production company with the name Chimerica Media. See https://chimericamedia.com/

6. Yuezhi Zhao, "The Life and Times of 'Chimerica': Global Press Discourses

on U.S.-China Economic Integration, Financial Crisis, and Power Shifts," *International Journal of Communication* 8 (January 2, 2014): 439.

7. Bishnupriya Ghosh, *Global Icons: Apertures to the Popular* (Durham: Duke University Press, 2011), 42.

8. Ghosh, *Global Icons*, 45–46.

9. Robert Hariman and John Louis Lucaites, *No Caption Needed: Iconic Photographs, Public Culture, and Liberal Democracy* (Chicago: University of Chicago Press, 2007), 209.

10. See, for example, Jane Chi Hyun Park, *Yellow Future* (Minneapolis: University of Minnesota Press, 2010).

11. Sara Ahmed, *Queer Phenomenology: Orientations, Objects, Others* (Durham: Duke University Press, 2006), 158; emphasis mine.

12. Christine Kiehl, "From Chimera to Reality: Lucy Kirkwood's *Chimerica* or 'What State Are We In?,'" *Journal of Contemporary Drama in English* 6, no. 1 (2018): 194, https://doi.org/10.1515/jcde-2018-0020. Kiehl also offers a more detailed plot summary and analysis of the play as extending the "state-of-the-nation" genre in British theater; i.e., "political theatre pieces probing the crises and chaos which jeopardize the stability of the state's institutions, the identity of the nation, and, in the process, urging the individual to redefine his/her place in the community" (192).

13. Featuring Tiananmen in 1989, there is also Nobel Laureate Gao Xingjian's play *Taowang* (Escape), discussed in Belinda Kong's *Tiananmen Fictions outside the Square: The Chinese Literary Diaspora and the Politics of Global Culture*, American Literatures Initiative ed. (Philadelphia: Temple University Press, 2012).

14. Kiehl, "From Chimera to Reality," 197.

15. Niall Ferguson and Moritz Schularick, "'Chimerica' and the Global Asset Market Boom," *International Finance* 10, no. 3 (December 27, 2007): 215–39.

16. Niall Ferguson and Moritz Schularick, "The End of Chimerica," *International Finance* 14, no. 1 (Spring 2011): 1–26.

17. Niall Ferguson and Xiang Xu, "Make Chimerica Great Again," Hoover Institution, May 3, 2018, 4–5, https://www.hoover.org/research/make-chimerica-great-again

18. Ferguson and Xu, "Make Chimerica Great Again," 20.

19. Zhao, "Life and Times of 'Chimerica,'" 425.

20. Zhao, "Life and Times of 'Chimerica,'" 436.

21. Kirkwood, *Chimerica*, 7.

22. Kirkwood, *Chimerica*, 7.

23. Tina Chen, "(The) Transpacific Turns," in *Oxford Research Encyclopedia of Literature* (Oxford: Oxford University Press, January 30, 2020), 9, https://doi.org/10.1093/acrefore/9780190201098.013.782

24. I thank an anonymous reviewer for reminding me to highlight this point.

25. Kiehl, "From Chimera to Reality," 201.

26. Mark Lawson, "*Chimerica* Playwright Lucy Kirkwood: 'The Whole of Democracy Looks Fragile and Farcical,'" *The Guardian*, November 14, 2016, sec. Stage, http://www.theguardian.com/stage/2016/nov/14/lucy-kirkwood-the-children-royal-court-theatre-chimerica

27. Yeside, "Chimerica," *StageWhisper* (blog), August 19, 2013, http://www.stagewhisper.net/chimerica/

28. Lloyd Evans, "Theatre Quest for Tank Man; ARTS—Exhibitions," *The Spectator*, August 31, 2013.

29. Paul Levy, "Holding Out for a Hero: A New Play in London Captures the Ambiguities of U.S.-China Relations," *Wall Street Journal*, August 22, 2013, http://www.wsj.com/articles/SB10001424127887324747104579022262640222686

30. Levy, "Holding Out for a Hero."

31. Peter Marks, "Review of 'Chimerica': A Sprawling Tale Is High on Dudgeon, Low on Insight," *Washington Post*, September 15, 2015, sec. Theater & Dance, https://www.washingtonpost.com/entertainment/theater_dance/review-of-chimerica-good-characters-forbidding-cities/2015/09/15/39b05488-5b33-11e5-8e9e-dce8a2a2a679_story.html

32. Levy, "Holding Out for a Hero"; Marks, "Review of 'Chimerica.'"

33. Kirkwood, *Chimerica*, 12.

34. Sarah Kember and Joanna Zylinska, *Life after New Media: Mediation as a Vital Process* (Cambridge, MA: MIT Press, 2012), xv.

35. Nick Couldry and Andreas Hepp, "Conceptualizing Mediatization: Contexts, Traditions, Arguments," *Communication Theory* 23, no. 3 (2013): 191–202. Couldry and Hepp distinguish "mediation" from "mediatization" by stating that "while 'mediation' refers to the process of communication in general—that is, how communication has to be understood as involving the ongoing mediation of meaning construction, 'mediatization' is a category designed to describe change"—that is, "how the overall consequences of multiple processes of mediation have changed with the emergence of different kinds of media" (197). In this formulation, which echoes Couldry's earlier work, it is implied that media and society are separate entities that act upon each other.

36. Kember and Zylinska, *Life after New Media*, 21.

37. Kember and Zylinska, *Life after New Media*, 71.

38. Kember and Zylinska, *Life after New Media*, 83.

39. One of the most exhaustive accounts of the 1989 events can be found in Carma Hinton's 1995 film, *The Gate of Heavenly Peace*, which aired on PBS's *Frontline* program.

40. Guobin Yang, "Power and Transgression in the Global Media Age: The Strange Case of Twitter in China," in *Communication and Power in the Global Era: Orders and Borders*, ed. Marwan M. Kraidy (London: Routledge, 2012), 167.

41. Craig Calhoun, "Tiananmen, Television, and the Public Sphere: Internationalization of Culture and the Beijing Spring of 1989," *Public Culture* 2, no. 1 (September 21, 1989): 59.

42. Yang, "Power and Transgression," 167.

43. Kirkwood, *Chimerica*, 14.

44. Kirkwood, *Chimerica*, 14–15.

45. Much of this material comes directly from the documentary *The Tank Man* by PBS, which Kirkwood lists as one of her sources. For a more recent documentation of firsthand accounts of the 1989 events, see Louisa Lim, *The People's Republic of Amnesia: Tiananmen Revisited* (New York: Oxford University Press, 2015).

46. Kember and Zylinska, *Life after New Media*, 13.

47. Kember and Zylinska, *Life after New Media*, 12.

48. Kirkwood, *Chimerica*, 107.

49. Kirkwood, *Chimerica*, 107.

50. Kirkwood, *Chimerica*, 108.

51. Kember and Zylinska, *Life after New Media*, 72.

52. Kember and Zylinska, *Life after New Media*, 83.

53. Kember and Zylinska, *Life after New Media*, 23.

54. Margaret Hillenbrand, *Negative Exposures: Knowing What Not to Know in Contemporary China* (Durham: Duke University Press, 2020), 195.

55. Hillenbrand, *Negative Exposures*, 204.

56. Hariman and Lucaites, *No Caption Needed*.

57. "Leica 'Tank Man' Ad Draws Online Anger," *South China Morning Post*, April 18, 2019, https://www.scmp.com/video/china/3006839/commercial-dep icting-tiananmen-squares-tank-man-creates-online-headache-leica

58. Kember and Zylinska, *Life after New Media*, 23.

59. Rey Chow, *Entanglements, or Transmedial Thinking about Capture* (Durham: Duke University Press Books, 2012), 10.

60. Chow, *Entanglements*, 10.

61. Chen, "Transpacific Turns," 3.

62. Ralph A Litzinger, "Screening the Political: Pedagogy and Dissent in *The Gate of Heavenly Peace*," *Positions: East Asia Cultures Critique* 7, no. 3 (December 21, 1999): 829.

63. Calhoun, "Tiananmen, Television, and the Public Sphere," 55.

64. Rantanen, *Media and Globalization*, 55; emphasis in original.

65. Scott McQuire, *The Media City: Media, Architecture, and Urban Space.* (London: Sage, 2008), 23.

66. Kirkwood, *Chimerica*, 23.

67. Kirkwood, *Chimerica*, 23.

68. Jack Linchuan Qiu, *Goodbye iSlave: A Manifesto for Digital Abolition* (Urbana: University of Illinois Press, 2017).

69. Cara Wallis, "'Immobile Mobility': Marginal Youth and Mobile Phones in Beijing," in *Mobile Communication: Bringing Us Together and Tearing Us Apart*, ed. Scott Campbell and Richard Seyler Ling (New Brunswick, NJ: Transaction, 2011), 62.

70. Chen, "Transpacific Turns."

71. Kirkwood, *Chimerica*, 33.

72. Kirkwood, *Chimerica*, 34–35.

73. Kirkwood, *Chimerica*, 85–86.

74. Kirkwood, *Chimerica*, 61.

75. Daniel C. Hallin, *The Uncensored War: The Media and Vietnam* (Berkeley: University of California Press, 1989).

76. See, for example, William M. Hammond, *Reporting Vietnam: Media and Military at War*, rev. ed. (Lawrence: University Press of Kansas, 1998).

77. Yuezhi Zhao, "The Media Matrix: China's Integration into Global Capitalism," in *The Empire Reloaded: Socialist Register 2005*, ed. Leo Panitch and Colin Leys (London: Merlin Press, 2004), 65–84.

78. See, for example, Chris Fenton, *Feeding the Dragon: Inside the Trillion Dollar Dilemma Facing Hollywood, the NBA, and American Business* (New York: Post Hill Press, 2020).

79. Rey Chow, "Violence in the Other Country: China as Crisis, Spectacle, and Woman," in *Third World Women and the Politics of Feminism*, ed. Chandra Talpade

Mohanty, Ann Russo, and Lourdes Torres (Bloomington: Indiana University Press, 1991), 87.

80. Chow, "Violence in the Other Country," 84.

81. Chow, "Violence in the Other Country," 84.

82. Kirkwood, *Chimerica*, 53.

83. Paul Yeung, "China Newspaper Editors Sacked over Tiananmen Ad," *Reuters*, June 7, 2007, accessed May 27, 2015, http://www.reuters.com/article/20 07/06/07/us-china-tiananmen-advertisement-idUSPEK17464820070607

84. Anne Anlin Cheng, *Ornamentalism* (New York: Oxford University Press, 2019), 14.

85. Cheng, *Ornamentalism*, 3.

86. Hillenbrand, *Negative Exposures*, 12.

87. Litzinger, "Screening the Political," 847.

88. Kirkwood, *Chimerica*, 114.

89. Kirkwood, *Chimerica*, 114.

90. Kirkwood, *Chimerica*, 114.

91. Kirkwood, *Chimerica*, 114.

92. Kirkwood, *Chimerica*, 115.

93. Kirkwood, *Chimerica*, 116.

94. This figure, embodied in such characters as the female lead in Sophia Coppola's film *Lost in Translation*, "is confronted with the world in a palpable way" in that "she may not have her bearings or feel at home in it, but it is precisely for this reason that she is aware of its existence." See Homay King, *Lost in Translation: Orientalism, Cinema, and the Enigmatic Signifier* (Durham: Duke University Press, 2010), 149.

95. King, *Lost in Translation*, 149.

96. McKenzie Wark, *Virtual Geography: Living with Global Media Events* (Bloomington: Indiana University Press, 1994), 159.

97. King, *Lost in Translation*, 149.

98. Kirkwood, *Chimerica*, 130.

99. Gilles Deleuze and Félix Guattari, *Anti-Oedipus: Capitalism and Schizophrenia* (Minneapolis: University of Minnesota Press, 1983), 246.

100. Daniel Vukovich, *China and Orientalism: Western Knowledge Production and the PRC* (Abingdon, Oxon, UK: Routledge, 2012), 1.

101. Zhao, "Life and Times of 'Chimerica,'" 425.

102. Kirkwood, *Chimerica*, 93.

103. Kirkwood, *Chimerica*, 72.

104. Kirkwood, *Chimerica*, 99.

105. Rebecca MacKinnon, *Consent of the Networked: The World-Wide Struggle for Internet Freedom* (New York: Basic Books, 2012).

106. Ralph Litzinger and Fan Yang, "Eco-media Events in China: From Yellow Eco-peril to Media Materialism," *Environmental Humanities* 12, no. 1 (May 1, 2020): 1–22, https://doi.org/10.1215/22011919-8142187

107. Kirkwood, *Chimerica*, 127.

108. Kirkwood, *Chimerica*, 27.

109. Kirkwood, *Chimerica*, 27.

110. In the production in Sydney, there were indeed multiple Tank Men with

the same look on stage to bring this critique of individualism to the fore. I thank writer Louisa Lim for first informing me about this.

111. Kirkwood, *Chimerica*, 20. As Christine Kiehl points out, Tess's line "ironically reverses Margaret Thatcher's 1987 notorious motto 'there is no such thing as society. There are individual men and women.'" Kiehl, "From Chimera to Reality," 198.

112. Listing Kirkwood as the creator, the miniseries retained the primary plots and lines of the play. But it reduces some of the nuances in the original script by overly dramatizing state oppression on both sides of the Pacific; i.e., the clamping down of human rights lawyers in China and arrests of anticapitalist protesters in the United States.

113. "*Chimerica*: Interview with Writer Lucy Kirkwood," Channel 4, April 9, 2019, https://www.channel4.com/press/news/chimerica-interview-writer-lucy -kirkwood

114. See, for example, Laura Mandaro, "Ferguson's 'Tank Man' Sparks Comparison with Tiananmen," USA Today, November 25, 2014, http://www.usatoday .com/story/news/nation-now/2014/11/25/ferguson-tank-man-tiananmen/70 078046/

115. Nick Visser, "This Black Lives Matter Photo Should Be Seen around the World," *Huffington Post*, July 10, 2016, http://www.huffingtonpost.com/entry/bl ack-lives-matter-protest-photo_us_5782d1ffe4b0344d514fdddc

116. Jayron, "#Baltimore #Tiananmen SQ Tank Man 2015. #Baltimore #FreddieGray #BlackLivesMatter"," *Twitter*, April 26, 2015, https://twitter.com/jayron 26/status/592353628792426496

117. Jennifer Hubbert, "Appropriating Iconicity: Why Tank Man Still Matters," *Visual Anthropology Review* 30, no. 2 (November 2014): 115, https://doi.org/10.11 11/var.12042. Hubbert's piece offers a more in-depth analysis of the Tank Man image and its global circulation. It is also worth mentioning that from 2020 to 2021, numerous protests were also carried out by antigovernment extremists and white supremacists, culminating in the storming of the US Capitol on January 6, 2021. Emerging there is the figure of a white male insurrectionist who also sees himself to be a Tank Man fighting the police force as he defends individual liberties and the creation of a reactionary mass movement. I thank Jessica Berman for pointing out the need to address this flipside of the BLM movement, which deserves more critical attention than what I am able to offer here.

118. Ghosh, *Global Icons*, 11.

119. Avery Gordon, *Ghostly Matters: Haunting and the Sociological Imagination* (Minneapolis: University of Minnesota Press, 1997), 195.

120. Almeida Theatre, "'Chimerica': A Thousand Words," *Almeida Theatre Blog*, May 24, 2013.

121. Ghosh, *Global Icons*, 5.

CHAPTER 2

1. Colin Dwyer, "China Says U.S. Has Begun 'Largest Trade War' in History, Retaliates with Tariffs," NPR.org, July 6, 2018, https://www.npr.org/2018/07/06 /626453571/china-says-u-s-has-begun-largest-trade-war-in-history-retaliates-with -tariffs

2. Thomas L. Friedman, "Biden: 'We're Going to Fight Like Hell by Investing in America First,'" *New York Times*, December 2, 2020, sec. Opinion, https://www.nytimes.com/2020/12/02/opinion/biden-interview-mcconnell-china-iran.html

3. Matt Egan, "US Tariffs on China Could Cost American Households $1,000 per Year, JPMorgan Says," CNN, August 20, 2019, https://www.cnn.com/2019/08/20/business/tariffs-cost-trade-war-consumers/index.html

4. Virginia Harrison, "US-China Trade War: 'We're All Paying for This,'" *BBC News*, August 1, 2019, sec. Business, https://www.bbc.com/news/business-4912 2849; David Goldman, "Apple 'Gut Punch': Trade War Will Cut iPhone Sales by 8 Million, Analyst Says," CNN, August 2, 2019, https://www.cnn.com/2019/08/02/tech/apple-iphone-trade-war/index.html

5. John Cavanagh, "Trump Trade Wars Have Led to Lost US Jobs and Factories. We Need a Worker-Centered Recovery," USA Today, September 17, 2020, https://www.usatoday.com/story/opinion/2020/09/17/donald-trump-trade-policies-damage-american-workers-column/5807633002/

6. Ho-fung Hung, *Clash of Empires: From "Chimerica" to the "New Cold War"* (Cambridge: Cambridge University Press, 2022), 61.

7. Hung, *Clash of Empires*, 63.

8. "Stephen Colbert's Pander Express," *The Late Show with Stephen Colbert* (October 7, 2015), YouTube. https://www.youtube.com/watch?v=V4WBsah U3X4

9. David Morley and Kevin Robins, "Techno-Orientalism: Japan Panic," *Spaces of Identity: Global Media, Electronic Landscapes and Cultural Boundaries* (London: Routledge, 1995), 147–73. Lisa Nakamura draws on an alternative formulation of techno-orientalism in a conference presentation by Greta Niu in 1998: "Techno-orientalism [is] a way of viewing (of making an object of knowledge) Asian Americans without attending to the relationships between Asian bodies and technology." See Lisa Nakamura, *Cybertypes: Race, Ethnicity, and Identity on the Internet* (New York: Routledge, 2002), 64; Stephen Hong Sohn, "Introduction: Alien/Asian: Imagining the Racialized Future," *MELUS* 33, no. 4 (2008): 19n5.

10. Morley and Robins, "Techno-Orientalism," 158–59.

11. Christopher T. Fan, "Techno-Orientalism with Chinese Characteristics: Maureen F. McHugh's *China Mountain Zhang*," *Journal of Transnational American Studies* 6, no. 1 (January 1, 2015), http://www.escholarship.org/uc/item/8n70 b1b6

12. Aimee Bahng, "The Cruel Optimism of Asian Futurity and the Reparative Practices of Sonny Liew's Malinky Robot," in *Techno-Orientalism: Imagining Asia in Speculative Fiction, History, and Media*, ed. David S. Roh, Betsy Huang, and Greta A. Niu (New Brunswick, NJ: Rutgers University Press, 2015), 165.

13. DefeatTheDebt, "Defeat The Debt Pledge Commercial," YouTube, August 31, 2009, https://www.youtube.com/watch?v=rRY5waZ4IbE

14. UpNorthLive, "Senate Candidate Pete Hoekstra under Fire for Ad," YouTube, 2012, http://www.youtube.com/watch?v=2-E2IhOc58k

15. First banned by major networks in 2010 during the midterm election, the ad was reenlisted by the Republican Party in 2012 to air after the October 22 presidential debate on Fox News, among other network channels like MSNBC

and AMC. Its YouTube link has accumulated over two million hits and continued to solicit comments from viewers to this day.

16. This is a federal-spending-cut advocacy group whose origin can be traced back to the Reagan era.

17. CampusProgressAction, "Chinese Professor," YouTube, accessed September 6, 2023, http://www.youtube.com/watch?v=OkRLxD-aZi0

18. The exact amount of US debt owed to China is updated monthly at the Department of the Treasury/Federal Reserve Board, "Major Foreign Holders of Treasury Securities," https://ticdata.treasury.gov/Publish/mfh.txt. In January 2023, China's ownership of US debt was $859.4 billion and the Grand Total national debt owed to foreign investors was $7402.5 billion.

19. Glenn Kessler, "No, China Does Not Hold More Than 50 Percent of U.S. Debt," *Washington Post*, December 29, 2014, http://www.washingtonpost.com/bl ogs/fact-checker/wp/2014/12/29/no-china-does-not-hold-more-than-50-percent -of-u-s-debt/

20. Morley and Robins, "Techno-Orientalism," 164.

21. Morley and Robins, "Techno-Orientalism," 171.

22. Johannes Fabian, *Time and the Other: How Anthropology Makes Its Object* (New York: Columbia University Press, 2002).

23. Morley and Robins, "Techno-Orientalism," 170.

24. David S. Roh, Betsy Huang, and Greta A. Niu, "Technologizing Orientalism: An Introduction," in Roh, Huang, and Niu, *Techno-Orientalism*, 4.

25. Roh, Huang, and Niu, "Technologizing Orientalism," 4–5.

26. Andrew Liu, "Lab-Leak Theory and the 'Asiatic' Form," *N+1*, Issue 22: Vanishing Act, March 10, 2022, https://www.nplusonemag.com/issue-42/politi cs/lab-leak-theory-and-the-asiatic-form/

27. Roh, Huang, and Niu, "Technologizing Orientalism," 4.

28. Roh, Huang, and Niu, "Technologizing Orientalism," 12.

29. Daniel Vukovich, *China and Orientalism: Western Knowledge Production and the PRC* (Abingdon, Oxon, UK: Routledge, 2012).

30. Ian Klinke, "Chronopolitics: A Conceptual Matrix," *Progress in Human Geography*, February 26, 2013, 676, https://doi.org/10.1177/0309132512472094

31. Morley and Robins, "Techno-Orientalism," 149.

32. Rita Raley, "eEmpires," *Cultural Critique* 57 (Spring 2004): 135, https://doi .org/10.1353/cul.2004.0014

33. Toshiya Ueno, "Techno-Orientalism and Media-Tribalism: On Japanese Animation and Rave Culture," *Third Text*, no. 47 (1999): 95.

34. Michael Pryke and John Allen, "Monetized Time-Space: Derivatives— Money's 'New Imaginary'?," *Economy & Society* 29, no. 2 (May 2000): 282, https:// doi.org/10.1080/030851400360497

35. Federal News Service, "Transcript and Audio: First Obama-Romney Presidential Debate," NPR, October 3, 2012, http://www.npr.org/2012/10/03/1622 58551/transcript-first-obama-romney-presidential-debate

36. Maurizio Lazzarato, *The Making of the Indebted Man: An Essay on the Neoliberal Condition*, Intervention Series, 13 (Los Angeles: Semiotext(e), 2012), 45–46.

37. See, for example, Maurice J. Meisner, *Mao's China and After: A History of the People's Republic*, 3rd ed. (New York: Free Press, 1999); Maurice J. Meisner, *The*

Deng Xiaoping Era: An Inquiry into the Fate of Chinese Socialism, 1978–1994 (New York: Hill and Wang, 1996).

38. See, among others, Wang Hui, *China's New Order: Society, Politics, and Economy in Transition*, trans. Rebecca E. Karl (Cambridge, MA: Harvard University Press, 2003).

39. Ho-fung Hung, *The China Boom: Why China Will Not Rule the World* (New York: Columbia University Press, 2016), 125.

40. Hung, *China Boom*, 125.

41. Mark Driscoll, "Debt and Denunciation in Post-Bubble Japan: On the Two Freeters," *Cultural Critique* 65, no. 1 (2007): 167.

42. Hung, *China Boom*, 125.

43. I cite dialogues primarily from the novel with comparison to the film and the screenplay by Drew Goddard. See Andy Weir, *The Martian* (New York: Broadway Books, 2014); Drew Goddard, *The Martian—Best Adapted Screenplay* (Twentieth Century Fox Film Corporation and TSG Entertainment Finance LLC, 2015), https://assets.scriptslug.com/live/pdf/scripts/the-martian-2015.pdf; *The Martian* (Twentieth Century Fox Film Corporation, 2015).

44. Weir, *The Martian*, 195. In the film, the introduction of this Chinese aid program is staged as a conversation between Guo and Zhu, labeled as "scientists" at China National Space Administration, who decide that "we need to keep this among scientists, a co-operation between space scientists." After the information was relayed to NASA, the Chinese American scientist Bruce says, "All right, thanks to my uncle Tommy in China, we get another chance at this." This differs from the screenplay, where Bruce's line is "All right, thanks to our friends in China, we get one more chance at this." See Goddard, *The Martian*, 66. When I first saw the film, I recall being amused by this seeming attempt to poke fun at the stereotype of Asian Americans as perpetual foreigners with foreign relatives or ties to foreign nation-states. (A case in point was the US Department of Justice's China Initiative launched in 2018 under the Trump administration, widely criticized for its racial profiling of Asian Americans. In response to such criticism, the program was reshaped in 2022 as a strategy to more broadly counter foreign threats.) It is also noteworthy that Benedict Wong, the actor who played Bruce, also starred in the London production of *Chimerica* as Zhang Lin/the Tank Man.

45. Weir, *The Martian*, 196. In the film, this particular segment is absent. Instead, at the end of the film, when *Ares 5* launches, a Chinese astronaut sits next to Martinez, implicitly conveying what is in the screenplay: "Wen Jiang. The first Chinese national to go to Mars." See Goddard, *The Martian*, 116.

46. Weir, *The Martian*, 215.

47. Weir, *The Martian*, 205.

48. Jenna Mullins, "This Is How Much Money Has Been Spent Saving Matt Damon," E! Online, December 28, 2015, http://www.eonline.com/news/7267 32/this-is-how-much-money-has-been-spent-saving-matt-damon

49. Randy Martin, *Financialization of Daily Life* (Philadelphia: Temple University Press, 2002), 119. Also see chap. 2, "When Finance Becomes You," 55–101.

50. Weir, *The Martian*, 282.

51. "Stephen Colbert's Pander Express."

52. Hung, *China Boom*, 128.

53. Hung, *China Boom*, 129.

54. For the complex relationship between Hollywood and China, see, for example, Aynne Kokas, *Hollywood Made in China* (Oakland: University of California Press, 2017); Ying Zhu, *Hollywood in China: Behind the Scenes of the World's Largest Movie Market* (New York: New Press, 2022).

55. Gang Meng and Zheneng Wu, *China's Belt and Road Initiative and RMB Internationalization,* Series on China's Belt and Road Initiative (New Jersey: World Scientific, 2019), https://doi.org/10.1142/11230

56. Fan, "Techno-Orientalism with Chinese Characteristics," 12; Eswar Prasad, *The Dollar Trap: How the U.S. Dollar Tightened Its Grip on Global Finance* (Princeton: Princeton University Press, 2014).

57. Guy Debord, "Society of the Spectacle," Marxists.org, 1967, http://www.marxists.org/reference/archive/debord/society.htm

58. Edward LiPuma and Benjamin Lee, *Financial Derivatives and the Globalization of Risk*, Public Planet Books (Durham: Duke University Press, 2004), 180.

59. Nancy Fraser, "Legitimation Crisis? On the Political Contradictions of Financialized Capitalism," *Critical Historical Studies* 2, no. 2 (2015): 159.

60. James Fallows, "The Phenomenal 'Chinese Professor' Ad," *The Atlantic*, October 21, 2010, http://www.theatlantic.com/politics/archive/2010/10/the-phenomenal-chinese-professor-ad/64982/

61. As Ho-fung Hung points out, the effect of this stimulus program was at best short-lived, for despite its boost for investment and exports, it "exacerbated China's internal imbalances and indebtedness, which will severely inhibit its growth in the years to come." See Hung, *China Boom*, 12.

62. Fallows subsequently confirmed that the actors were "DC-area college students." Fallows, "Phenomenal 'Chinese Professor' Ad."

63. Fallows, "Phenomenal 'Chinese Professor' Ad."

64. James M. Fallows, *More Like Us: Making America Great Again* (Boston: Houghton Mifflin, 1990), referenced in David Palumbo-Liu, *Asian/American: Historical Crossings of a Racial Frontier* (Stanford: Stanford University Press, 1999), 204.

65. Benjamin Lee and Edward LiPuma, "Cultures of Circulation: The Imaginations of Modernity," *Public Culture* 14, no. 1 (2002): 191–213, https://doi.org/10.1215/08992363-14-1-191

66. LiPuma and Lee, *Financial Derivatives and the Globalization of Risk*, 175. Speaking in more specific reference to the subjugation of state to capital in the form of sovereign debt among especially Southern European countries, Jerome Roos similarly suggests "that the making of the indebted state under the neoliberal condition has led to an unraveling of state sovereignty and political representation, thus presenting a major challenge to traditional democratic processes." See Jerome Roos, "The Making of the Indebted State Under Neoliberalism," *PopularResistance.Org* (blog), September 7, 2013, https://popularresistance.org/the-making-of-the-indebted-state-under-neoliberalism/. For a discussion on the cultural and political impact of derivative trading in the context of South Korea, see Joseph Jonghyun Jeon, "Neoliberal Forms: CGI, Algorithm, and Hegemony in Korea's IMF Cinema," *Representations* 126 (May 2014): 85–111, https://doi.org/10.1525/rep.2014.126.1.85

67. Lazzarato, *Making of the Indebted Man*, 8.

68. In this sense, fiscal orientalism shares an ideological function with what Colleen Lye calls "Asiatic racial form," produced within late-nineteenth- to mid-twentieth-century American literature in conjunction with national policy. See Colleen Lye, *America's Asia: Racial Form and American Literature, 1893–1945* (Princeton: Princeton University Press, 2004).

69. See Benedict R. O'G. Anderson, *Imagined Communities: Reflections on the Origin and Spread of Nationalism*, rev. and extended ed. (London: Verso, 1991).

70. James Fallows, "How America Can Rise Again," *The Atlantic*, January 1, 2010, http://www.theatlantic.com/magazine/archive/2010/01/how-america-can-rise-again/307839/?single_page=true

71. Lazzarato, *Making of the Indebted Man*, 46.

72. Fallows, "Phenomenal 'Chinese Professor' Ad."

73. Richard Dienst, *The Bonds of Debt* (London: Verso Books, 2011), 29–30.

74. Dienst, *Bonds of Debt*, 29.

75. The original video is no longer available but a redacted clip can be seen at otoleranceorg, "Jimmy Kimmel—Kid's Table—'Kill Everyone in China,'" *Jimmy Kimmel Live!*, October 29, 2013, YouTube, https://www.youtube.com/watch?v=PHR2ErH9HuI/

76. We the People: Your Voice in the White House, "Investigate Jimmy Kimmel Kid's Table Government Shutdown Show on ABC Network," October 19, 2013, https://petitions.obamawhitehouse.archives.gov/petition/investigate-jimmy-kimmel-kids-table-government-shutdown-show-abc-network/

77. "Investigate Jimmy Kimmel Kid's Table."

78. Yong Xu, "American Broadcaster Urged to Acknowledge Misconduct," *Xinhua*, November 11, 2013, http://news.xinhuanet.com/english/world/2013–11/11/c_132879051.htm

79. The Associated Press, "ABC Apologizes for 'Kill Everyone in China' Joke on 'Jimmy Kimmel Live,'" *Hollywood Reporter*, October 28, 2013, http://www.hollywoodreporter.com/news/abc-apologizes-kill-china-joke-651387

80. Lee Edelman, *No Future: Queer Theory and the Death Drive*, Series Q (Durham: Duke University Press, 2004), 11.

81. "Defeat the Debt Pledge Commercial."

82. Shawn Shimpach, "Realty Reality: HGTV and the Subprime Crisis," *American Quarterly* 64, no. 3 (September 2012): 538.

83. See Jacob S. Rugh and Douglas S. Massey, "Racial Segregation and the American Foreclosure Crisis," *American Sociological Review* 75, no. 5 (October 2010): 629–51.

84. An interesting parallel to this commercial is Strike Debt, "a nationwide movement of debt resisters fighting for economic justice and democratic freedom" that began in 2012 to challenge the neoliberal logic of debt accumulation in higher education. I thank the anonymous reviewer who reminded me of this movement, and I discuss the connection between China and US neoliberalized higher education further in chapter 4. See Folks from Strike Debt, "Strike Debt!," Strike Debt!, April 4, 2019, https://strikedebt.org/

85. Robert Samuelson, "Great Wall of Unknowns," *Washington Post*, May 26, 2004.

86. Julia Carrie Wong, "Asian Americans Decry 'Whitewashed' Great Wall Film Starring Matt Damon," *The Guardian*, July 30, 2016, sec. Film, https://www

.theguardian.com/film/2016/jul/29/the-great-wall-china-film-matt-damon-wh itewashed. Wong's article also features an image from the #StarringJohnCho movement on Twitter, which replaces Damon's image in a poster for *The Martian* with that of Cho's, stating, "John Cho as Mark Watney in The Martian? I'd see it!"

87. This is most clearly illustrated in the segment where Kimmel asks the Asian girl, "When you owe someone money, should you pay them back?" The girl answers, "Never!" Kimmel then follows up: "Well, then they won't lend you any money anymore. . . ." "Oh . . . and that's the problem," responds the girl, with a precocious gesture.

88. As he emphasizes in an apology, "I thought it was obvious that I didn't agree with that statement." See CNN Wire, "Jimmy Kimmel Apologizes for 'Killing Everyone in China' Skit," KTLA 5, October 29, 2013, http://ktla.com/2013/10/29/jimmy-kimmel-apologizes-for-killing-everyone-in-china-skit/#axzz2jFHpHPyA

89. Quoted in Morley and Robins, "Techno-Orientalism," 159.

90. I thank Kara Hunt for the inspiration to make this point.

91. This linkage is also highlighted in David Graeber's wide-ranging account on debt. See David Graeber, *Debt: The First 5,000 Years* (New York: Melville House, 2011).

92. Debord, "Society of the Spectacle." Also, compare Sheng-mei Ma's argument that Asian American resistance to orientalist/racist discourses inevitably has to invoke, and thus in some ways perpetuates, Orientalism. See Sheng-mei Ma, *The Deathly Embrace: Orientalism and Asian American Identity* (Minneapolis: University of Minnesota Press, 2000).

93. Cathy Park Hong, *Minor Feelings: An Asian American Reckoning*, reprint ed. (New York: Random House, 2021), 186.

94. Hong, *Minor Feelings*, 185.

95. For a critical account that connects this politics of indebtedness to American war and imperialism, see Mimi Thi Nguyen, *The Gift of Freedom: War, Debt, and Other Refugee Passages* (Durham: Duke University Press, 2012).

96. Dienst, *Bonds of Debt*, 63.

97. Dienst, *Bonds of Debt*, 176.

98. Weir, *The Martian*, 368–69.

99. Martin, *Financialization of Daily Life*, 190.

CHAPTER 3

1. Like many others, I recognize the challenge of discussing a show so closely associated with a complex figure like Whedon, given the more recent accusations of misogyny that contradicted the many influential feminist interventions in his previous work. See, for example, Lila Shapiro, "The Undoing of Joss Whedon," *Vulture*, January 17, 2022, https://www.vulture.com/article/joss-whedon-allegati ons.html/. At the same time, I believe it remains important not to presume a cultural artifact's significance stems solely from the ideas of its creator. Indeed, the focus of this chapter is the wide-ranging meaning-making practices that produce and are generated by the show in an environment characterized by Chimerican entanglements.

2. For example, in 2019 a parent from my daughter's Montessori school in a

Maryland suburb, upon hearing that the name of a classmate is Inara, the same as the empowered if not orientalized "companion" character on *Firefly*, immediately asked the mother if the naming was inspired by the show. The mother responded, "That's usually how I make friends." Relatedly, a former student of mine whom I ran into in 2022 on campus sported a T-shirt featuring *Firefly* imagery, including the Chinese characters for "Serenity," and told me he was a fan of the show and got it from a Comic-Con he attended that year.

3. Michael Shaara, *The Killer Angels: The Classic Novel of the Civil War* (New York: Ballantine Books, 1987), referenced in Emily Nussbaum, "Must-See Metaphysics," *New York Times*, September 22, 2002, sec. Magazine, http://www.nytim es.com/2002/09/22/magazine/must-see-metaphysics.html

4. Nussbaum, "Must-See Metaphysics."

5. Whedon quoted in Nussbaum, "Must-See Metaphysics."

6. Josh Whedon, "Re-Lighting the Firefly," documentary short, *Serenity* DVD, Universal Pictures, 2005.

7. Chinese, of course, is a character-based language with many regional dialects that sound very different from one another. It is, in other words, a multiphonic language with a shared script. In this chapter, however, I focus on the *sonic* performance of Chinese speaking more so than the *visual* aspect of Chinese writing. For a critical study of the Chinese script in relation to empire and authority, see Christopher Leigh Connery, *The Empire of the Text* (Lanham, MD: Rowman & Littlefield, 1999).

8. Another example is Chinese science fiction writer Liu Cixin's Hugo Award–winning trilogy, *The Three-Body Problem* (*Santi*), which also imagines a future world language that amalgamates Chinese and English.

9. Lucy Kirkwood, *Chimerica*, rev. ed. (London: Nick Hern Books, 2013), 24.

10. Kirkwood, *Chimerica*, 26.

11. Two decades after *Firefly*'s initial release, films featuring Asian and Asian American producers and casts, such as *Crazy Rich Asians* (2018), *Shang-Chi and the Legend of the Ten Rings* (2021) and *Everything Everywhere All at Once* (2022), have gained immense global popularity, deserving critical attention on their own, perhaps also in relation to "rising" China (as at least a major market for Hollywood if not also a source of capital and cultural identification). I shall leave this work to other scholars, but for a reading of a connected phenomenon in the literary realm, see Sunny Xiang, "Global China as Genre," *Post45*, no. 2 (July 16, 2019), https://post45.org/2019/07/global-china-as-genre/

12. Simon Denyer, "Trump's Granddaughter Gets Praise and Sympathy for Singing for Chinese President," *Washington Post*, November 9, 2017, sec. WorldViews, https://www.washingtonpost.com/news/worldviews/wp/2017/11/09 /trumps-granddaughter-gets-praise-and-sympathy-for-singing-for-chinese-presid ent/

13. Denyer, "Trump's Granddaughter Gets Praise and Sympathy."

14. Ollie Gillman, "Facebook Boss Mark Zuckerberg Spoke Mandarin with Chinese President," *Mail Online*, September 25, 2015, http://www.dailymail.co .uk/news/article-3248459/Zuckerberg-s-FaceTime-China-Facebook-boss-revea ls-spoke-Mandarin-rare-meeting-President-Xi-despite-Beijing-blocking-website .html

15. Xianying Tang, "Meiguo 'Hanyu Re' Beihou de 'Zhongguo Re' (The

'China Fad' behind America's 'Chinese Fad')," *Guangming Ribao (Guangming Daily)*, December 19, 2017, sec. 10, http://epaper.gmw.cn/gmrb/html/2017–12/19/nw.D110000gmrb_20171219_1–10.htm

16. Tang, "Meiguo 'Hanyu Re' Beihou de 'Zhongguo Re'."

17. Bethany Allen-Ebrahimian, "Can 1 Million American Students Learn Mandarin?," *Foreign Policy*, September 25, 2015, https://foreignpolicy.com/2015/09/25/china-us-obamas-one-million-students-chinese-language-mandarin/

18. Tang, "Meiguo 'Hanyu Re' Beihou de 'Zhongguo Re'."

19. "Kan Waiguo Mingxing Xiu Zhongwen, Yeshi Zuile (Watch Foreign Celebrities Show Chinese, Mesmerizing)" (Beijing, 2015), https://www.facebook.com/watch/?v=1473446559416305

20. "Ni Kanguo Zhexie Dianying Me? Neng Tingdong Limian de Zhongwen Me? (Have You Seen These Movies? Can You Understand the Chinese in Them?)" (Beijing, 2017), https://www.facebook.com/watch/?v=1473446559416305

21. "Kankan Sheldon Zenme Xue Zhongwen (How Does Sheldon Learn Chinese?)" (Beijing, 2015), https://www.facebook.com/watch/?v=1473446559416305

22. I thank May Chung for sharing this Chinese American experience as an inspiration for her dissertation. See May Chung, "Mandarin-English Dual Language Education: Understanding Parental Ideologies and Expectations," Dissertation, University of Maryland, Baltimore County, Baltimore, Maryland, 2021.

23. "Ni Kanguo Zhexie Dianying Me?"

24. Geoffrey Sant, "Is Jon Huntsman Fluent in Chinese?", Slate.com, October 31, 2011, http://www.slate.com/articles/news_and_politics/explainer/2011/10/is_jon_huntsman_fluent_in_chinese_.single.html#pagebreak_anchor_2

25. CNN, "Jon Huntsman Talks China, Speaks Chinese," YouTube, August 22, 2011, https://www.youtube.com/watch?v=IPb-5AZuzXo/

26. Sant, "Is Jon Huntsman Fluent in Chinese?"

27. It is important to note that with a Chinese-Hawaiian father, Reeves is often read by Asian Americans as "Asian Pacific passing as white." For a critical analysis of the complex racial dynamics of "passing," see Peter X. Feng, "False and Double Consciousness: Race, Virtual Reality, and the Assimilation of Hong Kong Action Cinema in *The Matrix*," in *Aliens R Us: The Other in Science Fiction Cinema*, ed. Ziauddin Sardar and Sean Cubitt (London: Pluto Press, 2002), 155–56. Ali Wong, the comedian and star of *Always Be My Maybe*, cast him in this 2019 Asian American romantic comedy, stating, "I was very aware that Keanu was Asian American because my family and community wouldn't shut up about it." Reeves is also noted to be supportive of the Asian community in white-dominant Hollywood, even though his success likely benefited from his white(-passing) privilege associated with a Caucasian name. See Megan C. Hills, "What Keanu Reeves Taught Me about White-Passing Privilege," *Evening Standard*, September 5, 2020, https://www.standard.co.uk/insider/celebrity/keanu-reeves-chinese-hawaiian-asian-heritage-white-passing-a4539726.html

28. Shilpa Davé, *Indian Accents: Brown Voice and Racial Performance in American Television and Film* (Urbana: University of Illinois Press, 2013), 2.

29. Jennifer Lynn Stoever, *The Sonic Color Line: Race and the Cultural Politics of Listening* (New York: NYU Press, 2016), 2.

30. US Census Bureau, "Nearly 3 Million U.S. Residents Speak Chinese at Home," United States Census Bureau, September 11, 2013, https://www.census.gov/newsroom/press-releases/2013/cb13-r90.html

31. "Chinese: The Language of the Future?," *The Asia Society* (blog), December 15, 2010, https://asiasociety.org/blog/asia/chinese-language-future

32. "Make Zakeboge Qinghua Yanjiang Quancheng Xiu Zhongwen (Mark Zuckerberg Showing off Chinese during the Entire Tsing-Hua Speech: 'I Want to Challenge Myself')," YouTube, 2014, https://www.youtube.com/watch?v=xFk_R5ltjoA

33. Hanban/Confucius Institute Headquarters, "Li Changchun and Liu Yandong Inspect Confucius Institute Headquarters and Call on the Staff of Hanban," Hanban, December 14, 2012, http://english.hanban.org/article/2012-12/14/content_476760.htm

34. Will Wachter, "The Language of Chinese Soft Power in the US," *Asia Times*, October 11, 2014, http://hsktests.com/language-chinese-soft-power-us/

35. Joseph Nye, *Soft Power: The Means to Success in World Politics* (New York: Public Affairs, 2004), 3.

36. Maria Repnikova, *Chinese Soft Power*, new ed. (Cambridge: Cambridge University Press, 2022), 1.

37. Lisi Ma, "Guanyu Woguo Jiaqiang Ruanshili Jianshe de Chubu Sikao (Preliminary Thoughts on Strengthening Our Nation's Soft Power)," *Dangde Wenxian (Literature of Chinese Communist Party)* 5 (2007): 35.

38. J. Wang, ed., "Introduction: China's Search of Soft Power," in *Soft Power in China: Public Diplomacy through Communication* (New York: Palgrave Macmillan, 2010), 5.

39. Wang, "Introduction: China's Search of Soft Power," 6.

40. Shiju Zhao, ed., *Yuyan Yu Guojia (Language and Nation)* (Beijing: Commercial Press, 2015).

41. Li Yuming, "Qiangguo de Yuyan Yu Yuyan Qiangguo (Nation-Strengthening Language and Linguistic Power)," *Guangming Ribao (Guangming Daily)*, August 24, 2004, http://www.people.com.cn/GB/wenhua/27296/27338 03.html

42. Li, "Qiangguo de Yuyan Yu Yuyan Qiangguo."

43. Terry Flew, "Entertainment Media, Cultural Power, and Post-Globalization: The Case of China's International Media Expansion and the Discourse of Soft Power," *Global Media and China* 1, no. 4 (December 1, 2016): 280, https://doi.org/10.1177/2059436416662037

44. Flew, "Entertainment Media, Cultural Power, and Post-Globalization," 281.

45. David Crystal, *English as a Global Language* (Cambridge: Cambridge University Press, 2003), 7.

46. National Research Centre for State Language Capacity, "Yuyan zhanlue yu guojia anquan gaoceng luntan (Language Strategy and National Security High-Level Forum Held in Beijing)," October 31, 2019, http://gynf.bfsu.edu.cn/?p=183

47. National Research Centre for State Language Capacity, "Yuyan zhanlue yu guojia anquan gaoceng luntan."

48. Wang Gengnian, "Shijie Geju Bianhua Zhong de Wenhua Guoji Chuanbo Zhanlue (The International Communication Strategy for Culture in the Chang-

ing World Order)," *Renmin wang (People Net)*, December 2, 2011, http://theory.pe ople.com.cn/GB/16480463.html

49. Ripei Zhang, "Yuyan Shi Ruanshili Yeshi Yingshili—Ping Yuyan Yu Guojia (Language Is Soft Power as Well as Hard Power—A Review of Language and Nation)," *Renmin Ribao (People's Daily)*, March 25, 2015, http://www.guoxue.co m/?p=27495

50. "Yong Kexue Taidu Weihu Zuguo Yuyan Wenzi Zhuquan (Protecting Our Nation's Linguistic and Literary Sovereignty with a Scientific Attitude)," *Zhongguo Jiaoyu Bao (China Education Daily)*, September 15, 2004, http://hnyycs.org/ar ticle-look-46.html

51. Li, "Qiangguo de Yuyan Yu Yuyan Qiangguo."

52. Nye, *Soft Power*, 15.

53. Hanban/Confucius Institute Headquarters, "Li Changchun and Liu Yan-dong Inspect Confucius Institute Headquarters and Call on the Staff of Hanban."

54. Lionel M. Jensen, "Culture Industry, Power, and the Spectacle of China's 'Confucius Institutes,'" in *China in and beyond the Headlines*, ed. Timothy B. Weston and Lionel M. Jensen (Lanham, MD: Rowman & Littlefield, 2012), 273.

55. See, for example, Christopher Walker, "What Is 'Sharp Power'?," *Journal of Democracy* 29, no. 3 (2018): 9–23, https://doi.org/10.1353/jod.2018.0041

56. Jensen, "Culture Industry, Power, and the Spectacle," 272.

57. Ingrid Hall, "Confucius Institutes and U.S. Exchange Programs: Public Diplomacy through Education," *World Education News & Reviews*, April 3, 2018, https://wenr.wes.org/2018/04/confucius-institutes-and-u-s-exchange-programs -public-diplomacy-through-education

58. Hall, "Confucius Institutes and U.S. Exchange Programs."

59. Austin Ramzy, "Get Ahead, Learn Mandarin," *Time.com*, June 26, 2006, http://content.time.com/time/world/article/0,8599,2047305-4,00.html

60. As of July 5, 2020, the official Hanban website announced, "The Confucius Institute brand will be fully operated by the 'China International Chinese Education Foundation.'" It remains to be seen whether this constitutes a mere name change or complete transformation of the CIs as a nongovernmental entity. See http://www.hanban.org/article/2020-07/05/content_810091.htm

61. Ministry of Education of the People's Republic of China, "What We Do," Ministry of Education of the People's Republic of China, 2018, http://en.moe .gov.cn/about_MOE/what_we_do/

62. Rachelle Peterson, *Outsourced to China: Confucius Institutes and Soft Power in American Higher Education* (New York: National Association of Scholars, 2017).

63. Hanban/Confucius Institute Headquarters, "Hanban—About Us— Confucius Institute Headquarters," Hanban, 2014, http://english.hanban.org /node_7716.htm

64. Hanban/Confucius Institute Headquarters, "Hanban—About Us— Confucius Institute Headquarters."

65. Hanban/Confucius Institute Headquarters, "Li Changchun and Liu Yan-dong Inspect Confucius Institute Headquarters and Call on the Staff of Hanban."

66. "Xi Jinping: Further Liberating Thoughts, Deepening the Reform, and Solidifying the Work to Promote Comprehensive Reform and Achieve New Breakthroughs at a New Starting Point," *People Net*, January 23, 2018, http://poli tics.people.com.cn/n1/2018/0123/c1024-29782294.html

67. "Xi Jinping: Further Liberating Thoughts."

68. Magnus Fiskesjö, "Confucius Institutes Serve Diplomacy," MCLC Resource Center, March 3, 2018, https://u.osu.edu/mclc/2018/03/03/confucius-institut es-serve-diplomacy/

69. Magnus Fiskesjö, "Who's Afraid of Confucius? Fear, Encompassment, and the Global Debates over the Confucius Institutes," in *Yellow Perils: China Narratives in the Contemporary World*, ed. Sören Urbansky and Franck Billé (Honolulu: University of Hawaii Press, 2018), 227.

70. Repnikova, *Chinese Soft Power*, 3.

71. Peterson, *Outsourced to China*, 20.

72. Peter Wood, Preface to Peterson, *Outsourced to China*, 12–14.

73. Peterson, *Outsourced to China*, 20.

74. Peterson, *Outsourced to China*, 12.

75. Marshall Sahlins, *Confucius Institutes: Academic Malware* (Chicago: University of Chicago Press, 2015), 1.

76. See, for example, Tao Xie, "China's Confucius Institutes: Self-Promotion or Cultural Imperialism?," CNN, October 21, 2014, https://www.cnn.com/2014 /10/21/opinion/china-confucius/index.html

77. Colin Sparks, "Media and Cultural Imperialism Reconsidered," *Chinese Journal of Communication* 5, no. 3 (September 2012): 293.

78. Jensen, "Culture Industry, Power, and the Spectacle," 283.

79. Peterson, *Outsourced to China*, 19.

80. This also means increased non-Chinese private funding with problematic ideological agendas for US universities, which is often obscured in the criticisms targeted at China. See Ivan Franceschini and Nicholas Loubere, *Global China as Method* (Cambridge: Cambridge University Press, 2022), 53.

81. David Morley, "Globalisation and Cultural Imperialism Reconsidered: Old Questions in New Guises," in *Media and Cultural Theory*, ed. James Curran and David Morley (London: Routledge, 2006), 30–43.

82. Jennifer Hubbert, *China in the World: An Anthropology of Confucius Institutes, Soft Power, and Globalization* (Honolulu: University of Hawaii Press, 2019), 114.

83. Jennifer Hubbert, "Ambiguous States: Confucius Institutes and Chinese Soft Power in the U.S. Classroom," *PoLAR: Political & Legal Anthropology Review* 37, no. 2 (November 2014): 333, https://doi.org/10.1111/plar.12078.

84. Hubbert, "Ambiguous States," 335.

85. Hubbert, "Ambiguous States," 340.

86. Robert Albro, "The Disjunction of Image and Word in US and Chinese Soft Power Projection," *International Journal of Cultural Policy* 21, no. 4 (September 2015): 392, https://doi.org/10.1080/10286632.2015.1042471.

87. Nianshen Song, "Chongtu de Shi Quanli, Jianshe de Shi Wenhua: Zhongmei Boyi Zhongde 'Wenhua Chongtu' (The Struggle of Power and the Construction of Culture: The 'Cultural Conflict' in Sino-U.S. Interactions)," *Waijiao Pinglun (Foreign Affairs Review)* 2 (2010): 55.

88. Randolph Kluver, "The Sage as Strategy: Nodes, Networks, and the Quest for Geopolitical Power in the Confucius Institute," *Communication, Culture & Critique* 7, no. 2 (June 2014): 201.

89. Jennifer Hubbert, "Authenticating the Nation: Confucius Institutes and

Soft Power," in *Confucius Institutes and the Globalization of China's Soft Power* (Los Angeles: Figueroa Press, 2014), 42.

90. Hubbert, "Ambiguous States," 345.

91. Jensen, "Culture Industry, Power, and the Spectacle," 272.

92. Jensen, "Culture Industry, Power, and the Spectacle," 281.

93. Chen Jinyu, quoted in Don Starr, "Chinese Language Education in Europe: The Confucius Institutes," *European Journal of Education* 44, no. 1 (2009): 69.

94. Inderpal Grewal, *Transnational America: Feminisms, Diasporas, Neoliberalisms* (Durham: Duke University Press, 2005), 2.

95. Fan Yang, *Faked in China: Nation Branding, Counterfeit Culture, and Globalization*, Framing the Global (Bloomington: Indiana University Press, 2016).

96. Aynne Kokas, *Hollywood Made in China* (Oakland: University of California Press, 2017), 54.

97. Referenced in Sahlins, *Confucius Institutes*, 38.

98. Song, "Chongtu de Shi Quanli, Jianshe de Shi Wenhua," 56.

99. Robert Phillipson, *Linguistic Imperialism* (Oxford: Oxford University Press, 1992); Robert Phillipson, *Linguistic Imperialism Continued* (Hyderabad, India: Orient Blackswan, 2009).

100. Daniel Immerwahr, *How to Hide an Empire: A History of the Greater United States* (New York: Farrar, Straus and Giroux, 2019), 629.

101. Vicente L. Rafael, "Linguistic Currencies: The Translative Power of English in Southeast Asia and the United States," *The Translator* 25, no. 2 (April 3, 2019): 149, https://doi.org/10.1080/13556509.2019.1654061

102. I analyze the film and the discourses around it in relation to the globalizing intellectual property rights regime and cultural imperialism in Yang, *Faked in China*, 169–202.

103. Phillipson, *Linguistic Imperialism*, 47.

104. Walter Mignolo, *Local Histories/Global Designs: Coloniality, Subaltern Knowledges, and Border Thinking* (Princeton: Princeton University Press, 2000).

105. Leigh Adams Wright, "Asian Objects in Space," in *Finding Serenity: Anti-Heroes, Lost Shepherds, and Space Hookers in Joss Whedon's* Firefly, ed. Jane Espenson and Glenn Yeffeth (Dallas: BenBella Books, 2005), 33.

106. Wright, "Asian Objects in Space," 31.

107. Douglas Ishii, "Palimpsestic Orientalisms and Antiblackness, or, Joss Whedon's Grand Vision of an Asian/American Tomorrow," in *Techno-Orientalism: Imagining Asia in Speculative Fiction, History, and Media*, ed. David S. Roh, Betsy Huang, and Greta A. Niu (New Brunswick, NJ: Rutgers University Press, 2015), 181. I also appreciate the media studies member of the faculty executive committee at the University of Michigan Press for pointing out that in this sense, *Firefly* has more in common with *Blade Runner* than does *The Martian*, examined in chapter 2.

108. I thank the anonymous reviewer who brought up this point.

109. Susan Mandala, "Representing the Future: Chinese and Codeswitching in *Firefly*," in *Investigating* Firefly *and* Serenity: *Science Fiction on the Frontier*, ed. Rhonda V. Wilcox and Tanya Cochran (London: I. B. Tauris, 2008), 38.

110. According to translator Jenny Lynn, the translation process involved

"making several phone calls to a group of people and it was always a back and forth trying to get the right words." It also entailed checking with her friends who were "more up on the current colloquialisms and curse words in China or Taiwan" when it came to "more current slang" like 'baboon's ass crack.'"

111. Rebecca M. Brown, "Orientalism in *Firefly* and *Serenity*," *Slayage: The Online International Journal of Buffy Studies* 7, no. 1 (2008): 7.

112. Brown, "Orientalism in *Firefly* and *Serenity*," 7.

113. Brown, "Orientalism in *Firefly* and *Serenity*," 7; emphasis mine.

114. Ishii, "Palimpsestic Orientalisms and Antiblackness," 183.

115. Rafael, "Linguistic Currencies," 152.

116. The actual translation turned out to be *houzi de pigu*, or "monkey's ass," which is not common at all at least in mainland China.

117. "*Firefly* behind the Scenes" (Twentieth Century Fox Home Entertainment Inc., 2003), https://www.youtube.com/watch?v=uLy_g1-ED1E

118. Alton L. Becker, *Beyond Translation: Essays toward a Modern Philology* (Ann Arbor: University of Michigan Press, 2000), 9.

119. Kevin Sullivan, "Chinese Words in the Verse," in *Finding Serenity: Anti-Heroes, Lost Shepherds, and Space Hookers in Joss Whedon's* Firefly, ed. Jane Espenson and Glenn Yeffeth (Dallas: BenBella Books, 2005), 201–2.

120. "*Firefly* behind the Scenes."

121. "*Firefly* behind the Scenes."

122. "*Firefly*—Chinese Curses," 2012, https://www.summer-glau.com/video/vip/494/interviews/2012/firefly_chinese_curses

123. Rey Chow, *Not Like a Native Speaker: On Languaging as a Postcolonial Experience* (New York: Columbia University Press, 2014), 15.

124. Chow, *Not Like a Native Speaker*, 56.

125. Chow, *Not Like a Native Speaker*, 56–57.

126. "*Firefly* behind the Scenes."

127. Brown, "Orientalism in *Firefly* and *Serenity*," 5.

128. Sullivan, "Chinese Words in the Verse," 199.

129. See, for example, Sarah Bunin Benor, "Ethnolinguistic Repertoire: Shifting the Analytic Focus in Language and Ethnicity," *Journal of Sociolinguistics* 14, no. 2 (2010): 159–83, https://doi.org/10.1111/j.1467-9841.2010.00440.x; Jonathan Rosa, *Looking Like a Language, Sounding like a Race: Raciolinguistic Ideologies and the Learning of Latinidad* (New York: Oxford University Press, 2019); Rosina Lippi-Green, "Accent, Standard Language Ideology, and Discriminatory Pretext in the Courts," *Language in Society* 23, no. 2 (1994): 163–98. I thank sociolinguist Britta Ingebretson for sharing this connection with me. Ingebretson also pointed out that such "mixing" often triggers anxieties from both mainstream white American society and native speakers from the home countries.

130. Shu-mei Shih, "Introduction: What Is Sinophone Studies?," in *Sinophone Studies: A Critical Reader*, ed. Shu-mei Shih, Chien-hsin Tsai, and Brian Bernards (New York: Columbia University Press, 2013), 9–10.

131. P. Gardner Goldsmith, "Freedom in an Unfree World," in *Serenity Found: More Unauthorized Essays on Joss Whedon's* Firefly *Universe*, ed. Jane Espenson and Leah Wilson (Dallas: BenBella Books, 2007), 55–66.

132. Amy H. Sturgis, "'Just Get Us a Little Further': Liberty and the Frontier in

Firefly and *Serenity*," in *The Philosophy of Joss Whedon*, ed. Dean Kowalski (Lexington: University Press of Kentucky, 2011), 24–38.

133. Joseph J. Foy, "The State of Nature and Social Contracts on Spaceship *Serenity*," in *The Philosophy of Joss Whedon*, ed. Dean Kowalski (Lexington: University Press of Kentucky, 2011), 39–54.

134. Goldsmith, "Freedom in an Unfree World."

135. Goldsmith, "Freedom in an Unfree World," 64.

136. Whedon quoted in Nussbaum, "Must-See Metaphysics."

137. Codeswitching can be understood as "the rapid succession of several languages in a single speech event," which differs from "code-mixing"; i.e., "where lexical items and grammatical features from two languages appear in one sentence." See Pieter Muysken, *Bilingual Speech: A Typology of Code-Mixing* (Cambridge: Cambridge University Press, 2005), 1. Again, I thank Ingebretson for her suggestion of the source here.

138. Mandala, "Representing the Future," 37.

139. Rafael, "Linguistic Currencies," 152.

140. Sullivan, "Chinese Words in the Verse," 204.

141. Sullivan, "Chinese Words in the Verse," 205.

142. "*Firefly* behind the Scenes."

143. Aimee Bahng, *Migrant Futures: Decolonizing Speculation in Financial Times* (Durham: Duke University Press, 2018), 8.

144. A 2022 episode of the Showtime series *Billions* (season 6, episode 11), in which Mike Prince, the main character, intends to leave his hedge fund business behind to join the US presidential race, provides yet another example of the Chinese-speaking non-Chinese phenomenon. At a meeting with Chinese delegates about a deal for infrastructure development in the Global South, Prince "demonstrates" his Mandarin ability (by speaking incomprehensible sentences) before chastising China for its human rights violation and rejecting the collaboration. Later it is revealed that this act is meant for generating publicity around his soon-to-be-announced presidential campaign. Again, "rising" China is invoked as a nonhuman Other to not only heighten a white protagonist's linguistic prowess but to also legitimize a kind of political righteousness that would allow a character like Prince to become a worthy presidential candidate.

145. Hubbert, *China in the World*, 61.

146. Bahng, *Migrant Futures*, 16.

147. Vicente L. Rafael, "Mutant Tongues: Translating English in the Postcolonial Humanities," *CR: The New Centennial Review* 16, no. 1 (2016): 107, https://doi.org/10.14321/crnewcentrevi.16.1.0093

148. Immerwahr, *How to Hide an Empire*, 598.

149. Immerwahr, *How to Hide an Empire*, 618.

150. May Chung, "'I Call Them My Little Chinese Kids': Parents' Identities and Language Ideologies in Mandarin-English Dual Language Immersion Schools," *Journal of Culture and Values in Education* 3, no. 2 (2020): 179–95.

151. Mandala, "Representing the Future," 40.

152. John H. McWhorter, "What the World Will Speak in 2115," *Wall Street Journal*, January 2, 2015, http://www.wsj.com/articles/what-the-world-will-speak-in-2115-1420234648

153. While I have primarily focused on the operation of racialization through language in the US context, it is important to recognize that the intersectional workings of race and language can manifest themselves differently beyond Chimerica, through distinct permutations in Afro-Chinese encounters, for example. See Jay Ke-Schutte, *Angloscene: Compromised Personhood in Afro-Chinese Translations* (Oakland: University of California Press, 2023).

154. Edward Wong, "U.S. Labels Chinese Language Education Group a Diplomatic Mission," *New York Times*, August 13, 2020, sec. U.S., https://www.nytimes .com/2020/08/13/us/politics/state-department-confucius-institutes.html

CHAPTER 4

1. Evan Osnos, "A Breakout Hit Sweeps China," *Chicago Tribune*, January 18, 2007, http://articles.chicagotribune.com/2007-01-18/news/0701180056_1_pri son-break-official-chinese-statistics-web-users/

2. Evan Osnos, "'Prison Break' Catches on in China," *Seattle Times*, January 25, 2007, http://www.seattletimes.com/nation-world/prison-break-catches-on -in-china/

3. Xinyan Chen, "Shuju Jiushi Shengchanli (Data Is Productivity)," *Jilin Yixue Xinxi (Jilin Medical Information)* 30, no. 9 (2014): 35.

4. Yao Wang, "Qiantan Meiju 'Zhipaiwu' Zhong de Kuawenhua Chuanbo—Yi Dashuju Wei Shijiao (On the Cross-Cultural Communication in the American TV Show *House of Cards*—from the Perspective of Big Data)," *Jingying Guanlizhe (Manager Journal)* 8 (March 2015): 352.

5. Kuanmian Nie, "Zhipaiwu 'gongdou' Kanzhe Bie Dangzhen, Shili Weiji Weina Taiduo Jiang (Don't Take the 'Palace Infighting' of *House of Cards* Seriously, Not Enough Strength to Obtain That Many Awards)," *Renmin wang (People Net)*, February 25, 2014, http://media.people.com.cn/n/2014/0225/c40606-24 452852.html

6. Qiuqi Qian, "OTT TV Zai Zhongguo Yingshi Chanye de Yanjiu (A Study of OTT TV in the Chinese Film and Television Industry)," *Shengping Shijie (Voice and Screen World)* 14 (December 2014): 12.

7. Contrasting this statement, I have personally encountered a great number of female viewers of Chinese descent who are fans of the show, both in China and the United States.

8. Chen, "Shuju Jiushi Shengchanli (Data Is Productivity)," 35.

9. Steven Jiang, "'House of Cards' in China: Surprisingly Available and Popular," CNN, February 19, 2014, http://www.cnn.com/2014/02/19/world/asia/ch ina-house-of-cards-jiang/

10. Andrew Stevens, "China's Xi Jinping in 'House of Cards' Joke," CNN, September 23, 2015, http://www.cnn.com/2015/09/23/asia/xi-jinping-us-visit-hou se-of-cards/index.html

11. Mareike Jenner, "Is This TVIV? On Netflix, TVIII, and Binge-Watching," *New Media & Society* 18, no. 2 (February 2016): 267–68.

12. Aynne Kokas, *Hollywood Made in China* (Oakland: University of California Press, 2017).

13. Jenner, "Is This TVIV?," 259.

14. Hui Zhang, "Zhipaiwu Weihe Zai Zhongguo Shou Zhuipeng? (Why Was

House of Cards Chased after in China?)," *Qingnian Cankao (Elite Reference)*, February 26, 2014, sec. B.

15. Xinyin Liu, "Meiju, Kanshangqu Hen Mei (American TV Shows, Looking Good)," *Guoji Renwen Lishi (National Humanity History)*, June 2016, 123.

16. Zhipeng Xu, "'Zipai Moshi' Yi Qidong—Cong Baidu Aiqiyi Kan Shipin Wangzhan de Yingshi Fazhan Zhilu (Selfie Mode Is Activated—The Film and Television Developmental Path of Video Streaming Sites through the Case of Baidu IQiyi)," *Dangdai Dianying (Contemporary Cinema)* 1 (2015): 153.

17. Lin Zhao, "Cong Zhipaiwu Re Toushi Xifang Fada Guojia Fubai Xianxiang (Probing the Corruption Phenomena in Western Developed Countries through the Popularity of House of Cards)," Guoji Fanfu Liaowang (International Anticorruption Outlook), June 16, 2014, http://www.ccdi.gov.cn/special /hwfb/tbbd_hwfb/201406/t20140617_24251.html

18. Bree Feng, "China Uses 'House of Cards' as Illustration of West's Corruption," *New York Times*, June 19, 2014, http://sinosphere.blogs.nytimes.com/2014 /06/19/china-uses-house-of-cards-as-illustration-of-wests-corruption/

19. James Areddy, "How Corrupt Is the U.S.? Just Watch 'House of Cards,' China Party Arm Says," *Wall Street Journal*, June 17, 2014, http://blogs.wsj.com /chinarealtime/2014/06/17/how-corrupt-is-the-u-s-just-watch-house-of-cards -china-party-arm-says/

20. Ping Bai, "US Political Drama Tells Much about Us," *China Daily*, February 24, 2014, http://usa.chinadaily.com.cn/2014-02/24/content_17300030.htm

21. Chunling Dong, "Bei Xishuo de Meiguo Zhengzhi—Xiezai Zhipaiwu Dierji Bochu Zhihou (American Politics Dramatized—Writing after the Release of the Second Season of House of Cards)," *Shijie Zhishi (World Affairs)* 7 (2014), 71.

22. Areddy, "How Corrupt Is the U.S.?"

23. Chedan Xia, "Womende Zhenhuanzhuan, Tamende Zhipaiwu (Our Legends of Empress Zhen, Their House of Cards)," *Yidu (IRead)* (blog), March 27, 2013, http://blog.sina.com.cn/s/blog_aa875eee0101asa3.html

24. Zhihu, "Zhipaiwu He Zhenhuanzhuan, Shui Geng Lihai? (House of Cards and Legends of Zhenhuan, Which One Is More Powerful?)," 2014–16, https:// www.zhihu.com/question/22833198

25. Erliang Li, "Zhongguo Weihe Meiyou Zhengzhiju? (Why Aren't There Any Political Shows in China?)," *Zhonghua Ernu (China Profiles)*, 2014, 42.

26. Ruoyun Bai, *Staging Corruption: Chinese Television and Politics*, Contemporary Chinese Studies (Vancouver: University of British Columbia Press, 2014), 5, http://www.washington.edu/uwpress/search/books/BAISTA.html#contents

27. Yin Cao, "China's 'House of Cards' to Focus on Graft Fight," *China Daily*, June 16, 2016, http://www.chinadaily.com.cn/china/2016-06/16/content_2572 6484.htm

28. CGTN, "Why Is the Chinese 'House of Cards' So Popular?," 2017, https:// www.youtube.com/watch?v=8JQyV54grrU

29. Chang Ye Chen, "Lingdaoren Xihuan Zhipaiwu, Dan Women Zhineng Pai Renminde Mingyi (The Leaders Like House of Cards, but We Can Only Make In the Name of the People)," huxiu.com, April 17, 2017, https://www.huxiu.com/ar ticle/190660.html

30. Alexander LaCasse, "How Accurate Is 'House of Cards?' Very, Says Presi-

dent Clinton," *Christian Science Monitor*, March 31, 2015, http://www.csmonitor
.com/The-Culture/Culture-Cafe/2015/0331/How-accurate-is-House-of-Cards
-Very-says-President-Clinton.-video

31. Seth Masket, "'House of Cards' Is the Worst Show about American Politics.
Ever," *Washington Post*, March 8, 2015, https://www.washingtonpost.com/news
/monkey-cage/wp/2015/03/08/house-of-cards-is-the-worst-show-about-americ
an-politics-ever/

32. Dong Chunling quoted in "Bei Xishuo de Meiguo Zhengzhi," 71.

33. Weiyu Zhang, *The Internet and New Social Formation in China: Fandom Publics
in the Making*, Media, Culture and Social Change in Asia (London: Routledge,
2016), 83.

34. The season features the newly inaugurated vice president Frank Underwood plotting to replace President Walker in the Oval Office. Part of Underwood's efforts consist of contending with Walker's longtime advisor, the billion-
aire Raymond Tusk, while making use of Feng, Tusk's business partner.

35. Zhang, "Zhipaiwu Weihe Zai Zhongguo Shou Zhuipeng?"

36. Qiongyuan Zhou and Hao Lu, "Zhipaiwu Zhongguo Shangren Feng
Banyanzhe: Buzhi Zhongguo Zhuxi Zongli Shi Shui (The Actor for the Chinese
Businessman Feng in House of Cards Doesn't Know Who the Chairman and
President of China Are)," guancha.cn, March 6, 2014, http://www.guancha.cn
/america/2014_03_06_211342.shtml

37. Yajie Zhang, "Dui Zhipaiwu Zhonguo Yuansu de Shenceng Sikao (An In-
Depth Consideration of the Chinese Elements in House of Cards)," *Mingzuo
Xinshang (Masterpieces Review)* 6 (2015): 172.

38. Ying Zhu, "Why Frank Underwood Is Great for China's Soft Power," ChinaFile, February 27, 2014, https://www.chinafile.com/Frank-Underwood-Great
-Chinas-Soft-Power

39. Kenneth Lin quoted in Wayne Ma, "'House of Cards' Writer on China,
U.S., and Power," *China Real Time Report—Wall Street Journal* (blog), February
19, 2014, http://blogs.wsj.com/chinarealtime/2014/02/19/house-of-cards-writ
er-on-china-u-s-and-power/

40. E.g., Jiang, "'House of Cards' in China"; Yu Liu, "Dianshi Hen Malatang,
Xianshi Hen Baikaishui—Dui Zhipaiwu de Zhengzhixue Jiedu (TV Is Very Hot
and Spicy, Reality Is Bland like Water—A Reading of House of Cards through
Political Science)," *Nanfang Renwu Zhoukan (Southern People Weekly)*, March 10,
2014, http://www.nfpeople.com/story_view.php?id=5253

41. "Chapter 18," *House of Cards*, Netflix, February 14, 2014.

42. "Chapter 15," *House of Cards*, Netflix, February 14, 2014.

43. Indeed, almost everyone I have spoken to about the show who lives in the
United States and has some interest in China has raised related questions about
the sex scene.

44. Bee Vang and Louisa Schein, "The Wretched from the East: Geopolitical
Perversions of Asian Manhood," unpublished manuscript, June 11, 2017, 13.

45. See, for example, Chiung Hwang Chen, "Feminization of Asian (American) Men in the U.S. Mass Media: An Analysis of *The Ballad of Little Jo*," *Journal of
Communication Inquiry* 20, no. 2 (October 1, 1996): 57–71, https://doi.org/10.11
77/019685999602000204

46. Vang and Schein, "Wretched from the East," 15.

47. David Palumbo-Liu, *Asian/American: Historical Crossings of a Racial Frontier* (Stanford, CA: Stanford University Press, 1999), 290.

48. Palumbo-Liu, *Asian/American*, 290.

49. Palumbo-Liu, *Asian/American*, 290.

50. Zhou and Lu, "Zhipaiwu Zhongguo Shangren Feng Banyanzhe."

51. Zhang, "Dui Zhipaiwu Zhonguo Yuansu de Shenceng Sikao," 172.

52. "Chapter 18," *House of Cards*, 18.

53. Karen Michelle Barad, *Meeting the Universe Halfway: Quantum Physics and the Entanglement of Matter and Meaning* (Durham: Duke University Press, 2007), 89.

54. Reed Hastings, Netflix—Keynote address, Consumer Technology Association, Las Vegas, Nevada, 2016, https://www.youtube.com/watch?v=l5R3E6jsICA

55. Reed Hastings, Netflix—Keynote address, 2016.

56. Reed Hastings, Netflix—Keynote address, 2016.

57. Roman Lobato, *Netflix Nations: The Geography of Digital Distribution* (New York: NYU Press, 2019), 70.

58. Taina Bucher, *If . . . Then: Algorithmic Power and Politics* (Oxford: Oxford University Press, 2018), 1.

59. Shoshana Zuboff, *The Age of Surveillance Capitalism: The Fight for a Human Future at the New Frontier of Powe* (New York: Public Affairs, 2019).

60. Nick Srnicek, *Platform Capitalism* (Cambridge: Polity, 2016).

61. Sarah Myers West, "Data Capitalism: Redefining the Logics of Surveillance and Privacy," *Business & Society* 58, no. 1 (January 1, 2019): 20–41, https://doi.org/10.1177/0007650317718185.

62. Nick Couldry and Ulises A. Mejias, *The Costs of Connection: How Data Is Colonizing Human Life and Appropriating It for Capitalism* (Stanford: Stanford University Press, 2019).

63. Xin Fu, "Zhipaiwu Ni Xuebuhui (House of Cards Can't Be Learned)," *Zhongguo Qiyejia (Chinese Entrepreneurs)* 7 (2013): 97.

64. Derrick Harris, "Netflix Analyzes a Lot of Data about Your Viewing Habits," *GigaOm* (blog), June 14, 2012, available at https://www.benton.org/headlines/netflix-analyzes-lot-data-about-your-viewing-habits/

65. Bucher, *If . . . Then*, 2.

66. Nellie Andreeva, "Netflix to Enter Original Programming with Mega Deal for David Fincher–Kevin Spacey Series 'House of Cards,'" *Deadline* (blog), March 15, 2011, https://deadline.com/2011/03/netflix-to-enter-original-programming-with-mega-deal-for-david-fincher-kevin-spacey-drama-series-house-of-cards-114184/

67. Ed Finn, *What Algorithms Want: Imagination in the Age of Computing* (Cambridge, MA: MIT Press, 2018), 98.

68. Finn, *What Algorithms Want*, 98.

69. Janko Roettgers, "For *House of Cards* and *Arrested Development*, Netflix Favors Big Data over Big Ratings," *GigaOm* (blog), February 12, 2013, https://gigaom.com/2013/02/12/netflix-ratings-big-data-original-content/ (no longer accessible).

70. David Carr, "For 'House of Cards,' Using Big Data to Guarantee Its Popularity," *New York Times*, February 24, 2013, sec. Media, https://www.nytimes.com

/2013/02/25/business/media/for-house-of-cards-using-big-data-to-guarantee-its-popularity.html

71. Bucher, *If . . . Then*, 2.

72. Nicole Laporte, "Netflix: The Red Menace," *Fast Company*, January 17, 2014, https://www.fastcompany.com/3024158/netflix-the-red-menace

73. Jean Baudrillard, "Simulation and Simulacra," in *Selected Writings*, ed. Mark Poster (Stanford: Stanford University Press, 1988), 166–84.

74. Fredrick Kunkle, "Creepy 'House of Cards' Ad on Metro Station Platform: 'A Push in the Right Direction,'" *Washington Post*, February 25, 2016, https://www.washingtonpost.com/news/tripping/wp/2016/02/25/creepy-house-of-cards-ad-on-metro-station-platform-a-push-in-the-right-direction/

75. Sarah Arnold, "Netflix and the Myth of Choice/Participation/Autonomy," in *The Netflix Effect: Technology and Entertainment in the 21st Century*, ed. Kevin McDonald and Daniel Smith-Rowsey, reprint ed. (New York: Bloomsbury Academic, 2018), 55.

76. Arnold, "Netflix and the Myth of Choice," 55.

77. Zuboff, *Age of Surveillance Capitalism*, 377–78.

78. Antoinette Rouvroy, "The End(s) of Critique: Data Behaviourism versus Due Process," in *Privacy, Due Process and the Computational Turn: The Philosophy of Law Meets the Philosophy of Technology*, ed. Mireille Hildebrandt and Katja de Vries (London: Routledge, 2013), 145.

79. Rouvroy, "End(s) of Critique," 143.

80. Rouvroy, "End(s) of Critique," 153.

81. Chen, "Shuju Jiushi Shengchanli."

82. Jodi Dean, *Democracy and Other Neoliberal Fantasies: Communicative Capitalism and Left Politics* (Durham: Duke University Press, 2009), 36.

83. Finn, *What Algorithms Want*, 103–5.

84. Lin quoted in Ma, "'House of Cards' Writer on China, U.S., and Power."

85. Zhou and Lu, "Zhipaiwu Zhongguo Shangren Feng Banyanzhe."

86. Joe Conway, "After Politics/After Television," *Studies in American Humor* 2, no. 2 (July 2016): 187.

87. Alan Kirby quoted in Conway, "After Politics/After Television," 186.

88. Conway, "After Politics/After Television," 186–87.

89. Conway, "After Politics/After Television," 185.

90. Lynne Joyrich, "Reality TV Trumps Politics," *Contemporary Condition* (blog), 2016, http://contemporarycondition.blogspot.com/2016/11/reality-tv-trumps-politics.html.

91. Joyrich, "Reality TV Trumps Politics."

92. Yingtuan Liu, "Zhipaiwu Li Kui Zhengzhi (Probing Politics in House of Cards)," *Zhongguo Renli Ziyuan Shehui Baozhang* (*China Human Resources and Social Security*), 2014, 60.

93. Conway, "After Politics/After Television," 192.

94. Jianfeng Cai, "Paoqi Xuyao Huanxiang de Chujing—Dui Zhipaiwu Rebo Xianxiang de Yidian Fansi (Abandon the Condition That Depends on Illusion—Some Thoughts on the Popularity of House of Cards)," *Shu Cheng* (*Book Town*) 5 (2014): 73.

95. Dingkun Wang and Xiaochun Zhang, "Ideological Manipulation of Controversial Information: The Unusual Case of the Chinese-Subtitled Version of

House of Cards," *Altre Modernità* 0, no. 0 (February 18, 2016): 3, https://doi.org/10.13130/2035-7680/6845

96. Wang Hui, *China's Twentieth Century: Revolution, Retreat and the Road to Equality* (London: Verso Books, 2016), 152–58.

97. Wang, *China's Twentieth Century*, 157.

98. Wang, *China's Twentieth Century*. 158.

99. Couldry and Mejias, *Costs of Connection*, xii.

100. Couldry and Mejias, *Costs of Connection*, 199.

101. Couldry and Mejias, *Costs of Connection*, 199.

102. Interestingly, the Netflix documentary *The Great Hack* offers an in-depth look into this colonialization of politics by algorithmic media, focusing on the role of key individuals in the Cambridge Analytica scandal. Yet, not unlike *HoC*, the film also becomes self-referential of Netflix as a company by dramatizing the effects of data mining on political subjectivity without sufficiently accounting for the economic and cultural conditions that inform widespread depoliticization (as reflected in low voter turnouts, among other things) in the United States and elsewhere.

103. Maria Repnikova, *Media Politics in China: Improvising Power under Authoritarianism*, reprint ed. (Cambridge: Cambridge University Press, 2018), 220.

104. Repnikova, *Media Politics in China*, 220–21.

105. Clare Birchall, *Radical Secrecy: The Ends of Transparency in Datafied America* (Minneapolis: University of Minnesota Press, 2021), 39.

106. Chris Hastings, "President Putin Thinks House of Cards Is a Documentary," *Daily Mail*, May 28, 2017, http://www.dailymail.co.uk/~/article-4549000/index.html

107. Daniel R. Coats, "Statement for the Record: Worldwide Threat Assessment of the US Intelligence Community" (Washington, DC: Senate Select Committee on Intelligence, January 29, 2019), 5, https://www.dni.gov/files/ODNI/documents/2019-ATA-SFR-SSCI.pdf

108. For a detailed analysis of the Chimerican entanglements in the realm of data, see Aynne Kokas, *Trafficking Data: How China Is Winning the Battle for Digital Sovereignty* (New York: Oxford University Press, 2022).

109. Zuboff, *Age of Surveillance Capitalism*, 388–95.

110. Couldry and Mejias, *Costs of Connection*, xxi.

111. Couldry and Mejias, *Costs of Connection*, 17.

112. Couldry and Mejias, *Costs of Connection*, 20.

113. Bucher, *If . . . Then*, 3.

114. Annemarie Mol, "Ontological Politics. A Word and Some Questions," *Sociological Review* 47, no. S1 (1999): 75, https://doi.org/10.1111/j.1467-954X.1999.tb03483.x

115. Bucher, *If . . . Then*, 38.

CONCLUSION

1. Fang Fang, *Wuhan Diary: Dispatches from a Quarantined City*, trans. Michael Berry (New York: HarperVia, 2020), 401. It should be noted that Fang Fang's diary, which not only records daily experiences but also calls for government accountability, generated a wave of online attacks that, upon its translation

into English, elevated into ultranationalist hate speech against both her and the translator. This event points to the complex manifestation of transpacific entanglements in the Chinese context that exceeds the scope of this book but deserves closer examination on its own. See, for instance, an engaged analysis by international relations scholar Chenchen Zhang, "Contested Disaster Nationalism in the Digital Age: Emotional Registers and Geopolitical Imaginaries in COVID-19 Narratives on Chinese Social Media," *Review of International Studies* 48, no. 2 (April 2022): 219–42, https://doi.org/10.1017/S0260210522000018

2. Nicholas Bogel-Burroughs, "Prosecutors Say Derek Chauvin Knelt on George Floyd for 9 Minutes 29 Seconds, Longer Than Initially Reported.," *New York Times*, March 30, 2021, sec. US, https://www.nytimes.com/2021/03/30/us/derek-chauvin-george-floyd-kneel-9-minutes-29-seconds.html

3. Evan Hill et al., "8 Minutes and 46 Seconds: How George Floyd Was Killed in Police Custody," *New York Times*, May 31, 2020, sec. US, https://www.nytimes.com/2020/05/31/us/george-floyd-investigation.html

4. See, for example, Guobin Yang, *The Wuhan Lockdown* (New York: Columbia University Press, 2022).

5. Lindsey Dillon and Julie Sze, "Equality in the Air We Breathe: Police Violence, Pollution, and the Politics of Sustainability," in *Sustainability: Approaches to Environmental Justice and Social Power*, ed. Julie Sze (New York: NYU Press, 2018), 255.

6. See, for example, Luke W. Cole and Sheila R. Foster, eds., *From the Ground Up: Environmental Racism and the Rise of the Environmental Justice Movement* (New York: NYU Press, 2001).

7. Edward Wong, "On Scale of 0 to 500, Beijing's Air Quality Tops 'Crazy Bad' at 755," *New York Times*, January 12, 2013, sec. Science, https://www.nytimes.com/2013/01/13/science/earth/beijing-air-pollution-off-the-charts.html. Arguably, this kind of dramatized description also obfuscates inequalities around the capacity to breathe in the United States.

8. Associated Press, "Air Pollution in China Is Killing 4,000 People Every Day, a New Study Finds," *The Guardian*, August 14, 2015, sec. World News, http://www.theguardian.com/world/2015/aug/14/air-pollution-in-china-is-killing-4000-people-every-day-a-new-study-finds

9. Beth Gardiner, "Pollution Made COVID-19 Worse. Now, Lockdowns Are Clearing the Air," *National Geographic*, April 8, 2020, https://www.nationalgeographic.com/science/2020/04/pollution-made-the-pandemic-worse-but-lockdowns-clean-the-sky/

10. John F. Kennedy, "'We All Breathe the Same Air,'" American University Commencement Ceremony, Washington, DC, June 10, 1963, http://www.humanity.org/voices/commencements/john.f.kennedy-american-university-speech-1963. I thank Louisa Schein for pointing me to this speech.

11. Julie Sze, *Fantasy Islands: Chinese Dreams and Ecological Fears in an Age of Climate Crisis* (Oakland: University of California Press, 2015), 26.

12. Jerry Zee, "Downwind: Three Phases of an Aerosol Form," in *Voluminous States: Sovereignty, Materiality, and the Territorial Imagination*, ed. Franck Billé (Durham: Duke University Press, 2020), 126.

13. Likewise, a speech by Xi Jinping in 2013 also emphasized that the CCP

must "never change the position of breathing together and sharing the common fate with the people at any time and under any circumstances." Xi Jinping, "Qunzhong Luxian Shi Dang de Shengmingxian He Genben Gongzuo Luxian—Zhuanti Baodao (The Mass Line Is the Party's Lifeline and Fundamental Work Line—Special Report)," *People's Daily Online*, June 18, 2013, http://cpc.people.com.cn/xuexi/n/2015/0721/c397563-27338348.html

14. Fan Yang, "Under the Dome: 'Chinese' Smog as a Viral Media Event," *Critical Studies in Media Communication* 33, no. 3 (April 26, 2016): 232–44, https://doi.org/10.1080/15295036.2016.1170172

15. Oliver Wainwright, "Inside Beijing's Airpocalypse—A City Made 'Almost Uninhabitable' by Pollution," *The Guardian*, December 16, 2014, https://www.theguardian.com/cities/2014/dec/16/beijing-airpocalypse-city-almost-uninhabitable-pollution-china

16. Ralph Litzinger and Fan Yang, "Eco-media Events in China: From Yellow Eco-peril to Media Materialism," *Environmental Humanities* 12, no. 1 (May 1, 2020): 1–22, https://doi.org/10.1215/22011919-8142187

17. Litzinger and Yang, "Eco-media Events in China," 8.

18. This conflation was particularly salient during the 2020 Republican National Convention.

19. Here, I'm drawing on a talk by political scientist Christian Sorace, available at "Brainwashed: The Legacies and Perils of American Sinophobia," Made in China Journal, Colorado Springs, Colorado, October 9, 2020, https://www.youtube.com/watch?v=kTxZYXqEsgU&fbclid=IwAR18jbArwIFtqSELIdFsTqiXjCRsmfS8QnkPzYfzFCsLUz9AeLPVHa3VtPM

20. Here it is important to recognize that relationality in itself does not always form the foundation for generating meaningful ethics and politics; thus, it is often necessary to discern what possibilities (such as alternative visions of state and citizenship) are excluded in the making of entangled realities. See Eva Haifa Giraud, *What Comes after Entanglement?: Activism, Anthropocentrism, and an Ethics of Exclusion* (Durham: Duke University Press, 2019).

21. Stefanie R. Fishel, *The Microbial State: Global Thriving and the Body Politic* (Minneapolis: University of Minnesota Press, 2017), 28.

22. Fishel, *Microbial State*, 75.

23. Fishel, *Microbial State*, 43.

24. Fishel, *Microbial State*, 76.

25. Fishel, *Microbial State*, 61.

26. See, for example, Raka Shome, "Thinking through the Diaspora: Call Centers, India, and a New Politics of Hybridity," *International Journal of Cultural Studies* 9, no. 1 (March 1, 2006): 105–124, https://doi.org/10.1177/1367877906061167

27. Sarah T. Roberts, *Behind the Screen: Content Moderation in the Shadows of Social Media* (New Haven: Yale University Press, 2019).

28. Christian Fuchs, *Digital Labour and Karl Marx* (New York: Routledge, 2014).

29. Paul Musgrave, "The Slip That Revealed the Real Trump Doctrine," *Foreign Policy* (blog), May 2, 2019, https://foreignpolicy.com/2019/05/02/the-slip-that-revealed-the-real-trump-doctrine/; Cedric J. Robinson, *Black Marxism: The*

Making of the Black Radical Tradition, 2nd ed. (Chapel Hill: University of North Carolina Press, 2000), 3.

30. Jodi Melamed, "Racial Capitalism," *Critical Ethnic Studies* 1, no. 1 (2015): 78, https://doi.org/10.5749/jcritethnstud.1.1.0076

31. Melamed, "Racial Capitalism," 78 (emphasis in original).

32. Ruth Wilson Gilmore, "Partition" (Keynote, Decolonize the City! Decoloniale Perspektiven auf die Neoliberal Stadt, Berlin, September 21, 2012); cited in Melamed, "Racial Capitalism," 78.

33. Melamed, "Racial Capitalism," 79.

34. Jack Linchuan Qiu, *Goodbye iSlave: A Manifesto for Digital Abolition* (Urbana: University of Illinois Press, 2017), 10.

35. Qiu, *Goodbye iSlave,* 9.

36. Nick Couldry and Ulises A. Mejias, *The Costs of Connection: How Data Is Colonizing Human Life and Appropriating It for Capitalism* (Stanford: Stanford University Press, 2019), 45.

37. Christina Sharpe, *In the Wake: On Blackness and Being* (Durham: Duke University Press, 2016), 106.

38. Dillon and Sze, "Equality in the Air We Breathe," 247.

39. Sean Metzger, *The Chinese Atlantic: Seascapes and the Theatricality of Globalization* (Bloomington: Indiana University Press, 2020).

40. Elspeth Probyn, "Doing Cultural Studies in Rough Seas: The COVID-19 Ocean Multiple," *Cultural Studies* 35, no. 2–3 (May 4, 2021): 558, https://doi.org/10.1080/09502386.2021.1898032

41. Melody Jue, *Wild Blue Media: Thinking through Seawater* (Durham: Duke University Press, 2020), 6.

42. Jue, *Wild Blue Media,* 67.

43. Jue, *Wild Blue Media,* 67.

44. I thank Judy Callow for this phrase.

45. Timothy Choy, *Ecologies of Comparison: An Ethnography of Endangerment in Hong Kong* (Durham: Duke University Press, 2011), 145.

46. Jamieson Webster, "On Breathing," *New York Review of Books* (blog), April 2, 2021, https://www.nybooks.com/daily/2021/04/02/on-breathing/

47. Dillon and Sze, "Equality in the Air We Breathe," 248.

48. Dillon and Sze, "Equality in the Air We Breathe," 257.

49. For example, activist Lincoln Mondy's documentary, tellingly named *Black Lives/Black Lungs,* demonstrates the detrimental effects of the tobacco industry on the African American community. See *Black Lives/Black Lungs* (2017), https://www.youtube.com/watch?v=Eeg5BNx–uQ&t=8s/

50. An estimated six million people suffer from the illness, which makes up almost "90 percent of the occupational disease population in China," see Litzinger and Yang, "Eco-media Events in China," 12–13.

51. David Theo Goldberg, "Racial Comparisons, Relational Racisms: Some Thoughts on Method," *Ethnic and Racial Studies* 32, no. 7 (July 27, 2009): 1279, https://doi.org/10.1080/01419870902999233

52. Darren Byler, "How China's 'Xinjiang Mode' Draws from US, British, and Israeli Counterinsurgency Strategy," *Lausan* (blog), October 2, 2020, http://lausan.hk/2020/chinas-xinjiang-mode-counterinsurgency-strategy/; also see Dar-

ren Byler, *Terror Capitalism: Uyghur Dispossession and Masculinity in a Chinese City* (Durham: Duke University Press, 2022).

53. Goldberg, "Racial Comparisons, Relational Racisms."

54. Choy, *Ecologies of Comparison*, 157.

55. Choy, *Ecologies of Comparison*, 151.

56. Choy, *Ecologies of Comparison*, 152.

57. Howey Ou, "欧泓奕 Howey Ou #FightFor1Point5 (@howey_ou)," Twitter, https://twitter.com/howey_ou

58. Bruno Latour, "Is This a Dress Rehearsal?," *In the Moment* (blog), March 26, 2020, https://critinq.wordpress.com/2020/03/26/is-this-a-dress-rehearsal/

59. Achille Mbembe, "The Universal Right to Breathe," *In the Moment* (blog), April 13, 2020, https://critinq.wordpress.com/2020/04/13/the-universal-right-to-breathe/

60. The two nations "are responsible for over 40 percent of global CO_2 emissions, though China's per capita emissions are still less than half those of the United States." See Barbara Finamore, *Will China Save the Planet?* (Cambridge: Polity, 2018), 4.

61. Robyn Eckersley, *The Green State: Rethinking Democracy and Sovereignty* (Cambridge, MA: MIT Press, 2004), 3.

62. Sze, *Fantasy Islands*, 25.

63. Sze, *Fantasy Islands*, 26.

64. Sze, *Fantasy Islands*, 25–26.

65. Yifei Li and Judith Shapiro, *China Goes Green: Coercive Environmentalism for a Troubled Planet* (Cambridge: Polity, 2020), 24.

66. Li and Shapiro, *China Goes Green*, 27.

67. Li and Shapiro, *China Goes Green*, 27–28.

68. Justin Worland, "Donald Trump Called Climate Change a Hoax. Now He's Awkwardly Boasting about Fighting It," *Time*, July 8, 2019, https://time.com/5622374/donald-trump-climate-change-hoax-event/

69. Coral Davenport and Lisa Friedman, "Biden, in a Burst of Climate Orders, Rejoins the Paris Agreement," *New York Times*, January 20, 2021, sec. Climate, https://www.nytimes.com/2021/01/20/climate/biden-paris-climate-agreement.html

70. See, for example, Eyck Freymann, *One Belt One Road: Chinese Power Meets the World* (Cambridge, MA: Harvard University Asia Center, 2020).

71. John Durham Peters, *The Marvelous Clouds: Toward a Philosophy of Elemental Media* (Chicago: University of Chicago Press, 2015).

72. I thank Lily Wong for alerting me to this connection.

73. Some of the thinking for this section came from Ralph Litzinger and Fan Yang, "Rethinking the Eco-Media Event in Pandemic Times," Sci-Tech Asia Webinar, February 24, 2023, https://scitechasia.org/webinars/rethinking-the-eco-media-event-in-pandemic-times/. I thank Gonçalo Santos for the invitation as well as Ralph Litzinger and other participants in this event for sharing their observations.

74. Chang Che and Amy Chang Chien, "Protest in Xinjiang against Lockdown after Fire Kills 10," *New York Times*, November 25, 2022, sec. World, https://www.nytimes.com/2022/11/25/world/asia/china-fire.html. The report states: "Chi-

nese commenters also pointed to video footage of what appeared to be attempts at putting out the fire as evidence that a lockdown had stalled the effort. The footage showed pressurized water from a fire hose spraying just out of reach of the burning building, suggesting that fire trucks were unable to get closer to the building. Some users said that cars that had been parked in the area could not be moved because their batteries were dead from having not been used for so long because of the lockdown. Li Wensheng, the head of Urumqi's Fire Rescue Detachment, acknowledged that fire trucks had been obstructed by parked cars in the neighborhood. He said fire doors in the apartment building had been open, and some residents had been unable to save themselves because they were not familiar with safety exits."

75. It should be noted that Hua Chunying, the spokesperson of the Chinese Foreign Ministry, tweeted "I Can't Breathe" in response to her US State Department counterpart's critique of China's suppression of the Hong Kong protests. For an engaged analysis of this exchange, which reflects additional layers of Chimerican entanglements, see Mitchell Reiss and Claudia Coscia, "The Global Stakes on Why Black Lives Matter," Wilson Center, September 21, 2020, https://www.wilsoncenter.org/article/global-stakes-why-black-lives-matter.

76. See, for example, the livestream comments recorded on "The China Show Special Report: EMERGENCY—China Has Erupted—REVOLUTION!!!" (2022), https://www.youtube.com/watch?v=vPRDLqggwQU

77. Lily Kuo and Theodora Yu, "One Man's Bold Protest against China's Leaders Inspires Global Copycats," *Washington Post*, November 10, 2022, https://www.washingtonpost.com/world/2022/11/10/china-protest-sitong-hong-kong/

78. Christian Shepherd, "'New Tank Man': Rare Protest in Beijing Mars Xi Jinping's Moment," *Washington Post*, October 19, 2022, https://www.washingtonpost.com/world/2022/10/14/china-protest-sitong-bridge-haidian/

79. Kuo and Yu, "One Man's Bold Protest."

80. Allissa V. Richardson, *Bearing Witness while Black: African Americans, Smartphones, and the New Protest #Journalism* (New York: Oxford University Press, 2020), 4.

81. Kuo and Yu, "One Man's Bold Protest."

82. Kuo and Yu, "One Man's Bold Protest."

83. See Jade Zhou and Bin Xu, "Where Performance Meets Pandemic: Bin Xu on Anti-COVID Policy in the U.S. and China," *U.S.-China Perception Monitor*, October 25, 2022, https://uscnpm.org/2022/10/25/bin-xu-on-performance-politics-disasters-and-covid-19/. Xu commented on social media during the November protests on the need to move beyond a facile 1989–2022 comparison and is conducting research on BLM in relation to China and the transnational public sphere.

84. Eli Friedman, "Foxconn's Great Escape," *Asian Labour Review* (blog), November 8, 2022, https://labourreview.org/foxconns-great-escape/

85. Friedman, "Foxconn's Great Escape."

86. Friedman, "Foxconn's Great Escape."

87. Amy Goodman and Eli Friedman, "From Xinjiang to Shanghai, Protests Grow in China over COVID Restrictions after Fatal Apartment Fire," *Democracy Now!*, November 28, 2022, https://www.democracynow.org/2022/11/28/protests_erupt_china_strict_zero_covid

88. This is a point of comparison shared by several participants in an online discussion cosponsored by the Critical China Scholars Collective and the Central New York Humanities Corridor. Many also highlighted the role of young women activists in the Chinese protests. Others pointed to the singing of not just China's national anthem but the *Internationale* during the protests. Roundtable discussion, "Protests in China Today: Perspectives from the Left," November 30, 2022.

89. Elsewhere, I have also argued that the transnational characteristic of the internet also challenges the national frame of "Chinese" censorship. See Fan Yang, "Rethinking China's Internet Censorship: The Practice of Recoding and the Politics of Visibility," *New Media & Society* 18, no. 7 (August 1, 2016): 1364–81, https://doi.org/10.1177/1461444814555951

90. Chang Che and Amy Chang Chien, "Memes, Puns, and Blank Sheets of Paper: China's Creative Acts of Protest," *New York Times*, November 28, 2022, sec. World, https://www.nytimes.com/2022/11/28/world/asia/china-protests-bla nk-sheets.html

91. Che and Chien, "Memes, Puns, and Blank Sheets of Paper."

92. For a more thoroughgoing analysis of the 2019–2020 Hong Kong movement, see Daniel F. Vukovich, *After Autonomy: A Post-Mortem for Hong Kong's First Handover, 1997–2019* (New York: Palgrave Macmillan, 2022).

93. Quoted in Che and Chien, "Memes, Puns, and Blank Sheets of Paper."

94. For a critical analysis of the potential problems of such "memeification of social justice activism," see Mariah L. Wellman, "Black Squares for Black Lives? Performative Allyship as Credibility Maintenance for Social Media Influencers on Instagram," *Social Media + Society* 8, no. 1 (January 1, 2022): 1–10, https://doi .org/10.1177/20563051221080473

95. Andrew Barry, *Political Machines: Governing a Technological Society* (London: Athlone Press, 2001), 195.

96. Peters, *Marvelous Clouds*, 127.

97. Christian Sorace and Nicholas Loubere, "Biopolitical Binaries (or How Not to Read the Chinese Protests)," *Made in China Journal* (blog), December 2, 2022, https://madeinchinajournal.com/2022/12/02/biopolitical-binaries-or -how-not-to-read-the-chinese-protests/

98. Sorace and Loubere, "Biopolitical Binaries."

99. A precursor for this is the netizens' recoding of an online interview using various scripts with the deceased doctor Li Wenliang, who died from COVID-19 after being silenced for his attempt to warn the public about the danger of the virus in Wuhan in December 2019. See Thomas Chen, *Made in Censorship: The Tiananmen Movement in Chinese Literature and Film* (New York: Columbia University Press, 2022), 165.

100. A special issue in *American Quarterly* called "The Chinese Factor: Reorienting Global Imaginaries in American Studies," edited by Chih-Ming Wang and Yu-Fang Cho, for example, offers insightful perspectives in this regard. See Chih-Ming Wang and Yu-Fang Cho, "Introduction: The Chinese Factor and American Studies, Here and Now," *American Quarterly* 69, no. 3 (September 19, 2017): 443–63.

Bibliography

otolerance.org. "Jimmy Kimmel—Kid's Table—'Kill Everyone in China.'" *Jimmy Kimmel Live!* YouTube: ABC, October 29, 2013. Available at https://www.yout ube.com/watch?v=PHR2ErH9HuI/

Ahmed, Sara. *Queer Phenomenology: Orientations, Objects, Others.* Durham: Duke University Press, 2006.

Albro, Robert. "The Disjunction of Image and Word in US and Chinese Soft Power Projection." *International Journal of Cultural Policy* 21, no. 4 (September 2015): 382–99. https://doi.org/10.1080/10286632.2015.1042471

Allen-Ebrahimian, Bethany. "Can 1 Million American Students Learn Mandarin?" *Foreign Policy*, September 25, 2015. https://foreignpolicy.com/2015/09 /25/china-us-obamas-one-million-students-chinese-language-mandarin/

Almeida Theatre. "'Chimerica': A Thousand Words." *Almeida Theatre Blog*, May 24, 2013. http://blog.almeida.co.uk/2013/05/24/chimerica-a-thousand-wo rds/

Anderson, Benedict R. O'G. *Imagined Communities: Reflections on the Origin and Spread of Nationalism.* Rev and extended ed. London: Verso, 1991.

Andreeva, Nellie. "Netflix to Enter Original Programming with Mega Deal for David Fincher–Kevin Spacey Series 'House of Cards.'" *Deadline* (blog), March 15, 2011. https://deadline.com/2011/03/netflix-to-enter-original-programm ing-with-mega-deal-for-david-fincher-kevin-spacey-drama-series-house-of-car ds-114184/

Appadurai, Arjun. *Modernity at Large: Cultural Dimensions of Globalization*, vol. 1: *Public Worlds.* Minneapolis: University of Minnesota Press, 1996.

Areddy, James. "How Corrupt Is the U.S.? Just Watch 'House of Cards,' China Party Arm Says." *Wall Street Journal*, June 17, 2014. http://blogs.wsj.com/ch inarealtime/2014/06/17/how-corrupt-is-the-u-s-just-watch-house-of-cards-ch ina-party-arm-says/

Arnold, Sarah. "Netflix and the Myth of Choice/Participation/Autonomy." In *The Netflix Effect: Technology and Entertainment in the 21st Century*, edited by

Kevin McDonald and Daniel Smith-Rowsey. Reprint ed., 49–62. New York: Bloomsbury Academic, 2018.

Associated Press. "ABC Apologizes for 'Kill Everyone in China' Joke on 'Jimmy Kimmel Live.'" *Hollywood Reporter*, October 28, 2013. http://www.hollywoodr eporter.com/news/abc-apologizes-kill-china-joke-651387/

Associated Press. "Air Pollution in China Is Killing 4,000 People Every Day, a New Study Finds." *The Guardian*, August 14, 2015, sec. World News. http:// www.theguardian.com/world/2015/aug/14/air-pollution-in-china-is-killing -4000-people-every-day-a-new-study-finds

Bahng, Aimee. "The Cruel Optimism of Asian Futurity and the Reparative Practices of Sonny Liew's Malinky Robot." In *Techno-Orientalism: Imagining Asia in Speculative Fiction, History, and Media*, edited by David S. Roh, Betsy Huang, and Greta A. Niu, 163–79. New Brunswick, NJ: Rutgers University Press, 2015.

Bahng, Aimee. *Migrant Futures: Decolonizing Speculation in Financial Times*. Durham: Duke University Press, 2018.

Bai, Ping. "US Political Drama Tells Much about Us." *China Daily*, February 24, 2014. http://usa.chinadaily.com.cn/2014-02/24/content_17300030.htm

Bai, Ruoyun. *Staging Corruption: Chinese Television and Politics*. Contemporary Chinese Studies. Vancouver: University of British Columbia Press, 2014. http:// www.washington.edu/uwpress/search/books/BAISTA.html#contents

Barad, Karen Michelle. *Meeting the Universe Halfway: Quantum Physics and the Entanglement of Matter and Meaning*. Durham: Duke University Press, 2007.

Barry, Andrew. *Political Machines: Governing a Technological Society*. London: Athlone Press, 2001.

Baudrillard, Jean. "Simulation and Simulacra." In *Selected Writings*, edited by Mark Poster, 166–84. Stanford: Stanford University Press, 1988.

Becker, Alton L. *Beyond Translation: Essays toward a Modern Philology*. Ann Arbor: University of Michigan Press, 2000.

Benor, Sarah Bunin. "Ethnolinguistic Repertoire: Shifting the Analytic Focus in Language and Ethnicity." *Journal of Sociolinguistics* 14, no. 2 (2010): 159–83. https://doi.org/10.1111/j.1467-9841.2010.00440.x

Benson-Allott, Caetlin. *The Stuff of Spectatorship: Material Cultures of Film and Television*. Oakland: University of California Press, 2021.

Birchall, Clare. *Radical Secrecy: The Ends of Transparency in Datafied America*. Minneapolis: University of Minnesota Press, 2021.

Black Lives/Black Lungs. 2017. https://www.youtube.com/watch?v=Eeg5BNx–uQ &t=8s/

Bogel-Burroughs, Nicholas. "Prosecutors Say Derek Chauvin Knelt on George Floyd for 9 Minutes 29 Seconds, Longer Than Initially Reported." *New York Times*, March 30, 2021, sec. U.S. https://www.nytimes.com/2021/03/30/us /derek-chauvin-george-floyd-kneel-9-minutes-29-seconds.html

Botsford, Jabin. "Close up of President @realDonaldTrump Notes Is Seen Where He Crossed out 'Corona' and Replaced It with 'Chinese' Virus as He Speaks with His Coronavirus Task Force Today at the White House. #trump #trumpnotes." *Twitter*, March 19, 2020. https://twitter.com/jabinbotsford/status/12 40701140141879298

"Brainwashed: The Legacies and Perils of American Sinophobia." Made in China Journal, Colorado Springs, Colorado, 2020. https://www.youtube.com/wat

ch?v=kTxZYXqEsgU&fbclid=IwAR18jbArwIFtqSELIdFsTqiXjCRsmfS8QnkP
zYfzFCsLUz9AeLPVHa3VtPM

Branch, John. "Eileen Gu Is Trying to Soar over the Geopolitical Divide." *New York Times*, February 3, 2022, sec. Sports. https://www.nytimes.com/2022/02/03/sports/olympics/eileen-gu-china-freeski.html

Brown, Kate. "The Pandemic Is Not a Natural Disaster." *The New Yorker*, April 13, 2020. https://www.newyorker.com/culture/annals-of-inquiry/the-pandemic-is-not-a-natural-disaster

Brown, Rebecca M. "Orientalism in *Firefly* and *Serenity*." *Slayage: The Online International Journal of Buffy Studies* 7, no. 1 (2008): 13.

Bucher, Taina. *If . . . Then: Algorithmic Power and Politics*. Oxford: Oxford University Press, 2018.

Budds, Diana. "The Fascinating History of 'Designed in California.'" *Fast Company*, June 14, 2017. https://www.fastcompany.com/90129351/the-history-of-designed-in-california

Byler, Darren. "How China's 'Xinjiang Mode' Draws from US, British, and Israeli Counterinsurgency Strategy." *Lausan* (blog), October 2, 2020. http://lausan.hk/2020/chinas-xinjiang-mode-counterinsurgency-strategy/

Byler, Darren. *Terror Capitalism: Uyghur Dispossession and Masculinity in a Chinese City*. Durham: Duke University Press Books, 2022.

Cai, Jianfeng. "Paoqi Xuyao Huanxiang de Chujing—Dui Zhipaiwu Rebo Xianxiang de Yidian Fansi (Abandon the Condition That Depends on Illusion—Some Thoughts on the Popularity of House of Cards)." *Shu Cheng (Book Town)*, 5 (2014): 69–88.

Calhoun, Craig. "Tiananmen, Television and the Public Sphere: Internationalization of Culture and the Beijing Spring of 1989." *Public Culture* 2, no. 1 (September 21, 1989): 54–71. https://doi.org/10.1215/08992363-2-1-54

Campus Progress Action. "Chinese Professor." YouTube. Accessed October 26, 2013. http://www.youtube.com/watch?v=OkRLxD-aZi0/

Cao, Yin. "China's 'House of Cards' to Focus on Graft Fight." *China Daily*, June 16, 2016. http://www.chinadaily.com.cn/china/2016-06/16/content_25726484.htm

Carr, David. "For 'House of Cards,' Using Big Data to Guarantee Its Popularity." *New York Times*, February 24, 2013, sec. Media. https://www.nytimes.com/2013/02/25/business/media/for-house-of-cards-using-big-data-to-guarantee-its-popularity.html

Casado, Juan Alberto Ruiz. "It Is Not Sheer Racism against 'Asian-Americans,' but Sinophobia Due to a Dehumanizing Anti-China Narrative—The Invisible Armada." *The Invisible Armada* (blog), March 20, 2021. https://invisiblearmada.web.nctu.edu.tw/2021/03/20/it-is-not-racism-against-asians-americans-but-sinophobia-due-to-a-dehumanizing-anti-china-narrative/

Castells, Manuel. *The Information Age: Economy, Society and Culture*. Vol. 1. Oxford: Blackwell, 1996.

Cavanagh, John. "Trump Trade Wars Have Led to Lost US Jobs and Factories. We Need a Worker-Centered Recovery." *USA Today*, September 17, 2020. https://www.usatoday.com/story/opinion/2020/09/17/donald-trump-trade-policies-damage-american-workers-column/5807633002/

CGTN. "Why Is the Chinese 'House of Cards' So Popular?" 2017. https://www.yo utube.com/watch?v=8JQyV54grrU/

Chang, Gordon H. "Chinese Americans and China: A Fraught and Complicated Relationship by Gordon H. Chang." *US-China Perception Monitor* (blog), July 18, 2019. https://uscnpm.org/2019/07/18/chinese-americans-china-fraug ht-complicated-relationship/

"Chapter 15." *House of Cards.* Netflix, February 14, 2014.

"Chapter 18." *House of Cards.* Netflix, February 14, 2014.

Che, Chang, and Amy Chang Chien. "Memes, Puns, and Blank Sheets of Paper: China's Creative Acts of Protest." *New York Times,* November 28, 2022, sec. World. https://www.nytimes.com/2022/11/28/world/asia/china-protests -blank-sheets.html

Che, Chang, and Amy Chang Chien. "Protest in Xinjiang against Lockdown after Fire Kills 10." *New York Times,* November 25, 2022, sec. World. https://www.ny times.com/2022/11/25/world/asia/china-fire.html

Chen, Chang Ye. "Lingdaoren Xihuan Zhipaiwu, Dan Women Zhineng Pai Ren-minde Mingyi (The Leaders like House of Cards, but We Can Only Make In the Name of the People)." huxiu.com, April 17, 2017. https://www.huxiu .com/article/190660.html

Chen, Chiung Hwang. "Feminization of Asian (American) Men in the U.S. Mass Media: An Analysis of *The Ballad of Little Jo.*" *Journal of Communication Inquiry* 20, no. 2 (October 1, 1996): 57–71. https://doi.org/10.1177/019685999602 000204

Chen, Kuan-Hsing. *Asia as Method: Toward Deimperialization.* Durham: Duke University Press, 2010.

Chen, Mel. *Animacies: Biopolitics, Racial Mattering, and Queer Affect.* Durham: Duke University Press, 2012.

Chen, Thomas. *Made in Censorship: The Tiananmen Movement in Chinese Literature and Film.* New York: Columbia University Press, 2022.

Chen, Tina. "(The) Transpacific Turns." In *Oxford Research Encyclopedia of Literature.* Oxford: Oxford University Press, January 30, 2020. https://doi.org/10 .1093/acrefore/9780190201098.013.782

Chen, Xinyan. "Shuju Jiushi Shengchanli (Data Is Productivity)." *Jilin Yixue Xinxi (Jilin Medical Information)* 30, no. 9 (2014): 34–37.

Cheng, Anne Anlin. *Ornamentalism.* New York: Oxford University Press, 2019.

Cheng, Yinghong. *Discourses of Race and Rising China.* New York: Palgrave Macmillan, 2019.

"*Chimerica:* Interview with Writer Lucy Kirkwood," Channel4, April 9, 2019. https://www.channel4.com/press/news/chimerica-interview-writer-lucy-kir kwood/

The China Show Special Report. "EMERGENCY—China Has Erupted—REVOLUTION!!!" 2022. https://www.youtube.com/watch?v=vPRDLqg gwQU

"Chinese: The Language of the Future?" The Asia Society (blog), December 15, 2010. https://asiasociety.org/blog/asia/chinese-language-future/

Chow, Rey. *Entanglements, or Transmedial Thinking about Capture.* Durham: Duke University Press Books, 2012.

Chow, Rey. *Not Like a Native Speaker: On Languaging as a Postcolonial Experience.* New York: Columbia University Press, 2014.

Chow, Rey. "Violence in the Other Country: China as Crisis, Spectacle, and Woman." In *Third World Women and the Politics of Feminism,* edited by Chandra Talpade Mohanty, Ann Russo, and Lourdes Torres, 81–100. Bloomington: Indiana University Press, 1991.

Choy, Timothy. *Ecologies of Comparison: An Ethnography of Endangerment in Hong Kong.* Durham: Duke University Press, 2011.

Chung, May. "'I Call Them My Little Chinese Kids': Parents' Identities and Language Ideologies in Mandarin-English Dual Language Immersion Schools." *Journal of Culture and Values in Education* 3, no. 2 (2020): 179–95.

Chung, May. "Mandarin-English Dual Language Education: Understanding Parental Ideologies and Expectations." Dissertation, University of Maryland, Baltimore County, Baltimore, Maryland, 2021.

CNBC Television. "President Donald Trump: Calling It the 'Chinese Virus' Is Not Racist at All, It Comes from China." YouTube. March 18, 2020. https://www.youtube.com/watch?v=dl78PQGJpiI/

CNN. "Jon Huntsman Talks China, Speaks Chinese." YouTube, August 22, 2011. https://www.youtube.com/watch?v=IPb-5AzuzXo/

CNN Wire. "Jimmy Kimmel Apologizes for 'Killing Everyone in China' Skit." KTLA 5, October 29, 2013. http://ktla.com/2013/10/29/jimmy-kimmel-apologizes-for-killing-everyone-in-china-skit/#axzz2jFHpHPyA

Coats, Daniel R. "Statement for the Record: Worldwide Threat Assessment of the US Intelligence Community." Washington, DC: Senate Select Committee on Intelligence, January 29, 2019. https://www.dni.gov/files/ODNI/documents/2019-ATA-SFR-SSCI.pdf

Cole, Luke W., and Sheila R. Foster, eds. *From the Ground Up: Environmental Racism and the Rise of the Environmental Justice Movement.* New York: NYU Press, 2001.

Connery, Christopher Leigh. *The Empire of the Text.* Lanham, MD: Rowman & Littlefield, 1999.

Conway, Joe. "After Politics/After Television." *Studies in American Humor* 2, no. 2 (July 2016): 182–207.

Couldry, Nick, and Andreas Hepp. "Conceptualizing Mediatization: Contexts, Traditions, Arguments." *Communication Theory* 23, no. 3 (2013): 191–202.

Couldry, Nick, and Ulises A. Mejias. *The Costs of Connection: How Data Is Colonizing Human Life and Appropriating It for Capitalism.* Stanford: Stanford University Press, 2019.

Crystal, David. *English as a Global Language.* Cambridge: Cambridge University Press, 2003.

Davé, Shilpa. *Indian Accents: Brown Voice and Racial Performance in American Television and Film.* Urbana: University of Illinois Press, 2013.

Davenport, Coral, and Lisa Friedman. "Biden, in a Burst of Climate Orders, Rejoins the Paris Agreement." *New York Times,* January 20, 2021, sec. Climate. https://www.nytimes.com/2021/01/20/climate/biden-paris-climate-agreement.html

Dean, Jodi. *Democracy and Other Neoliberal Fantasies: Communicative Capitalism and Left Politics.* Durham: Duke University Press, 2009.

Debord, Guy. "Society of the Spectacle." Marxists.org, 1967. http://www.marxis
ts.org/reference/archive/debord/society.htm

DeCook, Julia R. "A [White] Cyborg's Manifesto: The Overwhelmingly Western Ideology Driving Technofeminist Theory." *Media, Culture & Society* 43, no. 6 (September 2021): 1158–67. https://doi.org/10.1177/0163443720957891

DefeatTheDebt. "Defeat the Debt Pledge Commercial." YouTube, August 31, 2009. https://www.youtube.com/watch?v=rRY5waZ4IbE

DeHart, Monica. *Transpacific Developments*. Ithaca: Cornell University Press, 2021.

Deleuze, Gilles, and Félix Guattari. *Anti-Oedipus: Capitalism and Schizophrenia*. Minneapolis: University of Minnesota Press, 1983.

Denyer, Simon. "Trump's Granddaughter Gets Praise and Sympathy for Singing for Chinese President." *Washington Post*, November 9, 2017, sec. WorldViews. https://www.washingtonpost.com/news/worldviews/wp/2017/11/09/tru mps-granddaughter-gets-praise-and-sympathy-for-singing-for-chinese-presid ent/

Deuze, Mark. *Media Life*. Cambridge, UK: Polity, 2012.

Dienst, Richard. *The Bonds of Debt*. London: Verso Books, 2011.

Dikötter, Frank. *The Discourse of Race in Modern China*. Oxford: Oxford University Press, 2015.

Dillon, Lindsey, and Julie Sze. "Equality in the Air We Breathe: Police Violence, Pollution, and the Politics of Sustainability." In *Sustainability: Approaches to Environmental Justice and Social Power*, edited by Julie Sze, 246–70. New York: NYU Press, 2018.

Dirlik, Arif. *Complicities: The People's Republic of China in Global Capitalism*. Chicago: Prickly Paradigm Press, 2017.

Dong, Chunling. "Bei Xishuo de Meiguo Zhengzhi—Xiezai Zhipaiwu Dierji Bochu Zhihou (American Politics Dramatized—Writing after the Release of the Second Season of House of Cards)." *Shijie Zhishi* (*World Affairs*) 7 (2014): 69–71.

Driscoll, Mark. "Debt and Denunciation in Post-Bubble Japan: On the Two Freeters." *Cultural Critique* 65, no. 1 (2007): 164–87.

Dwyer, Colin. "China Says U.S. Has Begun 'Largest Trade War' in History, Retaliates with Tariffs." NPR.org, July 6, 2018. https://www.npr.org/2018/07/06 /626453571/china-says-u-s-has-begun-largest-trade-war-in-history-retaliates -with-tariffs

Eban, Katherine. "As Trump Administration Debated Travel Restrictions, Thousands Streamed in from China." *Reuters*, April 5, 2020. https://www.reuters .com/article/us-health-coronavirus-nsc-idUSKBN21N0EJ

Eckersley, Robyn. *The Green State: Rethinking Democracy and Sovereignty*. Cambridge, MA: MIT Press, 2004.

Edelman, Lee. *No Future: Queer Theory and the Death Drive*. Series Q. Durham: Duke University Press, 2004.

Egan, Matt. "US Tariffs on China Could Cost American Households $1,000 per Year, JPMorgan Says." CNN, August 20, 2019. https://www.cnn.com/2019 /08/20/business/tariffs-cost-trade-war-consumers/index.html

Espiritu, Yến Lê, Lisa Lowe, and Lisa Yoneyama. "Transpacific Entanglements." In *Flashpoints for Asian American Studies*, edited by Cathy Schlund-Vials, 175–89. New York: Fordham University Press, 2017.

Evans, Lloyd. "Theatre Quest for Tank Man; ARTS—Exhibitions." *The Spectator*, August 31, 2013.

Fabian, Johannes. *Time and the Other: How Anthropology Makes Its Object*. New York: Columbia University Press, 2002.

Fallows, James. "How America Can Rise Again." *The Atlantic*, January 1, 2010. http://www.theatlantic.com/magazine/archive/2010/01/how-america-can-rise-again/307839/?single_page=true

Fallows, James. *More Like Us: Making America Great Again*. Boston: Houghton Mifflin, 1990.

Fallows, James. "The Phenomenal 'Chinese Professor' Ad." *The Atlantic*, October 21, 2010. http://www.theatlantic.com/politics/archive/2010/10/the-pheno menal-chinese-professor-ad/64982/

Fan, Christopher T. "Techno-Orientalism with Chinese Characteristics: Maureen F. McHugh's China Mountain Zhang." *Journal of Transnational American Studies* 6, no. 1 (January 1, 2015). http://www.escholarship.org/uc/item/8n70 b1b6

Fang, Fang. *Wuhan Diary: Dispatches from a Quarantined City*. Translated by Michael Berry. New York: HarperVia, 2020.

Federal News Service. "Transcript and Audio: First Obama-Romney Presidential Debate." NPR, October 3, 2012. http://www.npr.org/2012/10/03/1622585 51/transcript-first-obama-romney-presidential-debate

Feng, Bree. "China Uses 'House of Cards' as Illustration of West's Corruption." *New York Times*, June 19, 2014. http://sinosphere.blogs.nytimes.com/2014 /06/19/china-uses-house-of-cards-as-illustration-of-wests-corruption/

Feng, Peter X. "False and Double Consciousness: Race, Virtual Reality, and the Assimilation of Hong Kong Action Cinema in *The Matrix*." In *Aliens R Us: The Other in Science Fiction Cinema*, edited by Ziauddin Sardar and Sean Cubitt, 140–63. London: Pluto Press, 2002.

Fenton, Chris. *Feeding the Dragon: Inside the Trillion Dollar Dilemma Facing Hollywood, the NBA, and American Business*. New York: Post Hill Press, 2020.

Ferguson, Emily. "China Accused of Attempted Assassination after Trump Catches Covid—Not Coincidental." *Express*, October 4, 2020. https://www .express.co.uk/news/world/1343389/donald-trump-latest-news-china-assass ination-attempt-trump-health-update-deanna-lorraine

Ferguson, Niall, and Moritz Schularick. "'Chimerica' and the Global Asset Market Boom." *International Finance* 10, no. 3 (December 27, 2007): 215–39. https:// doi.org/10.1111/j.1468-2362.2007.00210.x

Ferguson, Niall, and Moritz Schularick. "The End of Chimerica." *International Finance* 14, no. 1 (Spring 2011): 1–26. https://doi.org/Article

Ferguson, Niall, and Xiang Xu. "Make Chimerica Great Again." Hoover Institution, May 3, 2018. https://www.hoover.org/research/make-chimerica-great -again

Finamore, Barbara. *Will China Save the Planet?* Cambridge: Polity, 2018.

Finn, Ed. *What Algorithms Want: Imagination in the Age of Computing*. Cambridge, MA: MIT Press, 2018.

"*Firefly*—Chinese Curses." 2012. https://www.summer-glau.com/video/vip/494 /interviews/2012/firefly_chinese_curses

"*Firefly* behind the Scenes." Twentieth Century Fox Home Entertainment Inc., 2003. https://www.youtube.com/watch?v=uLy_g1-ED1E

Fishel, Stefanie R. *The Microbial State: Global Thriving and the Body Politic*. Minneapolis: University of Minnesota Press, 2017.

Fiskesjö, Magnus. "Confucius Institutes Serve Diplomacy." MCLC Resource Center, March 3, 2018. https://u.osu.edu/mclc/2018/03/03/confucius-institut es-serve-diplomacy/

Fiskesjö, Magnus. "Who's Afraid of Confucius? Fear, Encompassment, and the Global Debates over the Confucius Institutes." In *Yellow Perils: China Narratives in the Contemporary World*, edited by Sören Urbansky and Franck Billé, 221–45. Honolulu: University of Hawaii Press, 2018.

Flew, Terry. "Entertainment Media, Cultural Power, and Post-Globalization: The Case of China's International Media Expansion and the Discourse of Soft Power." *Global Media and China* 1, no. 4 (December 1, 2016): 278–94. https:// doi.org/10.1177/2059436416662037

Folks from Strike Debt. "Strike Debt!" Strike Debt!, April 4, 2019. https://strik edebt.org/

Fox News. "The Wuhan Institute of Virology: The Mysterious Lab Where US Officials Believe the Coronavirus Started." InteractiveResource. Fox News, April 16, 2020. https://www.foxnews.com/health/the-wuhan-institute-of-vi rology-the-mysterious-chinese-lab-where-us-officials-believe-the-coronavirus -pandemic-may-have-begun

Foy, Joseph J. "The State of Nature and Social Contracts on Spaceship *Serenity*." In *The Philosophy of Joss Whedon*, edited by Dean Kowalski, 39–54. Lexington: University Press of Kentucky, 2011.

Franceschini, Ivan, and Nicholas Loubere. *Global China as Method*. Cambridge: Cambridge University Press, 2022.

Franceschini, Ivan, and Nicholas Loubere. *Global China as Method*. Cambridge [England]: Cambridge University Press, 2022. https://www.cambridge.org /core/elements/global-china-as-method/E384D0A1545B1DBC554C878C3 012011D

Fraser, Nancy. "Legitimation Crisis? On the Political Contradictions of Financialized Capitalism." *Critical Historical Studies* 2, no. 2 (2015): 157–89.

Frazier, Robeson. *The East Is Black: Cold War China in the Black Radical Imagination*. Durham: Duke University Press, 2015.

Freymann, Eyck. *One Belt One Road: Chinese Power Meets the World*. Cambridge, MA: Harvard University Asia Center, 2020.

Friedman, Eli. "Foxconn's Great Escape." *Asian Labour Review* (blog), November 8, 2022. https://labourreview.org/foxconns-great-escape/

Friedman, Thomas L. "Biden: 'We're Going to Fight Like Hell by Investing in America First.'" *New York Times*, December 2, 2020, sec. Opinion. https:// www.nytimes.com/2020/12/02/opinion/biden-interview-mcconnell-china -iran.html

Frum, David. "The Coronavirus Is Demonstrating the Value of Globalization." *The Atlantic*, March 27, 2020. https://www.theatlantic.com/ideas/archive/20 20/03/dont-abandon-globalizationmake-it-better/608872/

Fu, Xin. "Zhipaiwu Ni Xuebuhui (House of Cards Can't Be Learned)." *Zhongguo Qiyejia (Chinese Entrepreneurs)* 7 (2013): 96–98.

Fuchs, Christian. *Digital Labour and Karl Marx.* New York: Routledge, 2014.

Gabrys, Jennifer. *Digital Rubbish: A Natural History of Electronics.* Ann Arbor: University of Michigan Press, 2011.

Gardiner, Beth. "Pollution Made COVID-19 Worse. Now, Lockdowns Are Clearing the Air." *National Geographic,* April 8, 2020. https://www.nationalgeogra phic.com/science/2020/04/pollution-made-the-pandemic-worse-but-lockd owns-clean-the-sky/

Gergen, Kenneth J. "The Challenge of Absent Presence." In *Perpetual Contact: Mobile Communication, Private Talk, Public Performance,* edited by James E. Katz and Mark Aakhus, 227–41. Cambridge: Cambridge University Press, 2002. https://doi.org/10.1017/CBO9780511489471.018

Ghosh, Bishnupriya. *Global Icons: Apertures to the Popular.* Durham: Duke University Press, 2011.

Gillman, Ollie. "Facebook Boss Mark Zuckerberg Spoke Mandarin with Chinese President." *Mail Online,* September 25, 2015. http://www.dailymail.co.uk /news/article-3248459/Zuckerberg-s-FaceTime-China-Facebook-boss-revea ls-spoke-Mandarin-rare-meeting-President-Xi-despite-Beijing-blocking-websi te.html

Gilmore, Ruth Wilson. "Partition." Keynote presented at the Decolonize the City! Decoloniale Perspektiven auf die Neoliberal Stadt, Berlin, September 21, 2012.

Giraud, Eva Haifa. *What Comes after Entanglement? Activism, Anthropocentrism, and an Ethics of Exclusion.* Durham: Duke University Press, 2019.

Goddard, Drew. *The Martian—Best Adapted Screenplay.* Twentieth Century Fox Film Corporation and TSG Entertainment Finance LLC, 2015. https://assets .scriptslug.com/live/pdf/scripts/the-martian-2015.pdf

Goldberg, David Theo. "Racial Comparisons, Relational Racisms: Some Thoughts on Method." *Ethnic and Racial Studies* 32, no. 7 (July 27, 2009): 1271–82. https://doi.org/10.1080/01419870902999233

Goldman, David. "Apple 'Gut Punch': Trade War Will Cut iPhone Sales by 8 Million, Analyst Says." CNN, August 2, 2019. https://www.cnn.com/2019/08/02 /tech/apple-iphone-trade-war/index.html

Goldsmith, P. Gardner. "Freedom in an Unfree World." In *Serenity Found: More Unauthorized Essays on Joss Whedon's* Firefly *Universe,* edited by Jane Espenson and Leah Wilson, 55–66. Dallas: BenBella Books, 2007.

Goodman, Amy, and Eli Friedman. "From Xinjiang to Shanghai, Protests Grow in China over COVID Restrictions after Fatal Apartment Fire." *Democracy Now!,* November 28, 2022. https://www.democracynow.org/2022/11/28/pr otests_erupt_china_strict_zero_covid

Gordon, Avery. *Ghostly Matters: Haunting and the Sociological Imagination.* Minneapolis: University of Minnesota Press, 1997.

Gorman, James. "With Virus Origins Still Obscure, W.H.O. and Critics Look to Next Steps." *New York Times,* April 7, 2021, sec. Health. https://www.nytimes .com/2021/04/07/health/coronavirus-lab-leak-who.html

Graeber, David. *Debt: The First 5,000 Years.* New York: Melville House, 2011.

Grewal, Inderpal. *Transnational America: Feminisms, Diasporas, Neoliberalisms.* Durham: Duke University Press, 2005.

Hall, Ingrid. "Confucius Institutes and U.S. Exchange Programs: Public Diplomacy through Education." *World Education News & Reviews*, April 3, 2018. https://wenr.wes.org/2018/04/confucius-institutes-and-u-s-exchange-progr ams-public-diplomacy-through-education

Hallin, Daniel C. *The Uncensored War: The Media and Vietnam.* Berkeley: University of California Press, 1989.

Hammond, William M. *Reporting Vietnam: Media and Military at War.* Rev. ed. Lawrence: University Press of Kansas, 1998.

Hanban/Confucius Institute Headquarters. "Hanban—About Us—Confucius Institute Headquarters." Hanban, 2014. http://english.hanban.org/node _7716.htm

Hanban/Confucius Institute Headquarters. "Li Changchun and Liu Yandong Inspect Confucius Institute Headquarters and Call on the Staff of Hanban." Hanban, December 14, 2012. http://english.hanban.org/article/2012-12/14 /content_476760.htm

Haraway, Donna. "A Cyborg Manifesto." In *The Cultural Studies Reader*, edited by Simon During, 2nd ed. London: Routledge, 1999.

Hariman, Robert, and John Louis Lucaites. *No Caption Needed: Iconic Photographs, Public Culture, and Liberal Democracy.* Chicago: University of Chicago Press, 2007.

Harris, Derrick. "Netflix Analyzes a Lot of Data about Your Viewing Habits." *GigaOm*, June 14, 2012. https://gigaom.com/2012/06/14/netflix-analyzes -a-lot-of-data-about-your-viewing-habits/

Harrison, Virginia. "US-China Trade War: 'We're All Paying for This.'" *BBC News*, August 1, 2019, sec. Business. https://www.bbc.com/news/business-4912 2849

Hastings, Chris. "President Putin Thinks *House of Cards* Is a Documentary." *Daily Mail*, May 28, 2017. http://www.dailymail.co.uk/~/article-4549000/index .html

Hernández, Javier C., and Austin Ramzy. "China Confirms New Coronavirus Spreads from Humans to Humans." *New York Times*, January 20, 2020, sec. World. https://www.nytimes.com/2020/01/20/world/asia/coronavirus-chi na-symptoms.html

Hill, Evan, Ainara Tiefenthäler, Christiaan Triebert, Drew Jordan, Haley Willis, and Robin Stein. "8 Minutes and 46 Seconds: How George Floyd Was Killed in Police Custody." *New York Times*, May 31, 2020, sec. U.S. https://www.nytim es.com/2020/05/31/us/george-floyd-investigation.html

Hillenbrand, Margaret. *Negative Exposures: Knowing What Not to Know in Contemporary China.* Durham: Duke University Press, 2020.

Hills, Megan C. "What Keanu Reeves Taught Me about White-Passing Privilege." *Evening Standard*, September 5, 2020. https://www.standard.co.uk/insider /celebrity/keanu-reeves-chinese-hawaiian-asian-heritage-white-passing-a453 9726.html

Hoang, Kimberly Kay. "How the History of Spas and Sex Work Fits into the Conversation about the Atlanta Shootings." Vox, March 18, 2021. https://www .vox.com/first-person/22338462/atlanta-shooting-georgia-spa-asian-amer ican

Hong, Cathy Park. *Minor Feelings: An Asian American Reckoning.* Reprint ed. New York: Random House, 2021.

Huang, Yunte. *Transpacific Imaginations: History, Literature, Counterpoetics*. Cambridge, MA: Harvard University Press, 2008.

Hubbert, Jennifer. "Ambiguous States: Confucius Institutes and Chinese Soft Power in the U.S. Classroom." *PoLAR: Political & Legal Anthropology Review* 37, no. 2 (November 2014): 329–49. https://doi.org/10.1111/plar.12078

Hubbert, Jennifer. "Appropriating Iconicity: Why Tank Man Still Matters." *Visual Anthropology Review* 30, no. 2 (November 2014): 114–26. https://doi.org/10.1111/var.12042/

Hubbert, Jennifer. "Authenticating the Nation: Confucius Institutes and Soft Power." In *Confucius Institutes and the Globalization of China's Soft Power*, 33–46. Los Angeles: Figueroa Press, 2014.

Hubbert, Jennifer. *China in the World: An Anthropology of Confucius Institutes, Soft Power, and Globalization*. Honolulu: University of Hawaii Press, 2019.

Hung, Ho-fung. *The China Boom: Why China Will Not Rule the World*. New York: Columbia University Press, 2016.

Hung, Ho-fung. *Clash of Empires: From "Chimerica" to the "New Cold War."* Cambridge: Cambridge University Press, 2022.

Hung, Ho-fung. "Holding Beijing Accountable for the Coronavirus Is Not Racist." *Journal of Political Risk* 8, no. 3 (March 17, 2020). https://www.jpolrisk.com/holding-beijing-accountable-for-the-coronavirus-is-not-racist/

Immerwahr, Daniel. *How to Hide an Empire: A History of the Greater United States*. New York: Farrar, Straus and Giroux, 2019.

Ishii, Douglas. "Palimpsestic Orientalisms and Antiblackness, or, Joss Whedon's Grand Vision of an Asian/American Tomorrow." In *Techno-Orientalism: Imagining Asia in Speculative Fiction, History, and Media*, edited by David S. Roh, Betsy Huang, and Greta A. Niu, 180–92. New Brunswick, NJ: Rutgers University Press, 2015.

Jack, Simon. "Trump Official: Coronavirus Could Boost US Jobs." *BBC News*, January 31, 2020, sec. Business. https://www.bbc.com/news/business-51276323

James S. Brady Press Briefing Room. "Remarks by President Trump, Vice President Pence, and Members of the Coronavirus Task Force in Press Briefing." The White House, March 23, 2020. https://trumpwhitehouse.archives.gov/briefings-statements/remarks-president-trump-vice-president-pence-members-coronavirus-task-force-press-briefing-9/

Jayron. "#Baltimore #Tiananmen SQ Tank Man 2015. #Baltimore #FreddieGray #BlackLivesMatter." *Twitter*, April 26, 2015. https://twitter.com/jayron26/status/592353628792426496

Jenner, Mareike. "Is This TVIV? On Netflix, TVIII, and Binge-Watching." *New Media & Society* 18, no. 2 (February 2016): 257.

Jensen, Lionel M. "Culture Industry, Power, and the Spectacle of China's 'Confucius Institutes.'" In *China in and beyond the Headlines*, edited by Timothy B. Weston and Lionel M. Jensen, 271–99. Lanham, MD: Rowman & Littlefield, 2012.

Jeon, Joseph Jonghyun. "Neoliberal Forms: CGI, Algorithm, and Hegemony in Korea's IMF Cinema." *Representations* 126 (May 2014): 85–111. https://doi.org/10.1525/rep.2014.126.1.85

Jiang, Steven. "'House of Cards' in China: Surprisingly Available and Popular." CNN, February 19, 2014. http://www.cnn.com/2014/02/19/world/asia/china-house-of-cards-jiang/

Joyrich, Lynne. "Reality TV Trumps Politics." *Contemporary Condition* (blog), 2016. http://contemporarycondition.blogspot.com/2016/11/reality-tv-tru mps-politics.html

Jue, Melody. *Wild Blue Media: Thinking through Seawater.* Durham: Duke University Press, 2020. https://doi.org/10.2307/j.ctv11g97ph

Kafer, Alison. *Feminist, Queer, Crip.* Bloomington: Indiana University Press, 2013.

Kaiser, Jocelyn. "Federal Watchdog Finds Problems with NIH Oversight of Grant Funding Bat Virus Research in China." *Science,* January 25, 2023. https://www .science.org/content/article/federal-watchdog-finds-problems-nih-oversight -grant-funding-bat-virus-research-china

"Kan Waiguo Mingxing Xiu Zhongwen, Yeshi Zuile (Watch Foreign Celebrities Show Chinese, Mesmerizing)." Beijing, 2015. https://www.facebook.com/wa tch/?v=1473446559416305

Kandil, Caitlin Yoshiko. "Asian Americans Report over 650 Racist Acts over Last Week, New Data Says." NBC News, March 26, 2020. https://www.nbcnews .com/news/asian-america/asian-americans-report-nearly-500-racist-acts-over -last-week-n1169821

"Kankan Sheldon Zenme Xue Zhongwen (How Does Sheldon Learn Chinese?)." Beijing, 2015. https://www.facebook.com/watch/?v=1473446559416305

Kember, Sarah, and Joanna Zylinska. *Life after New Media: Mediation as a Vital Process.* Cambridge, MA: MIT Press, 2012.

Kennedy, John F. "'We All Breathe the Same Air.'" Presented at the American University Commencement Ceremony, Washington, DC, June 10, 1963. http://www.humanity.org/voices/commencements/john.f.kennedy-americ an-university-speech-1963

Ke-Schutte, Jay. *Angloscene: Compromised Personhood in Afro-Chinese Translations.* Oakland: University of California Press, 2023.

Kessler, Glenn. "No, China Does Not Hold More Than 50 Percent of U.S. Debt." *Washington Post,* December 29, 2014. http://www.washingtonpost.com/blogs /fact-checker/wp/2014/12/29/no-china-does-not-hold-more-than-50-perce nt-of-u-s-debt/

Kiehl, Christine. "From Chimera to Reality: Lucy Kirkwood's *Chimerica* or 'What State Are We In?'" *Journal of Contemporary Drama in English* 6, no. 1 (2018): 191–205. https://doi.org/10.1515/jcde-2018–0020

King, Homay. *Lost in Translation: Orientalism, Cinema, and the Enigmatic Signifier.* Durham: Duke University Press, 2010.

Kirkwood, Lucy. *Chimerica.* Rev. ed. London: Nick Hern Books, 2013.

Klinke, Ian. "Chronopolitics: A Conceptual Matrix." *Progress in Human Geography,* February 26, 2013. https://doi.org/10.1177/0309132512472094

Kluver, Randolph. "The Sage as Strategy: Nodes, Networks, and the Quest for Geopolitical Power in the Confucius Institute." *Communication, Culture & Critique* 7, no. 2 (June 2014): 192–209.

Kokas, Aynne. *Hollywood Made in China.* Oakland: University of California Press, 2017.

Kokas, Aynne. *Trafficking Data: How China Is Winning the Battle for Digital Sovereignty.* New York: Oxford University Press, 2022.

Kong, Belinda. "Pandemic as Method." *Prism* 16, no. 2 (October 1, 2019): 368–89. https://doi.org/10.1215/25783491-7978531

Kong, Belinda. "Recovering First Patients." *Boundary* 2 (blog), August 27, 2020. https://www.boundary2.org/2020/08/belinda-kong-recovering-first-patie nts/

Kong, Belinda. *Tiananmen Fictions outside the Square: The Chinese Literary Diaspora and the Politics of Global Culture.* American Literatures Initiative ed. Philadelphia: Temple University Press, 2012.

Kunkle, Fredrick. "Creepy 'House of Cards' Ad on Metro Station Platform: 'A Push in the Right Direction.'" *Washington Post*, February 25, 2016. https://www.washingtonpost.com/news/tripping/wp/2016/02/25/creepy-house-of -cards-ad-on-metro-station-platform-a-push-in-the-right-direction/

Kuo, Lily, and Theodora Yu. "One Man's Bold Protest against China's Leaders Inspires Global Copycats." *Washington Post*, November 10, 2022. https://www .washingtonpost.com/world/2022/11/10/china-protest-sitong-hong-kong/

LaCasse, Alexander. "How Accurate Is 'House of Cards?' Very, Says President Clinton." *Christian Science Monitor*, March 31, 2015. http://www.csmonitor .com/The-Culture/Culture-Cafe/2015/0331/How-accurate-is-House-of-Car ds-Very-says-President-Clinton.-video

Laporte, Nicole. "Netflix: The Red Menace." *Fast Company*, January 17, 2014. https://www.fastcompany.com/3024158/netflix-the-red-menace

Latour, Bruno. "Is This a Dress Rehearsal?" *In the Moment* (blog), March 26, 2020. https://critinq.wordpress.com/2020/03/26/is-this-a-dress-rehearsal/

Lawson, Mark. "*Chimerica* Playwright Lucy Kirkwood: 'The Whole of Democracy Looks Fragile and Farcical.'" *The Guardian*, November 14, 2016, sec. Stage. http://www.theguardian.com/stage/2016/nov/14/lucy-kirkwood-the-child ren-royal-court-theatre-chimerica

Lazzarato, Maurizio. *The Making of the Indebted Man: An Essay on the Neoliberal Condition.* Intervention Series 13. Los Angeles: Semiotext(e), 2012.

Lee, Benjamin, and Edward LiPuma. "Cultures of Circulation: The Imaginations of Modernity." *Public Culture* 14, no. 1 (2002): 191–213. https://doi.org/10.12 15/08992363-14-1-191

Lee, Ching Kwan. *The Specter of Global China: Politics, Labor, and Foreign Investment in Africa.* Illustrated ed. Chicago: University of Chicago Press, 2018.

"Leica 'Tank Man' Ad Draws Online Anger." *South China Morning Post*, April 18, 2019. https://www.scmp.com/video/china/3006839/commercial-depicting -tiananmen-squares-tank-man-creates-online-headache-leica/

Levenson, Michael. "Scale of China's Wuhan Shutdown Is Believed to Be without Precedent." *New York Times*, January 22, 2020, sec. World. https://www.nytim es.com/2020/01/22/world/asia/coronavirus-quarantines-history.html

Levy, Paul. "Holding Out for a Hero: A New Play in London Captures the Ambiguities of U.S.-China Relations." *Wall Street Journal*, August 22, 2013. http://www.wsj.com/articles/SB10001424127887324747104579022262640222686

Li, Erliang. "Zhongguo Weihe Meiyou Zhengzhiju? (Why Aren't There Any Political Shows in China?)." *Zhonghua Ernu (China Profiles)*, 2014.

Li, Yifei, and Judith Shapiro. *China Goes Green: Coercive Environmentalism for a Troubled Planet.* Cambridge, UK: Polity, 2020.

Li, Yuming. "Qiangguo de Yuyan Yu Yuyan Qiangguo (Nation-Strengthening Language and Linguistic Power)." *Guangming Ribao (Guangming Daily)*,

August 24, 2004. http://www.people.com.cn/GB/wenhua/27296/2733803.html

Lim, Louisa. *The People's Republic of Amnesia: Tiananmen Revisited*. New York: Oxford University Press, 2015.

Lippi-Green, Rosina. "Accent, Standard Language Ideology, and Discriminatory Pretext in the Courts." *Language in Society* 23, no. 2 (1994): 163–98.

LiPuma, Edward, and Benjamin Lee. *Financial Derivatives and the Globalization of Risk*. Public Planet Books. Durham: Duke University Press, 2004.

Litzinger, Ralph A. "Screening the Political: Pedagogy and Dissent in *The Gate of Heavenly Peace*." *Positions: East Asia Cultures Critique* 7, no. 3 (December 21, 1999): 827–50.

Litzinger, Ralph, and Fan Yang. "Eco-media Events in China: From Yellow Eco-peril to Media Materialism." *Environmental Humanities* 12, no. 1 (May 1, 2020): 1–22. https://doi.org/10.1215/22011919-8142187

Litzinger, Ralph, and Fan Yang. "Rethinking the Eco-Media Event in Pandemic Times." Presented at the Sci-Tech Asia Webinar, February 24, 2023. https://scitechasia.org/webinars/rethinking-the-eco-media-event-in-pandemic-times/

Liu, Andrew. "Lab-Leak Theory and the 'Asiatic' Form." *N+1* (blog), Issue 22: Vanishing Act, March 10, 2022. https://www.nplusonemag.com/issue-42/politics/lab-leak-theory-and-the-asiatic-form/

Liu, Catherine. "Inequality, Technocracy, and National Healthcare: Taiwan and COVID-19." In *The Pandemic: Perspectives on Asia*, edited by Vinayak Chaturvedi, 111–22. Asia Shorts. New York: Columbia University Press, 2020. https://www.asianstudies.org/wp-content/uploads/The-Pandemic-Perspectives-on-Asia.pdf

Liu, Xinyin. "Meiju, Kanshangqu Hen Mei (American TV Shows, Looking Good)." *Guoji Renwen Lishi (National Humanity History)*, June 2016.

Liu, Yingtuan. "Zhipaiwu Li Kui Zhengzhi (Probing Politics in House of Cards)." *China Human Resources and Social Security*, 2014.

Liu, Yu. "Dianshi Hen Malatang, Xianshi Hen Baikaishui—Dui Zhipaiwu de Zhengzhixue Jiedu (TV Is Very Hot and Spicy, Reality Is Bland like Water—A Reading of House of Cards through Political Science)." *Nanfang Renwu Zhoukan (Southern People Weekly)*, March 10, 2014. http://www.nfpeople.com/story_view.php?id=5253

Lobato, Roman. *Netflix Nations: The Geography of Digital Distribution*. New York: NYU Press, 2019.

Lowe, Lisa. *The Intimacies of Four Continents*. Durham: Duke University Press, 2015.

Lye, Colleen. *America's Asia: Racial Form and American Literature, 1893–1945*. Princeton: Princeton University Press, 2004.

Ma, Lisi. "Guanyu Woguo Jiaqiang Ruanshili Jianshe de Chubu Sikao" (Preliminary Thoughts on Strengthening Our Nation's Soft Power). *Dangde Wenxian (Literature of Chinese Communist Party)* 5 (2007): 35–38.

Ma, Sheng-mei. *The Deathly Embrace: Orientalism and Asian American Identity*. Minneapolis: University of Minnesota Press, 2000.

Ma, Wayne. "'House of Cards' Writer on China, U.S., and Power." *China Real Time Report—Wall Street Journal* (blog), February 19, 2014. http://blogs.wsj.com/chinarealtime/2014/02/19/house-of-cards-writer-on-china-u-s-and-power/

MacKinnon, Rebecca. *Consent of the Networked: The World-Wide Struggle for Internet Freedom.* New York: Basic Books, 2012.

"Make Zakeboge Qinghua Yanjiang Quancheng Xiu Zhongwen (Mark Zuckerberg Showing off Chinese during the Entire Tsing-Hua Speech: 'I Want to Challenge Myself')." YouTube, 2014. https://www.youtube.com/watch?v=x Fk_R5ltjoA

Mandala, Susan. "Representing the Future: Chinese and Codeswitching in *Firefly.*" In *Investigating* Firefly *and* Serenity*: Science Fiction on the Frontier,* edited by Rhonda V. Wilcox and Tanya Cochran, 31–40. London: I. B. Tauris, 2008.

Mandaro, Laura. "Ferguson's 'Tank Man' Sparks Comparison with Tiananmen," *USA Today,* November 25, 2014. http://www.usatoday.com/story/news/nati on-now/2014/11/25/ferguson-tank-man-tiananmen/70078046/

Marks, Peter. "Review of 'Chimerica': A Sprawling Tale Is High on Dudgeon, Low on Insight." *Washington Post,* September 15, 2015, sec. Theater & Dance. https://www.washingtonpost.com/entertainment/theater_dance/review-of -chimerica-good-characters-forbidding-cities/2015/09/15/39b05488-5b33 -11e5-8e9e-dce8a2a2a679_story.html

The Martian. Twentieth Century Fox Film Corporation, 2015.

Martin, Randy. *Financialization of Daily Life.* Philadelphia: Temple University Press, 2002.

Martina, Michael, and Trevor Hunnicutt. "Biden Says Trump Failed to Hold China Accountable on Coronavirus." *Reuters,* April 17, 2020. https://www.re uters.com/article/us-usa-election-china-idUSKBN21Z3DZ

Masket, Seth. "'House of Cards' Is the Worst Show about American Politics. Ever." *Washington Post,* March 8, 2015. https://www.washingtonpost.com/news/mo nkey-cage/wp/2015/03/08/house-of-cards-is-the-worst-show-about-americ an-politics-ever/

Mbembe, Achille. "The Universal Right to Breathe." *In the Moment* (blog), April 13, 2020. https://critinq.wordpress.com/2020/04/13/the-universal-right-to -breathe/

McQuire, Scott. *The Media City: Media, Architecture, and Urban Space.* London: Sage, 2008.

McWhorter, John H. "What the World Will Speak in 2115." *Wall Street Journal,* January 2, 2015. http://www.wsj.com/articles/what-the-world-will-speak-in -2115-1420234648

Meisner, Maurice J. *The Deng Xiaoping Era: An Inquiry into the Fate of Chinese Socialism, 1978–1994.* New York: Hill and Wang, 1996.

Meisner, Maurice J. *Mao's China and After: A History of the People's Republic.* 3rd ed. New York: Free Press, 1999.

Melamed, Jodi. "Racial Capitalism." *Critical Ethnic Studies* 1, no. 1 (2015): 76–85. https://doi.org/10.5749/jcritethnstud.1.1.0076

Meng, Gang, and Zheneng Wu. *China's Belt and Road Initiative and RMB Internationalization.* Series on China's Belt and Road Initiative. Hackensack, NJ: World Scientific, 2019. https://doi.org/10.1142/11230

Metzger, Sean. *The Chinese Atlantic: Seascapes and the Theatricality of Globalization.* Bloomington: Indiana University Press, 2020.

Mid-April Designs. "China Lied People Died, Coronavirus Shirts, Covid Shirt,

Trump 2020, MAGA Shirts, Trump Coronavirus Navy." Amazon, April 20, 2020. https://www.amazon.com/China-People-coronavius-Shirts-coronavir us/dp/B087C7FXJL

Mignolo, Walter. *Local Histories/Global Designs: Coloniality, Subaltern Knowledges, and Border Thinking.* Princeton, NJ: Princeton University Press, 2000.

Ministry of Education of the People's Republic of China. "What We Do." Ministry of Education of the People's Republic of China, 2018. http://en.moe.gov.cn /about_MOE/what_we_do/

Mol, Annemarie. "Ontological Politics. A Word and Some Questions." *Sociological Review* 47, no. S1 (1999): 74–89. https://doi.org/10.1111/j.1467-954X.1999 .tb03483.x

Morley, David. "Globalisation and Cultural Imperialism Reconsidered: Old Questions in New Guises." In *Media and Cultural Theory,* edited by James Curran and David Morley, 30–43. London: Routledge, 2006.

Morley, David, and Kevin Robins. "Techno-Orientalism: Japan Panic." *Spaces of Identity: Global Media, Electronic Landscapes and Cultural Boundaries,* 1995, 147–73.

Mullins, Jenna. "This Is How Much Money Has Been Spent Saving Matt Damon." E! Online, December 28, 2015. http://www.eonline.com/news/726732/this -is-how-much-money-has-been-spent-saving-matt-damon

Musgrave, Paul. "The Slip That Revealed the Real Trump Doctrine." *Foreign Policy* (blog), May 2, 2019. https://foreignpolicy.com/2019/05/02/the-slip-that -revealed-the-real-trump-doctrine/

Muysken, Pieter. *Bilingual Speech: A Typology of Code-Mixing.* Cambridge: Cambridge University Press, 2005.

Myers, Steven Lee. "Facing New Outbreaks, China Places over 22 Million on Lockdown." *New York Times,* January 13, 2021, sec. World. https://www.nytim es.com/2021/01/13/world/asia/china-covid-lockdown.html

Nakamura, Lisa. *Cybertypes: Race, Ethnicity, and Identity on the Internet.* New York: Routledge, 2002.

National Research Centre for State Language Capacity. "Yuyan zhanlue yu guojia anquan gaoceng luntan (Langage Strategy and National Security High-level Forum held in Beijing)," October 31, 2019. http://gynf.bfsu.edu.cn/?p=183

Nguyen, Mimi Thi. *The Gift of Freedom: War, Debt, and Other Refugee Passages.* Durham: Duke University Press, 2012.

Nguyen, Viet Thanh, and Janet Alison Hoskins. "Introduction: Transpacific Studies: Critical Perspectives on an Emerging Field." In *Transpacific Studies: Framing an Emerging Field,* edited by Janet Alison Hoskins and Viet Thanh Nguyen, 1–38. Honolulu: University of Hawaii Press, 2014.

"Ni Kanguo Zhexie Dianying Me? Neng Tingdong Limian de Zhongwen Me? (Have You Seen These Movies? Can You Understand the Chinese in Them?)." Beijing, 2017. https://www.facebook.com/watch/?v=1473446559416305

Nie, Kuanmian. "Zhipaiwu 'gongdou' Kanzhe Bie Dangzhen, Shili Weiji Weina Taiduo Jiang (Don't Take the 'Palace Infighting' of House of Cards Seriously, Not Enough Strength to Obtain That Many Awards)." *Renmin wang (People Net),* February 25, 2014. http://media.people.com.cn/n/2014/0225/c40606 -24452852.html

Nussbaum, Emily. "Must-See Metaphysics." *New York Times,* September 22, 2002, sec. Magazine. http://www.nytimes.com/2002/09/22/magazine/must-see -metaphysics.html

Nye, Joseph. *Soft Power: The Means to Success in World Politics*. New York: Public Affairs, 2004.

Ollstein, Alice Miranda. "Politico-Harvard Poll: Most Americans Believe Covid Leaked from Lab." Politico, July 9, 2021. https://www.politico.com/news/20 21/07/09/poll-covid-wuhan-lab-leak-498847

Ono, Kent A., and Joy Yang Jiao. "China in the US Imaginary: Tibet, the Olympics, and the 2008 Earthquake." *Communication and Critical/Cultural Studies* 5, no. 4 (December 1, 2008): 406–10. https://doi.org/10.1080/147914208 02416168

Orkin, Martin, and Alexa Alice Joubin. *Race*. The New Critical Idiom. New York: Routledge, 2019.

Osborne, Hannah. "Coronavirus Outbreak May Have Started as Early as September, Scientists Say." *Newsweek*, April 17, 2020. https://www.newsweek.com/co ronavirus-outbreak-september-not-wuhan-1498566

Osnos, Evan. "A Breakout Hit Sweeps China." *Chicago Tribune*, January 18, 2007. http://articles.chicagotribune.com/2007-01-18/news/0701180056_1_pris on-break-official-chinese-statistics-web-users

Osnos, Evan. "'Prison Break' Catches on in China." *Seattle Times*, January 25, 2007. http://www.seattletimes.com/nation-world/prison-break-catches-on -in-china/

Ou, Howey. "欧泓奕Howey Ou #FightFor1Point5 (@howey_ou)." Twitter. Accessed December 17, 2020. https://twitter.com/howey_ou

Ow, Jeffrey A. "The Revenge of the Yellow Faced Terminator: The Rape of Digital Geishas and the Colonization of Cyber Coolies in 3D Realms' Shadow Warrior." In *Asian America.Net: Ethnicity, Nationalism, and Cyberspace*, edited by Rachel C. Lee and Sau-Ling Cynthia Wong, 249–66. New York: Routledge, 2003.

Packer, George. "We Are Living in a Failed State." *The Atlantic*, April 20, 2020. https://www.theatlantic.com/magazine/archive/2020/06/underlying-cond itions/610261/

Palmer, James. "Winter Olympics: Eileen Gu and the Chimerican Dream," *Foreign Policy*, February 9, 2022. https://foreignpolicy.com/2022/02/09/eileen -gu-china-winter-olympics-chimerica/

Palumbo-Liu, David. *Asian/American: Historical Crossings of a Racial Frontier*. Stanford: Stanford University Press, 1999.

Park, Jane Chi Hyun. *Yellow Future*. Minneapolis: University of Minnesota Press, 2010.

Peters, John Durham. *The Marvelous Clouds: Toward a Philosophy of Elemental Media*. Chicago: University of Chicago Press, 2015.

Peterson, Rachelle. *Outsourced to China: Confucius Institutes and Soft Power in American Higher Education*. New York: National Association of Scholars, 2017.

Phillipson, Robert. *Linguistic Imperialism*. Oxford: Oxford University Press, 1992.

Phillipson, Robert. *Linguistic Imperialism Continued*. Hyderabad, India: Orient Blackswan, 2009.

Prasad, Eswar. *The Dollar Trap: How the U.S. Dollar Tightened Its Grip on Global Finance*. Princeton: Princeton University Press, 2014.

Probyn, Elspeth. "Doing Cultural Studies in Rough Seas: The COVID-19 Ocean Multiple." *Cultural Studies* 35, no. 2–3 (May 4, 2021): 557–71. https://doi.org/10.1080/09502386.2021.1898032

Pryke, Michael, and John Allen. "Monetized Time-Space: Derivatives—Money's 'New Imaginary'?" *Economy & Society* 29, no. 2 (May 2000): 264–84. https://doi.org/10.1080/030851400360497

Qian, Qiuqi. "OTT TV Zai Zhongguo Yingshi Chanye de Yanjiu (A Study of OTT TV in the Chinese Film and Television Industry)." *Shengping Shijie (Voice and Screen World)* 14 (December 2014).

Qin, Yaqing. *A Relational Theory of World Politics.* New York: Cambridge University Press, 2018.

Qiu, Jack Linchuan. *Goodbye iSlave: A Manifesto for Digital Abolition.* Urbana: University of Illinois Press, 2017.

Rafael, Vicente L. "Linguistic Currencies: The Translative Power of English in Southeast Asia and the United States." *The Translator* 25, no. 2 (April 3, 2019): 142–58. https://doi.org/10.1080/13556509.2019.1654061

Rafael, Vicente L. "Mutant Tongues: Translating English in the Postcolonial Humanities." *CR: The New Centennial Review* 16, no. 1 (2016): 93–114. https://doi.org/10.14321/crnewcentrevi.16.1.0093

Raley, Rita. "eEmpires." *Cultural Critique* 57 (Spring 2004): 111–50. https://doi.org/10.1353/cul.2004.0014

Ramzy, Austin. "Get Ahead, Learn Mandarin." *Time.com*, June 26, 2006. http://content.time.com/time/world/article/0,8599,2047305-4,00.html

Rancière, Jacques. *The Politics of Aesthetics: The Distribution of the Sensible.* London: Continuum, 2006.

Rantanen, Terhi. *The Media and Globalization.* London: Sage, 2005.

Reed Hastings, Netflix—Keynote address, Consumer Technology Association 2016. Las Vegas, Nevada, 2016. https://www.youtube.com/watch?v=l5R3E6jsICA

Reiss, Mitchell, and Claudia Coscia. "The Global Stakes on Why Black Lives Matter." Wilson Center, September 21, 2020. https://www.wilsoncenter.org/article/global-stakes-why-black-lives-matter

Repnikova, Maria. *Chinese Soft Power.* New ed. Cambridge: Cambridge University Press, 2022.

Repnikova, Maria. *Media Politics in China: Improvising Power under Authoritarianism.* Reprint ed. Cambridge: Cambridge University Press, 2018.

Richardson, Allissa V. *Bearing Witness while Black: African Americans, Smartphones, and the New Protest #Journalism.* New York: Oxford University Press, 2020.

Roberts, Brian Russell, and Michelle Ann Stephens. "Introduction: Archipelagic American Studies: Decontinentalizing the Study of American Culture." In *Archipelagic American Studies*, edited by Brian Russell Roberts and Michelle Ann Stephens. Illustrated ed., 1–54. Durham: Duke University Press, 2017.

Roberts, Sarah T. *Behind the Screen: Content Moderation in the Shadows of Social Media.* Illustrated ed. New Haven: Yale University Press, 2019.

Robinson, Cedric J. *Black Marxism: The Making of the Black Radical Tradition.* 2nd ed. Chapel Hill: University of North Carolina Press, 2000.

Roettgers, Janko. "For *House of Cards* and *Arrested Development*, Netflix Favors Big

Data over Big Ratings." *GigaOm* (blog), February 12, 2013. https://gigaom
.com/2013/02/12/netflix-ratings-big-data-original-content/

Roh, David S., Betsy Huang, and Greta A. Niu. "Technologizing Orientalism: An
Introduction." In *Techno-Orientalism: Imagining Asia in Speculative Fiction, His-
tory, and Media*, edited by David S. Roh, Betsy Huang, and Greta A. Niu, 1–19.
New Brunswick, NJ: Rutgers University Press, 2015.

Roos, Jerome. "The Making of the Indebted State Under Neoliberalism." *Popu-
larResistance.Org* (blog), September 7, 2013. https://popularresistance.org
/the-making-of-the-indebted-state-under-neoliberalism/

Rosa, Jonathan. *Looking Like a Language, Sounding Like a Race: Raciolinguistic Ideologies and the Learning of Latinidad.* New York: Oxford University Press, 2019.

Rouvroy, Antoinette. "The End(s) of Critique: Data Behaviourism versus Due
Process." In *Privacy, Due Process, and the Computational Turn: The Philosophy
of Law Meets the Philosophy of Technology*, edited by Mireille Hildebrandt and
Katja de Vries, 143–67. London: Routledge, 2013. https://www.routledge
.com/Privacy-Due-Process-and-the-Computational-Turn-The-Philosophy-of
-Law/Hildebrandt-de-Vries/p/book/9780415644815

Rugh, Jacob S., and Douglas S. Massey. "Racial Segregation and the American
Foreclosure Crisis." *American Sociological Review* 75, no. 5 (October 2010):
629–51.

Sahlins, Marshall. *Confucius Institutes: Academic Malware.* Chicago: University of
Chicago Press, 2015.

Said, Edward W. *Orientalism.* New York: Vintage Books, 1979.

Samuelson, Robert. "Great Wall of Unknowns." *Washington Post*, May 26, 2004.

Sant, Geoffrey. "Is Jon Huntsman Fluent in Chinese?" *Slate.com*, October 31, 2011.
http://www.slate.com/articles/news_and_politics/explainer/2011/10/is
_jon_huntsman_fluent_in_chinese_.single.html#pagebreak_anchor_2

Shapiro, Lila. "The Undoing of Joss Whedon." *Vulture*, January 17, 2022. https://
www.vulture.com/article/joss-whedon-allegations.html

Sharpe, Christina. *In the Wake: On Blackness and Being.* Durham: Duke University
Press, 2016.

Shepherd, Christian. "'New Tank Man': Rare Protest in Beijing Mars Xi Jinping's
Moment." *Washington Post*, October 19, 2022. https://www.washingtonpost
.com/world/2022/10/14/china-protest-sitong-bridge-haidian/

Shih, Shu-mei. "Introduction: What Is Sinophone Studies?" In *Sinophone Studies:
A Critical Reader*, edited by Shu-mei Shih, Chien-hsin Tsai, and Brian Bernards, 1–16. New York: Columbia University Press, 2013.

Shimpach, Shawn. "Realty Reality: HGTV and the Subprime Crisis." *American
Quarterly* 64, no. 3 (September 2012): 515–42.

Shome, Raka. "Thinking through the Diaspora: Call Centers, India, and a New
Politics of Hybridity." *International Journal of Cultural Studies* 9, no. 1 (March 1,
2006): 105–24. https://doi.org/10.1177/1367877906061167

Smith, Marion. "Blame the Chinese Communist Party for the Coronavirus Crisis." *USA Today*, April 5, 2020. https://www.usatoday.com/story/opinion/20
20/04/05/blame-chinese-communist-party-coronavirus-crisis-column/2940
486001/

So, Richard Jean. *Transpacific Community: America, China, and the Rise and Fall of a
Cultural Network.* New York: Columbia University Press, 2016.

Sohn, Stephen Hong. "Introduction: Alien/Asian: Imagining the Racialized Future." *MELUS* 33, no. 4 (2008): 5–22.

Song, Nianshen. "Chongtu de Shi Quanli, Jianshe de Shi Wenhua: Zhongmei Boyi Zhongde 'Wenhua Chongtu' (The Struggle of Power and the Construction of Culture: The 'Cultural Conflict' in Sino-U.S. Interactions)." *Waijiao Pinglun (Foreign Affairs Review)* 2 (2010): 48–56.

Sorace, Christian, and Nicholas Loubere. "Biopolitical Binaries (or How Not to Read the Chinese Protests)." *Made in China Journal* (blog), December 2, 2022. https://madeinchinajournal.com/2022/12/02/biopolitical-binaries-or-how-not-to-read-the-chinese-protests/

Sparks, Colin. "Media and Cultural Imperialism Reconsidered." *Chinese Journal of Communication* 5, no. 3 (September 2012): 281.

Srnicek, Nick. *Platform Capitalism.* Cambridge, UK: Polity, 2016.

Starr, Don. "Chinese Language Education in Europe: The Confucius Institutes." *European Journal of Education* 44, no. 1 (2009): 65–82.

"Stephen Colbert's Pander Express." *The Late Show with Stephen Colbert.* October 7, 2015, YouTube. https://www.youtube.com/watch?v=V4WBsahU3X4

Stevens, Andrew. "China's Xi Jinping in 'House of Cards' Joke." CNN, September 23, 2015. http://www.cnn.com/2015/09/23/asia/xi-jinping-us-visit-house-of-cards/index.html

Stoever, Jennifer Lynn. *The Sonic Color Line: Race and the Cultural Politics of Listening.* New York: NYU Press, 2016.

Sturgis, Amy H. "'Just Get Us a Little Further': Liberty and the Frontier in *Firefly* and *Serenity.*" In *The Philosophy of Joss Whedon,* edited by Dean Kowalski, 24–38. Lexington: University Press of Kentucky, 2011.

Sullivan, Kevin. "Chinese Words in the Verse." In *Finding Serenity: Anti-Heroes, Lost Shepherds, and Space Hookers in Joss Whedon's* Firefly, edited by Jane Espenson and Glenn Yeffeth, 197–207. Dallas: BenBella Books, 2005.

Sze, Julie. *Fantasy Islands: Chinese Dreams and Ecological Fears in an Age of Climate Crisis.* Oakland: University of California Press, 2015.

Tang, Xianying. "Meiguo 'Hanyu Re' Beihou de 'Zhongguo Re' (The 'China Fad' behind America's 'Chinese Fad')." *Guangming Ribao (Guangming Daily),* December 19, 2017, sec. 10. http://epaper.gmw.cn/gmrb/html/2017-12/19/nw.D110000gmrb_20171219_1-10.htm

"Trump Blames China for Acting Too Late in Coordinating U.S. Coronavirus Response." *The Onion,* May 4, 2020. https://www.theonion.com/trump-blames-china-for-acting-too-late-in-coordinating-1843243502

Trump, Donald. "Donald J. Trump on Twitter: 'The United States Will Be Powerfully Supporting Those Industries, like Airlines and Others, That Are Particularly Affected by the Chinese Virus. We Will Be Stronger than Ever Before!'" *Twitter,* March 16, 2020.

Ueno, Toshiya. "Techno-Orientalism and Media-Tribalism: On Japanese Animation and Rave Culture." *Third Text,* no. 47 (1999): 95–106.

UpNorthLive. "Senate Candidate Pete Hoekstra under Fire for Ad." YouTube, 2012. http://www.youtube.com/watch?v=2-E2IhOc58k/

US Census Bureau. "Nearly 3 Million U.S. Residents Speak Chinese at Home." United States Census Bureau, September 11, 2013. https://www.census.gov/newsroom/press-releases/2013/cb13-r90.html

Vang, Bee, and Louisa Schein. "The Wretched from the East: Geopolitical Perversions of Asian Manhood." Unpublished manuscript, June 11, 2017.

Visser, Nick. "This Black Lives Matter Photo Should Be Seen around the World." *Huffington Post*, July 10, 2016. http://www.huffingtonpost.com/entry/black-li ves-matter-protest-photo_us_5782d1ffe4b0344d514fdddc

Vukovich, Daniel. *China and Orientalism: Western Knowledge Production and the PRC*. Abingdon, Oxon, UK: Routledge, 2012.

Vukovich, Daniel F. *After Autonomy: A Post-Mortem for Hong Kong's First Handover, 1997–2019*. New York: Palgrave Macmillan, 2022.

Vukovich, Daniel F. *Illiberal China—The Ideological Challenge of the People's Republic of China*. New York: Palgrave Macmillan, 2018.

Wachter, Will. "The Language of Chinese Soft Power in the US." *Asia Times*, October 11, 2014. http://hsktests.com/language-chinese-soft-power-us/

Wadhams, Nick, and Jennifer Jacobs. "China Concealed Extent of Virus Outbreak, U.S. Intelligence Says." Bloomberg.com, April 1, 2020. https://www.bl oomberg.com/news/articles/2020-04-01/china-concealed-extent-of-virus-ou tbreak-u-s-intelligence-says

Wainwright, Oliver. "Inside Beijing's Airpocalypse—A City Made 'Almost Uninhabitable' by Pollution." *The Guardian*, December 16, 2014. https://www.the guardian.com/cities/2014/dec/16/beijing-airpocalypse-city-almost-uninha bitable-pollution-china

Wald, Priscilla. *Contagious: Cultures, Carriers, and the Outbreak Narrative*. Durham: Duke University Press Books, 2008.

Walker, Christopher. "What Is 'Sharp Power'?" *Journal of Democracy* 29, no. 3 (2018): 9–23. https://doi.org/10.1353/jod.2018.0041

Wallis, Cara. "'Immobile Mobility:' Marginal Youth and Mobile Phones in Beijing." In *Mobile Communication: Bringing Us Together and Tearing Us Apart*, edited by Scott Campbell and Richard Seyler Ling, 61–81. New Brunswick, NJ: Transaction, 2011.

Wang, Chih-Ming, and Yu-Fang Cho. "Introduction: The Chinese Factor and American Studies, Here and Now." *American Quarterly* 69, no. 3 (September 19, 2017): 443–63.

Wang, Dingkun, and Xiaochun Zhang. "Ideological Manipulation of Controversial Information: The Unusual Case of the Chinese-Subtitled Version of *House of Cards*." *Altre Modernità* 0, no. 0 (February 18, 2016): 1–20. https://doi .org/10.13130/2035-7680/6845

Wang, Gengnian. "Shijie Geju Bianhua Zhong de Wenhua Guoji Chuanbo Zhanlue (The International Communication Strategy for Culture in the Changing World Order)." *Renmin wang (People Net)*, December 2, 2011. http://theory.pe ople.com.cn/GB/16480463.html

Wang, Hui. *China's New Order: Society, Politics, and Economy in Transition*. Translated by Rebecca E. Karl. Cambridge, MA: Harvard University Press, 2003.

Wang, Hui. *China's Twentieth Century: Revolution, Retreat, and the Road to Equality*. London: Verso Books, 2016.

Wang, J., ed. "Introduction: China's Search of Soft Power." In *Soft Power in China: Public Diplomacy through Communication*, 1–18. New York: Palgrave Macmillan, 2010.

Wang, Yao. "Qiantan Meiju 'Zhipaiwu' Zhong de Kuawenhua Chuanbo—Yi

Dashuju Wei Shijiao (On the Cross-Cultural Communication in the American TV Show House of Cards—From the Perspective of Big Data)." *Jingying Guanlizhe (Manager Journal)* 8 (March 2015): 352–53.

Wark, McKenzie. *Virtual Geography: Living with Global Media Events.* Bloomington: Indiana University Press, 1994.

We the People: Your Voice in the White House. "Investigate Jimmy Kimmel Kid's Table Government Shutdown Show on ABC Network," October 19, 2013. https://petitions.obamawhitehouse.archives.gov/petition/investigate-jimmy-kimmel-kids-table-government-shutdown-show-abc-network/

Weber, Isabella. "Could the US and Chinese Economies Really 'Decouple'?" *The Guardian*, September 11, 2020, sec. Opinion. http://www.theguardian.com/commentisfree/2020/sep/11/us-china-global-economy-donald-trump

Webster, Jamieson. "On Breathing." *New York Review of Books* (blog), April 2, 2021. https://www.nybooks.com/daily/2021/04/02/on-breathing/

Weir, Andy. *The Martian.* New York: Broadway Books, 2014.

Wellman, Mariah L. "Black Squares for Black Lives? Performative Allyship as Credibility Maintenance for Social Media Influencers on Instagram." *Social Media + Society* 8, no. 1 (January 1, 2022): 1–10. https://doi.org/10.1177/20563051221080473

West, Sarah Myers. "Data Capitalism: Redefining the Logics of Surveillance and Privacy." *Business & Society* 58, no. 1 (January 1, 2019): 20–41. https://doi.org/10.1177/0007650317718185

Whedon, Josh. "Re-Lighting the Firefly." Documentary short. *Serenity* DVD. Universal Pictures, 2005.

Wilson, Shawn. *Research Is Ceremony: Indigenous Research Methods.* Black Point, N.S: Fernwood Publishing, 2008.

Wong, Edward. "On Scale of 0 to 500, Beijing's Air Quality Tops 'Crazy Bad' at 755." *New York Times*, January 12, 2013, sec. Science. https://www.nytimes.com/2013/01/13/science/earth/beijing-air-pollution-off-the-charts.html

Wong, Edward. "U.S. Labels Chinese Language Education Group a Diplomatic Mission." *New York Times*, August 13, 2020, sec. U.S. https://www.nytimes.com/2020/08/13/us/politics/state-department-confucius-institutes.html

Wong, Julia Carrie. "Asian Americans Decry 'Whitewashed' Great Wall Film Starring Matt Damon." *The Guardian*, July 30, 2016, sec. Film. https://www.theguardian.com/film/2016/jul/29/the-great-wall-china-film-matt-damon-whitewashed

Wong, Lily. *Transpacific Attachments: Sex Work, Media Networks, and Affective Histories of Chineseness.* New York: Columbia University Press, 2018.

Wood, Peter. Preface to Peterson, *Outsourced to China*, 12–14.

Worland, Justin. "Donald Trump Called Climate Change a Hoax. Now He's Awkwardly Boasting about Fighting It." *Time*, July 8, 2019. https://time.com/5622374/donald-trump-climate-change-hoax-event/

Wright, Leigh Adams. "Asian Objects in Space." In *Finding Serenity: Anti-Heroes, Lost Shepherds, and Space Hookers in Joss Whedon's* Firefly, edited by Jane Espenson and Glenn Yeffeth, 29–35. Dallas: BenBella Books, 2005.

"Xi Jinping: Further Liberating Thoughts, Deepening the Reform, and Solidifying the Work to Promote Comprehensive Reform and Achieve New Breakthroughs at a New Starting Point." *People Net,* January 23, 2018. http://politi cs.people.com.cn/n1/2018/0123/c1024-29782294.html/

Xi, Jinping. "Qunzhong Luxian Shi Dang de Shengmingxian He Genben Gong-zuo Luxian—Zhuanti Baodao (The Mass Line Is the Party's Lifeline and Fundamental Work Line-Special Report)." *People's Daily Online,* June 18, 2013. http://cpc.people.com.cn/xuexi/n/2015/0721/c397563-27338348.html

Xia, Chedan. "Womende Zhenhuanzhuan, Tamende Zhipaiwu (Our Legends of Empress Zhen, Their House of Cards)." *Yidu (IRead)* (blog), March 27, 2013. http://blog.sina.com.cn/s/blog_aa875eee0101asa3.html

Xiang, Biao. "The Pacific Paradox: The Chinese State in Transpacific Interac-tions." In *Transpacific Studies: Framing an Emerging Field,* edited by Janet Ali-son Hoskins and Viet Thanh Nguyen, 85–105. Honolulu: University of Hawaii Press, 2014.

Xiang, Sunny. "Global China as Genre." *Post45,* no. 2 (July 16, 2019). https://po st45.org/2019/07/global-china-as-genre/

Xie, Tao. "China's Confucius Institutes: Self-Promotion or Cultural Imperial-ism?" CNN, October 21, 2014. https://www.cnn.com/2014/10/21/opinion /china-confucius/index.html

Xu, Chelsea Wenzhu. "The Making of 'China's' First Skiing Princess: Neo-Liberal Feminism and Nationalism in Eileen Gu's Online Presence during the 2022 Winter Olympics." July 11, 2023. https://doi.org/10.1386/eapc_00103_1

Xu, Yong. "American Broadcaster Urged to Acknowledge Misconduct." *Xinhua,* November 11, 2013. http://news.xinhuanet.com/english/world/2013–11 /11/c_132879051.htm

Xu, Zhipeng. "'Zipai Moshi' Yi Qidong—Cong Baidu Aiqiyi Kan Shipin Wang-zhan de Yingshi Fazhan Zhilu (Selfie Mode Is Activated—The Film and Tele-vision Developmental Path of Video Streaming Sites through the Case of Baidu IQiyi)." *Dangdai Dianying (Contemporary Cinema)* 1 (2015): 153–56.

Yang, Fan. *Faked in China: Nation Branding, Counterfeit Culture, and Globalization.* Framing the Global. Bloomington: Indiana University Press, 2016.

Yang, Fan. "Learning from Lana: Netflix's *Too Hot to Handle,* COVID-19, and the Human-Nonhuman Entanglement in Contemporary Technoculture." *Cul-tural Studies,* March 10, 2021, 1–11. https://doi.org/10.1080/09502386.2021 .1898036

Yang, Fan. "Rethinking China's Internet Censorship: The Practice of Recoding and the Politics of Visibility." *New Media & Society* 18, no. 7 (August 1, 2016): 1364–81. https://doi.org/10.1177/1461444814555951

Yang, Fan. "Under the Dome: 'Chinese' Smog as a Viral Media Event." *Critical Studies in Media Communication* 33, no. 3 (April 26, 2016): 232–44. https://doi .org/10.1080/15295036.2016.1170172

Yang, Guobin. "Power and Transgression in the Global Media Age: The Strange Case of Twitter in China." In *Communication and Power in the Global Era: Orders and Borders,* edited by Marwan M. Kraidy, 166–83. London: Routledge, 2012.

Yang, Guobin. *The Wuhan Lockdown.* New York: Columbia University Press, 2022.

Yeside. "Chimerica." *StageWhisper* (blog), August 19, 2013. http://www.stagewhi sper.net/chimerica/

Yeung, Paul. "China Newspaper Editors Sacked over Tiananmen Ad," *Reuters,*

June 7, 2007. http://www.reuters.com/article/2007/06/07/us-china-tianan
men-advertisement-idUSPEK17464820070607

"Yong Kexue Taidu Weihu Zuguo Yuyan Wenzi Zhuquan (Protecting Our
Nation's Linguistic and Literary Sovereignty with a Scientific Attitude)."
Zhongguo jiaoyu bao (China Education Daily), September 15, 2004. http://hnyy
cs.org/article-look-46.html/

Zee, Jerry. "Downwind: Three Phases of an Aerosol Form." In *Voluminous States:
Sovereignty, Materiality, and the Territorial Imagination*, edited by Franck Billé,
119–30. Durham: Duke University Press, 2020.

Zhang, Chenchen. "Contested Disaster Nationalism in the Digital Age: Emotional Registers and Geopolitical Imaginaries in COVID-19 Narratives on
Chinese Social Media." *Review of International Studies* 48, no. 2 (April 2022):
219–42. https://doi.org/10.1017/S0260210522000018

Zhang, Hui. "Zhipaiwu Weihe Zai Zhongguo Shou Zhuipeng? (Why Was House
of Cards Chased after in China?)." *Qingnian Cankao (Elite Reference)*, February
26, 2014, sec. B.

Zhang, Ripei. "Yuyan Shi Ruanshili Yeshi Yingshili—Ping Yuyan Yu Guojia (Language Is Soft Power as Well as Hard Power—A Review of Language and
Nation)." *Renmin Ribao (People's Daily)*, March 25, 2015. http://www.guoxue
.com/?p=27495

Zhang, Weiyu. *The Internet and New Social Formation in China: Fandom Publics in
the Making*. Media, Culture, and Social Change in Asia Series. London: Routledge, 2016.

Zhang, Yajie. "Dui Zhipaiwu Zhonguo Yuansu de Shenceng Sikao (An In-Depth
Consideration of the Chinese Elements in House of Cards)." *Mingzuo Xinshang (Masterpieces Review)* 6 (2015).

Zhao, Lin. "Cong Zhipaiwu Re Toushi Xifang Fada Guojia Fubai Xianxiang
(Probing the Corruption Phenomena in Western Developed Countries
through the Popularity of House of Cards)." Guoji Fanfu Liaowang (International Anticorruption Outlook), June 16, 2014. http://www.ccdi.gov.cn/spec
ial/hwfb/tbbd_hwfb/201406/t20140617_24251.html

Zhao, Shiju, ed. *Yuyan Yu Guojia (Language and Nation)*. Beijing: Commercial
Press, 2015.

Zhao, Yuezhi. "The Life and Times of 'Chimerica': Global Press Discourses on
U.S.-China Economic Integration, Financial Crisis, and Power Shifts." *International Journal of Communication* 8 (January 2, 2014): 419–44.

Zhao, Yuezhi. "The Media Matrix: China's Integration into Global Capitalism."
In *The Empire Reloaded: Socialist Register 2005*, edited by Leo Panitch and Colin
Leys, 65–84. London: Merlin Press, 2004.

Zhihu. "Zhipaiwu He Zhenhuanzhuan, Shui Geng Lihai? (House of Cards and
Legends of Zhenhuan, Which One Is More Powerful?)," 2014–2016. https://
www.zhihu.com/question/22833198

Zhou, Jade, and Bin Xu. "Where Performance Meets Pandemic: Bin Xu on Anti-
COVID Policy in the U.S. and China." *U.S.-China Perception Monitor*, October
25, 2022. https://uscnpm.org/2022/10/25/bin-xu-on-performance-politics
-disasters-and-covid-19/

Zhou, Qiongyuan, and Hao Lu. "Zhipaiwu Zhongguo Shangren Feng Banyanzhe: Buzhi Zhongguo Zhuxi Zongli Shi Shui (The Actor for the Chinese

Businessman Feng in House of Cards Doesn't Know Who the Chairman and President of China Are)." guancha.cn, March 6, 2014. http://www.guancha .cn/america/2014_03_06_211342.shtml

Zhu, Ying. *Hollywood in China: Behind the Scenes of the World's Largest Movie Market.* New York: New Press, 2022.

Zhu, Ying. "Why Frank Underwood Is Great for China's Soft Power." ChinaFile, February 27, 2014. https://www.chinafile.com/Frank-Underwood-Great-Chi nas-Soft-Power

Zimmer, Carl. "Most New York Coronavirus Cases Came from Europe, Genomes Show." *New York Times*, April 8, 2020, sec. Science. https://www.nytimes.com /2020/04/08/science/new-york-coronavirus-cases-europe-genomes.html

Zuboff, Shoshana. *The Age of Surveillance Capitalism: The Fight for a Human Future at the New Frontier of Power.* New York: Public Affairs, 2019.

Index

Tank Man photo, 26–28, 30, 136–37, 153n117; Black Lives Matter movement and, 35, 48–49; in Kirkwood's *Chimerica*, 30–36, 38–50, 133–34, 156n44; in Leica commercial, 35–36

Tanner, Travis, 77

Taylor, Breonna, 48

techno-orientalism, 53, 55–57, 59–60, 68, 94, 129, 154n9

Telegram (social media platform), 136–37

Tesla, 52, 137–38

Thatcher, Margaret, 106, 153n111

The Three-Body Problem (*Santi*), 160n8

Tiananmen Square protests, 27, 33–37, 40, 136–37, 139. *See also* Tank Man photo

Tibet, 88, 97

TikTok, 122, 129

time: link between time of the Other and time of debt, 58–59, 65–68, 71; politics of, 57–58

Time magazine, 76

time-space compression, 26

time-space distanciation, 26

totalitarianism, 58, 95, 98

trade war, US-China, 51, 70–71, 113–14, 144n33

transnational media, 8

transpacific entanglements. *See* entanglements

transpacific media: defined, 8. *See also* Chimerican media artifacts

Trans-Pacific Partnership (TPP), 18–19

transpacific studies, 18–19

Trump, Donald, and administration: "China chanting" video, 4, 7; China Initiative and, 156n44; Chinese language and, 75, 80; COVID-19 and, 1–2, 4, 12–13, 15, 17, 102, 147n80; cyber threats and, 122; election of, 48, 116, 119, 121; tariffs on Chinese imports, 29, 51, 70

Tudyk, Alan, 96

2012, 62

Ueno, Toshiya, 57

Under the Dome (documentary film), 126

United States: Chinese Exclusion Act, 13, 66; as "declining" or "weakening," 6, 19, 39, 52, 57, 69, 89; entanglements with China (*see* Chimerica); imperialism, 20–21, 68, 99; inequalities in, 21, 174n7; January 6 Capitol riot (2021), 153n111; language education, 75, 86–90 (*see also*

Confucius Institutes); manufacturing sector, 52; minority populations, 67, 71, 125, 132–33 (*see also* African Americans; Asian Americans); nationalism, 65–66, 129; national security, 88, 112; neoliberal financialization, 57; public schools, 101; racial hierarchy, 68; racism in, 48–50, 125, 132; soft power, 83–85, 88–92, 100–102 (*see also* English language); state public spending, 58–61, 64, 69, 89

University of Chicago, 88

US Civil War, 74, 94

US Democratic National Committee, 112

US Department of Justice, China Initiative, 156n44

US Information Agency (USIA), 86

US National Institutes of Health, 3

US Office of War Information, 86

Uyghurs, 133

Vang, Bee, 111

Vietnam War, 39, 99

Virilio, Paul, 57

Vukovich, Dan, 12, 46, 56

Wallis, Cara, 38

Wang, Chih-Ming, 147n83, 179n100

Wang, Hui, 120–21

Wang, Jian, 82

Wang Gengnian, 84

Wang Qishan, 105

Wark, McKenzie, 45

Washington Consensus, 129

Washington Post, 109, 136

Webster, Jamieson, 132

WeChat, 122, 125, 129, 137, 143n25

Weir, Andy, 52

Whedon, Joss, 73–74, 94–95, 97–99, 159n1. See also *Firefly*

white supremacy, 80, 94, 153n117

whitewashing, 68

Willimon, Beau, 118

Wong, Ali, 161n27

Wong, Benedict, 156n44

Wong, Lily, 8

Wood, Peter, 88

workers: American, 146n72; border-crossing movement, 130. *See also* Chinese workers

World Bank, 60

World Health Organization (WHO), 1–2

Wright, Leigh Adams, 93